elf-pledged to vote for liberty,
And uphold the Liberal party;
But when to town this member got,
He with the Tories cast his lot,
And said the thing he knew was not,
And most completely turned his coat
Then all the voters of Dundee
Bewailed their fate most bitterly—
That they had sent in seventy-three
This foe to the Liberal party.

When at Lintrathen champagne flowed,
The member said that he'd be blowed
If he had broken the faith he owed
To the local Liberal party.
Some folks had said that he'd been scratched
Out of the list of those attached
To Hartington, because he'd snatched
A vote or two from those who watched
The conduct of the Government;
But whipper Adam was content,
And to him every notice sent
On behalf of the Liberal party.

But most of those who shared the spree
With the lame excuse could not agree,
And sighed that the Liberal party
Should have been saddled by Dundee
With a slippery old man of the sea,
Who thimblerigged the political pea,
And to the Tories bent the knee.
So ominous whispers ran around
That that was not the time nor ground
For the egotistical trump to sound
To deafen the Liberal party.

To meetings did the member call;
But at dinner, supper, or at ball
He'd praise himself till hours grew small,
And sneer at the Liberal party.
He nightly said he must confess
He couldn't see nor even guess
Why "ratting" caused such deep distress.
The slippery member went to toun
Prepared to vote against faction's froun;
In other words, when they were doon
To kick the Liberal party.

The member was a crafty man—
Divide et impera was his plan—
But his special friend was the publican,
Who to him was a Liberal party.
"Oh, friendly pubs, if you don't blench
In my support, my seat we'll wrench
From hands of 'Rads' then on the bench;
We'll seat some pubs, and the Court entrench
'Gainst Wilfrid Lawson and his crew,
And Templars led by Matthew, too;"
So the publics cheered till they were blue.

glows.

The other, a true veteran
pride the
of his t
bes, or '
Yet, conscious that his
He lays his trophies at th
Careful to hide the evils
Lest ill-won fame should p
And masks a wolfish ma
fleece.

Arrayed in tinsell'd might
While, aping greatness,
And, jackdaw-like, assume
The cast-off feathers fro
The jester at a show of f
His mimic wisdom but exc
One with a golden wreat
While laughter flies with e
For golden laurels fail to r

But how shall language gr
And prompt the secret o
Though I could drain the
I'd still lack language w
His eloquence glows like
Consuming all the chaff of
Humble in heart, let the
Whose spotless lives no err
Still in his power we can w

Beloved Gladstone! would
Thy praise in strains ser
Then would my muse with
And stir the echoes with
Thou well-proved rock in
On thee we build the fabric
Our hopes, our hearts we
Say, shall our building cru
We love thy virtue much, f

Such are the men whom Br
Between, once more to g
Peace now must prompt, o
The dim industrial prosp
Rise, Britons! rise in mi
The baneful influence of th
Bid mad ambition seek a
And whet her talons in sor
Then will prosperity shine

Dundee.

University
of Glasgow

Library

THE ASSOCIATION FOR SCOTTISH LITERARY STUDIES
NUMBER FORTY-FIVE

THE POETS OF THE
PEOPLE'S JOURNAL

Newspaper Poetry in Victorian Scotland

*

THE ASSOCIATION FOR SCOTTISH LITERARY STUDIES

The Association for Scottish Literary Studies aims to promote the study, teaching and writing of Scottish literature, and to further the study of the languages of Scotland.

To these ends, the ASLS publishes works of Scottish literature (of which this volume is an example); literary criticism and in-depth reviews of Scottish books in *Scottish Literary Review*; short articles, features and news in *ScotLit*; and scholarly studies of language in *Scottish Language*. It also publishes *New Writing Scotland*, an annual anthology of new poetry, drama and short fiction, in Scots, English and Gaelic. ASLS has also prepared a range of teaching materials covering Scottish language and literature for use in schools.

All the above publications are available as a single 'package', in return for an annual subscription. Enquiries should be sent to:

ASLS, Scottish Literature, 7 University Gardens, University of Glasgow, Glasgow G12 8QH. Telephone/fax +44 (0)141 330 5309 or visit our website at **www.asls.org.uk**

THE ASSOCIATION FOR SCOTTISH LITERARY STUDIES

THE POETS OF THE PEOPLE'S JOURNAL

Newspaper Poetry in Victorian Scotland

Edited by Kirstie Blair

GLASGOW

2016

Published in Great Britain, 2016
by The Association for Scottish Literary Studies
Scottish Literature
University of Glasgow
7 University Gardens
Glasgow G12 8QH

ASLS is a registered charity no. SC006535

www.asls.org.uk

ISBN: 978-1-906841-28-7

A catalogue record for this book
is available from the British Library.

Typeset by AFS Image Setters Ltd, Glasgow
Printed and bound by Bell & Bain Ltd, Glasgow

Contents

Acknowledgements x

Introduction xi

Poetry from the *People's Journal* 1
1. The Muir, 'Complaint and Petition of the Muir of Alyth'. 23 January 1858 3
2. Trebor, 'Consolation to the Muir of Alyth'. 30 January 1858 5
3. The Muir, 'Eik to Petition of the Muir of Alyth'. 27 February 1858 7
4. Apollo, 'A Young Rhymester's Address to the Editor'. 1 May 1858 9
5. A Son of St Tammas, 'I sigh not for greatness'. 26 June 1858 10
6. Apollo, 'The Dundee Maiden'. 3 July 1858 12
7. David M. Eli, 'Dialogue between the Auld Brig and the Burn'. 10 July 1858 14
8. J. M., 'Think For Yourselves'. 5 March 1859 16
9. Factorius, 'The Shepherd's Song'. 10 September 1859 17
10. Pro Libertate, 'The Subscription to Garibaldi'. 23 June 1860 18
11. Anon, 'Garibaldi's Soliloquy'. 17 November 1860 20
12. Anon, 'Poem on the Forfar Volunteers'. 3 August 1861 22
13. Hawthorn, 'Epistle to Tammas Bodkin'. 31 August 1861 24
14. Poute, 'Untitled [Letter to Editor]'. 5 October 1861 25
15. Poute, 'Odd to a Krokis'. 22 March 1862 27
16. G. D., 'The Lass o' Broughty Ferry'. 5 April 1862 29
17. E. J., A Factory Girl, 'To My Husband'. 9 August 1862 30
18. A. F. M., 'On Top of the Law'. 4 October 1862 ... 32
19. J. E. Watt, 'Nan Tamson's Wean'. 22 November 1862 33
20. D. Tasker, 'The Bairnies at Hame'. 6 June 1863.... 35

21. Iain Ban, 'The Author of "Bonny Strathtay's"
    Apology to the *People's Journal*'. 1 August 1863 37
22. James Watson, 'Home Recollections'.
    29 August 1863 40
23. Anon, 'Rouse, Brothers, Rouse'. 5 September 1863   41
24. E. J., The Factory Girl, 'The Opening of the
    Baxter Park'. 12 September 1863 43
25. Will Harrow, 'A Voice from Stanley Mills'.
    19 December 1863 45
26. Poute, 'Apostroffe to the Rainbow'.
    30 January 1864 46
27. A Missionary, 'The Chappin' Laddie'.
    30 January 1864 48
28. Anon, 'The Working Lasses'. 16 July 1864 49
29. J. F., 'A Voice from Parnassus'. 1 October 1864 .. 51
30. Poute, 'Kale-Wurms'. 26 August 1865 52
31. Moses Daylite, 'An Epissel to Poute'.
    10 March 1866 54
32. J. C., 'The Scottish Servant Maid'. 17 March 1866.. 56
33. A. L. B., 'A Scottish Servant Maid'. 19 May
    1866 57
34. John Taylor, 'The Navvies'. 17 July 1866 58
35. William Donaldson, 'A Lay of Reform'.
    11 August 1866 60
36. J. C., 'Song. (Dedicated to the Scottish Servant
    Maids)'. 18 August 1866 62
37. A. W., 'Reform'. 13 October 1866 64
38. Justitia, 'The Plague-Stricken Village'.
    8 December 1866 65
39. Fernogus, 'Hold Up Your Head'. 9 February 1867   67
40. James Gow, 'Despondency'. 13 July 1867 68
41. W. R. Mainds, 'Lines Addressed to James Gow'.
    20 July 1867 69
42. David Morrison, 'The Bard of Caldervale'.
    10 August 1867 70
43. J. G., 'Hard Times'. 16 November 1867 72
44. J. S. M., 'Lines on Receiving a *People's Journal*'.
    30 May 1868 73
45. James Winthrope, 'Woe'. Christmas 1868 74
46. John Pettigrew, 'What is Sweet'. 27 March 1869 .. 76
47. David Johnson, 'Co-operation'. 3 April 1869 77
48. A. A., 'John Keats'. 17 April 1869 79

49. Will Harrow, 'The Tory Lords'. 17 July 1869 81
50. Wolfhill, 'The Herd Laddie'. 11 September 1869 . 83
51. Harpoon, 'A Tale of a Whale'. 20 November 1869 . 84
52. J. D., 'The Charge of the Light Brigade (Apollo's)'.
    27 November 1869 86
53. J. B. M., 'The Tay Bridge'. 23 April 1870............ 88
54. John Pindar, 'To My Auld Knapsack'. 4 June 1870 . 90
55. Backwoodsman, 'The Land That Rear'd Us A''.
    24 September 1870.. 92
56. M. W. W., 'My Washing Machine'.
    14 January 1871.. 93
57. M., 'Lines on the Death of the Glenlivet Poet'.
    18 February 1871... 95
58. G. L., 'The Tailor's Protest'. 25 March 1871 97
59. T. N. D., 'Murder Most Foul'. 24 June 1871 99
60. Poute, 'Gouldings Manur'. 18 November 1871 101
61. Eriphos, 'Defeatit'. 2 December 1871 104
62. Matilda, 'To the Domestic Servants'. 4 May 1872 105
63. The Factory Muse, 'Athole's Pies'. 1 June 1872 ... 107
64. J. Doubleyou, 'The Evening Hours, A Homely
    Rhyme'. 1 June 1872 109
65. Anon, 'Address to J. Doubleyou'. 22 June 1872 ... 110
66. Will Harrow, 'Epistle to Tammas Bodkin'.
    13 July 1872 112
67. W. M., 'A Favourite Picture'. 3 August 1872 114
68. Eriphos, 'Oor Mill'. 15 February 1873................ 115
69. W. T. E., 'Coals'. 22 March 1873 117
70. Margaret Wallace, 'Lily of the Vale'. 30 May 1874 . 119
71. Wandering Willie, 'Happy Lamoo'.
    23 January 1875.. 120
72. John Stargazer, 'My First Attempt'. 15 May 1875. 122
73. Elizabeth Campbell, 'Three Score and Ten'.
    15 May 1875.. 126
74. Auld Betty, 'The Lassies o' Bonnie Dundee'.
    14 August 1875 127
75. Mistress Lapstane, 'Ane Strikeing Ballant'.
    28 August 1875 129
76. D. Taylor, 'Jute'. 10 March 1877 130
77. C., 'Rapidly, Rapidly. A Good Templar Song'.
    10 March 1877.. 132
78. Lisa M. Smith, 'Only'. 14 April 1877 134
79. Mrs Duthie, 'Naething New'. 28 July 1877.......... 135

80. William McGonagall, 'An Address to Thee Tay
Bridge'. 15 September 1877 138
81. W. S. T., 'Burns's Lament'. 2 March 1878......... 140
82. Auld C., 'King Jute'. 7 April 1878 142
83. An Old Stager, 'An Epistle to "Poet McGonagall!"'.
25 May 1878 144
84. W. W., 'The Millennium of Capital'.
20 July 1878 146
85. Mrs Duthie, 'The Poet's Wail'.
23 November 1878 148
86. E. Lindsay, 'The Sack-Sewers of Dundee'.
1 March 1879 149
87. James Y. Geddes, 'Died on the Street'.
22 March 1879.. 151
88. D. Taylor, 'Ring Up the Curtain'. 19 April 1879. 155
89. Per Mare Per Terram, 'Isandula'.
8 November 1879 157
90. Anon, 'Ketchwayo the Zulu'. 22 November 1879 160
91. G. W. Donald, 'Lines, Suggested by the
Melancholy Wreck of the Tay Bridge'.
3 January 1880... 162
92. J. S. M., 'In Memoriam'. 10 January 1880 164
93. John Rae, 'An Election Song'. 20 March 1880.... 165
94. Jacob Moon, 'An M.P. Non Est'. 27 March 1880.. 167
95. Jessie R. McIntyre, 'The Dogs of War'.
10 April 1880 169
96. P. Mitchell, 'Dakota'. 21 August 1880.............. 170
97. Grandfather, 'Reminiscences of the *People's
Journal*'. 29 March 1881 171
98. Jessie R. McIntyre, 'A Year Ago'. 21 May 1881.. 173
99. John Rae, 'Eviction'. 23 July 1881 174
100. Annie S. Swan, 'April Days'. 29 April 1882....... 177
101. Jas. Burns, 'Advice to Blue Ribboners at the
Fair Holidays'. 24 June 1882 178
102. J. M. K., 'Victory'. 23 September 1882............. 180
103. G. Bruce, 'The Battle of Tel-el-Kebir'.
14 October 1882 182
104. E. W., 'In the Net Factory'. 14 April 1883......... 184

Poetry from the *People's Friend*

105. Maggie, 'The Trappit Mouse'. 4 August 1869 189
106. Dorothea, 'With You'. 15 March 1871............. 191

107. Surfaceman, 'Jenny wi' the Airn Teeth'.
     26 November 1873 192
108. T. N. D., 'The Night Signalman'. 5 May 1875..... 194
109. J. W. R., 'I'll Hae My "Freen"'. 23 June 1875.... 197
110. Nisbet Noble, 'The Storming of Perth'.
     19 January 1876 198
111. James Nicholson, 'Jenny wi' the Lang Pock'.
     20 September 1876 202
112. Alexander G. Murdoch, 'The Thistle Yet'.
     20 December 1876.. 204
113. W. M. W., 'The Workmen's Cry to the
     Masters'. 13 June 1877 207
114. W. P. Crawford, 'Epistle to "Faither Fernie"
     (Jas. Nicholson)'. 19 January 1881 209
115. L. J. Nicolson, 'A Shetland Lullaby'.
     10 August 1881... 211
116. Nisbet Noble, 'Epistle to Robert Wanlock'.
     4 January 1882... 213
117. Sailon, 'A Song of the Clyde'. 10 May 1882....... 216
118. Alexander G. Murdoch, 'Song of the Clyde
     Workers'. 3 January 1883.............................. 217

Bibliography and further reading 221

Index of poems by subgenre 225

Acknowledgements

The research for this collection was enabled by a Curran Fellowship from the Research Society for Victorian Periodicals and two small grants from the Carnegie Trust for the Universities of Scotland. The anthology was completed while on research leave funded by a Leverhulme Research Fellowship. I am very grateful for this support. This volume emerged from a suggestion by Scott Hames, whose advice and encouragement has been invaluable. I am also highly indebted to David Goldie and Gerry Carruthers for their comments, and to Duncan Jones for assistance with the editorial process. Many scholars in the field of Victorian studies have enabled my study of newspaper poetry and shared their work in the field, including Alison Chapman, Linda Hughes, Caley Ehnes, Andrew Hobbs, Jason Rudy, Natalie Houston, Florence Boos and others. Erin Farley's ongoing PhD research into the literary and song cultures of Victorian Dundee has provided vital context, and she identified one of the pseudonymous poets here. I am also enormously grateful to the staff at Dundee Central Library, particularly Eileen Moran and Deirdre Sweeney.

Introduction

On 2 January 1858, a new weekly newspaper appeared in Dundee, the *Dundee, Perth and Forfar People's Journal*. Its opening advertisement described it as:

A Penny Saturday paper devoted to the interests of the Working Classes, and containing the latest telegraphic news, news of the week, interesting tales, extracts from books, poetry and anecdotes, fun without scurrility; pleasant and amusing miscellany, and capital family paper. To be had of all news agents.[1]

As this suggests, the *People's Journal* would fulfil two desires. It would supply news, as did the daily newspapers, but it would also supply entertainment, particularly in the form of fiction and poetry. And unlike other Dundee papers (such as the well-established and Tory-leaning *Dundee Courier*), it not only aimed to attract working-class readers in the rapidly growing town of Dundee, it would also be a paper constituted, from the outset, as for and about 'the people'.[2] In the aftermath of the repeal of the stamp duty and paper duties, which meant that selling papers for a penny was economically viable for the first time, hundreds if not thousands of new provincial newspapers were launched across Britain and Ireland. As Matthew Rubery has recently noted, 'From the province to the metropolis, the newspaper went in a remarkably short space of time from being an item few could afford to an item few could afford to be without.'[3] Some flourished, many folded. Arguably, none would be as successful or as culturally influential as the *People's Journal*.

The *Journal* was founded by John Leng, a newspaperman and radically inclined Liberal from Hull who would later become Liberal MP for Dundee. He began as editor of the *Dundee Advertiser* in 1851, when he was only twenty-three, rapidly transformed its fortunes and became a partner, and went on to launch several further newspaper enterprises, with the *Journal* and its more literary companion, the *People's Friend* – now owned by D. C. Thomson and still published today – by far the most successful. From 1860, the *Journal* was edited by William Latto, who was himself a newspaper poet (his early productions appeared in the *Fife News*) and, in the persona of the comic tailor 'Tammas Bodkin', an enormously successful writer of Scots prose. The *Journal* 'almost instantly became the greatest popular weekly title in Scotland' and helped Leng to establish 'one of the biggest newspaper empires in Britain during the second half of the nineteenth century'.[4] In the period I cover here, the first twenty-five years of the *Journal's* existence, the circulation reputedly reached nearly a quarter of a million readers.[5] Because most newspapers in this period were passed from hand to hand, read aloud in the workplace, posted to relatives overseas, ordered for communal reading rooms and generally treated as shared property, it does not seem an exaggeration for the *Journal* and *Friend*, after its foundation in 1869, to claim that they collectively reached a million readers. As William Donaldson, whose 1986 discussion of the *People's Journal* remains the most significant, notes, this success was partly due to an efficient distribution system which meant that 'country areas were properly served': from 1860 the *Journal* gradually established a number of regional versions, which syndicated national and international news and literary content (including poems) but incorporated suitable local news items.[6] But more important, as Donaldson notes, was the *Journal's* 'unique openness to its readers, its eagerness to act as a platform for their opinions and experiences, its genuine readiness to enter into dialogue with them.'[7]

From the outset, Leng, Latto and the *Journal* staff saw the literary productions of Scottish working men and women as essential to the newspaper's political mission. Indeed, literary works helped to sell politics – the *Journal's* Aberdeen agent, William Lindsay, recalled that in 1861, booksellers were disinclined 'to accept an agency for a paper promulgating Radical politics', as was the *Journal's* reputation, but that in finding news-agents, 'I found the nom de plume "Tammas Bodkin" a name to conjure with.'[8] Contemporary readers attested that they came for the fiction and poetry, and stayed for the news. While comic prose and fiction (as examined by Donaldson) was always an important feature of the *Journal*, and still more so of the *Friend*, it was poetry that attracted the most editorial commentary, the most reviews, and that responded more immediately than fiction to the political, social and economic concerns discussed in the news sections of the paper. By its second issue, the *Journal* was already running a poetry competition for readers, with a book, contributed by another reader, as a prize. Twenty-nine entries were received. 'Nothing has ever gratified us more,' the editor commented, 'than to have placed in our hands such a body of evidence attesting the intelligence of the classes whom we specially address, and the right feeling which pervades them' (16 January 1858). Readers took the hint. A decade later (in the year James Winthrope's 'Woe', included here, won a ten-shilling prize), the *Journal* Christmas poetry competition attracted four hundred and twenty entries and was internationally famous. Readers wrote in from as far afield as Australia to ask that competition deadlines were set early enough for them to enter.[9]

From its early years onwards, such large quantities of poems were allegedly received by the *Journal* ('we receive every week much more poetry than we can possibly insert' (21 August 1858)) that the paper launched one of its most striking features, a 'To Correspondents' column which was primarily devoted to assessing the merits, or otherwise, of poems received, and offering advice for their improvement, often in devastatingly scathing prose. 'The poem you have been ten years upon we have disposed of in as many minutes – verdict, rubbish,' was a not atypical comment.[10] As I have examined elsewhere, readers loved this, and an effective craze for the newspaper as a venue for literary criticism of readers' efforts spread through the Scottish press.[11] 'To Correspondents', although I do not feature extracts from it here, helped to create the impression that encouraging working-class poets was so important to the *Journal*'s mission, that the editor would risk insanity in wading through 'Three hundred "first attempts"' and 'ninety-nine pieces of sheer doggerel' to find 'one, with four lines, passable!'.[12] By 1869, the literary portions of the *Journal* had been so successful that Leng launched a spin-off, the *People's Friend*, edited by popular fiction writer David Pae with assistance from sub-editor Andrew Stewart. Starting as a 'monthly miscellany', by early 1870 it was issued weekly (on Wednesdays). The editor stated, in 'Our Design and Purpose', that the *Friend* was inspired by the success of the Christmas competitions in the *Journal* – which by this time included prose and fiction categories as well as poetry – and that its aim was 'to provide literary entertainment which the masses of the people would welcome with eager avidity' and 'to foster and encourage the literary talent which we know exists among the people' (5 January 1870).

From 1858 onwards, the *Journal* published, on average, around two poems a week. Sometimes weeks or even months would pass without much poetry; sometimes, especially in moments of excitement about a local, national or international cause or event, an edition might include four or five poems on related themes. This was not in itself exceptional. Most nineteenth-century newspapers published poetry, in two categories: firstly, poems reprinted from works by famous authors (Alfred Tennyson and Henry Wadsworth Longfellow were by far the most popular living authors here) or from other newspapers, and secondly, 'Original Verse', usually composed by writers who submitted their poems directly to the local paper.[13] For a writer like Tennyson, in this period, the London *Times* seemed an appropriate venue for new poems that took politics or current affairs as their theme. For most aspiring poets, however, their best chance of seeing their works in print was to send them to the editor of a provincial paper and hope for a favourable opinion. If the editor approved the poem, they would receive no payment – periodicals and magazines sometimes paid for poetry, newspapers did not – but they would have the kudos of seeing their relations and neighbours reading their work, and the satisfaction, particularly important to those whose daily lives consisted of relentless hard manual labour, of having shown that they were capable of something more than drudgery. 'I shall never forget the exquisite, the thrilling pleasure I experienced in these innocent years on beholding my effusions, time after time, adorning the "Poet's Corner" of the weekly city press,' Alexander Murdoch, who worked from the age of eleven as a shop assistant and then engineer in Glasgow, recalled ('The Laird's Lyke-wake', *Journal*, 21 February 1877). 'Tradesman' sent the *Journal* a 'poem of gratitude' on seeing his work in its columns:

I gave a great yell, and cried, 'Mither, come ben,
Your laddie's a poet, and it's weel you should ken';
And ben she cam' rinnin' as if I'd been shot,
In sic a great hurry she fell ower the kail pot. ('To
Correspondents', *Journal*, 19 October 1872)

Tradesman's use of Scots and his reference to the 'kail
pot' set up a comic scenario about the stereotypical poet
who sought inclusion in newspaper poetry columns; a
young aspirational working man from a provincial family,
as are many of the poets (or their personae) included in this
anthology.

The *Journal*'s importance for newspaper poetry – and
for working-class writing in this period – lies not in kind
but in degree. If most other weekly provincial papers
published poems by working men and women, few had so
explicitly made it part of their rationale to encourage the
writing of poetry. In one of the *Journal*'s regular reviews of
volumes of local verse, the reviewer noted that for working
men to learn reading, writing and the rules of grammar
and composition was laborious:

It is for the poets who perform this necessary drudgery
for themselves without enjoying the assistance of a pro-
fessor – it is, in short, for the poets of the people – the
self-taught singers of the hillside, the mill, and the
artizans' workshop – that we entertain a special respect
and regard. Dryasdust, M. A. writes a poem. Well, it is
very meritorious in him, providing it is a good one, but
Dryasdust has had hundreds of pounds expended on his
education, and it would be a shame to him if he could
not write in a scholarly way at least, if not as a man of
genius. With poor Tompkins, however, the case is alto-
gether different; he has only been six weeks at school
in his life, and when he writes a poem – even if it lacks in
some respects the graces which a poem ought to possess
– we are yet disposed to give him a hearty welcome, and
to read his simple unadorned poem in preference to the
learned poem of the erudite Dryasdust. ('A Couple of
New Poets', 25 January 1868)

'Dryasdust', after Walter Scott's imagined pedantic authority, was by this date a standard term for a learned but tedious literary figure or historian. Such commentary encouraged would-be working-class poets to see the *Journal* as a friendly venue, and indicated that their work would be publishable even if it did not reach the high standards they would be familiar with from cheap volumes of canonical authors. Poems that were metrically awkward or had infelicities of language or expression (which is true of many poems in this anthology), were still acceptable, though unless they were preserving errors deliberately for comic effect, editors silently corrected spelling and punctuation.[14] It was clear to contemporary readers that in this championing of self-taught poets, the *Journal* was enacting its commitment to reformist, at times radical, politics. In the common perception of the mid-Victorian period, writing poetry was a sign of aspirational culture and self-improvement. It showed that working men and women were educated, thoughtful and intelligent, plus it indicated that they possessed 'right feeling'. Therefore, it constituted direct evidence that nothing was to be feared from extending the franchise in their favour. The *Journal*'s championing of the people's poetry, and its fervent support for the Reform acts of 1867 and 1884, are part of the same cause. Not only did it thereby attract a more substantial number of politically engaged poets and poems than may be the case elsewhere, it also encouraged higher standards for newspaper verse.

Even when the *Journal* expanded its readership well beyond Scotland and set up its famous offices in Fleet Street, Scottish loyalty and Scottish interests were central to its image, and so a crucial part of its editorial stance (and an opinion repeated again and again by Victorian Scottish writers and editors) was that Scotland was a literary nation, producing, post-Burns, more 'people's poets' than any other country on earth, and that this should be an immense source of national pride. This attitude is nicely summed up in a letter from John Gibson, East Linton, Prestonkirk responding to a *Journal* article on the life of Elizabeth Campbell, the 'Lochee Poetess', a working woman living in poverty, which he read 'with tears in my eyes':

We need not despair of our country with such characters in our midst; they are a guarantee against its decay. I do

not know how your other readers feel; but, for myself, I
feel as if you conferred a great obligation on all who read
the Journal in bringing under their notice such a fine
example as that of Mrs E. Campbell; and that in doing so
you have done more to reach our hearts than if you had
written a dozen leading articles on the topics of the day
(10 April 1876).

The *Journal* was also known for its championing of the
Scots language. The first issue contained a letter from
'Sandy', a supposed working man (in fact Latto in another
guise), in Scots, which defiantly stated, 'I think my ain
hamely Scotch to be every bit as expressive, or even far
mair sae, than what is ca'd "pure" English' (2 January
1858). Almost every subsequent issue contained at least one
letter, prose piece or poem in Scots, justifying one reader's
sense that 'Singular to say, the only popular publication
that seems not ashamed to be the channel for the Scots
language is the *People's Journal*, where it is still cultivated in
all its native beauty of polish and sly pawky humour' ('A
Plea for Braid Scotch', 18 July 1863). As the Scots poems
included here show, writers celebrated the richness and
variation of Scots and expected readers to appreciate it.

From the perspective of Scottish literary studies, this
anthology of newspaper poetry sheds light on an aspect of
popular literature that has been frequently recognised as
significant and neglected, but seldom explored. It also dis-
proves the sentiment, still to some extent current, that 'in
Scottish Victorian literature industrialisation and the
Enlightenment are both missing. One would scarcely know
from it what was happening to the majority of Scots.'[15]
No-one who has explored the publishing venue where most
popular Scottish literature appeared – the local press –
could ever support such claims. The poems here speak for
themselves in showing just how much working people
engaged with 'what was happening' around them, naturally
including the rapid industrialisation of Scotland. As my
headnotes indicate, while some of these poems were re-
printed in published collections, most were not, or not that
we know of. Even when working-class poets managed to
find the support and patronage to publish a collection of
poetry, they often chose to exclude poems that espoused

party politics (and might thus damage their standing with certain readers), that dealt with purely local events and affairs, or that had been written with a specific newspaper venue in mind. While the newspaper press is still a highly mediated form, it does give more, and to some degree unique, insight into what working people were writing and reading and why they were doing so.

This leads to the second purpose of this anthology, which is to assist in an ongoing reassessment of Victorian popular poetry, and particularly working-class poetry, through study of the periodical and newspaper press. The mid-late Victorian era is the heyday of popular newspaper poetry, which gradually faded as the twentieth century progressed. Yet no other anthologies of newspaper verse exist – though we might note that most anthologies of working-class poetry could plausibly be described as such. Producing such an anthology is, of course, problematic because it inevitably involves extracting poems from their original format and context, and because newspaper poetry is such a vast and diverse field. By concentrating on one newspaper (and its associated literary 'miscellany'), and by focusing on only the first twenty-five years of its operation (January 1858– December 1883), I hope that this anthology gives a sense of the concerns of Scottish and British regional newspaper verse more broadly, while retaining a tight focus that enables careful contextualisation of the poems in relation to the events they reference. Because the *Journal* and *Friend* are products of a rapidly growing Victorian city with strong links to imperial trade and commerce, and one which had a vibrant, politicised, artisanal tradition that supported various forms of literary culture, they also show 'bardic culture' at work in the heart of Victorian industry.[16]

Scholars and historians of the newspaper press rarely mention the presence of poetry in newspapers, and the third aim of this anthology is to show that poems are not merely filler. They are as engaged in promoting – and sometimes contradicting – the mission of a newspaper as are the editorials or lead articles, and they frequently serve as reportage and commentary on local events. As Linda Hughes has noted in an important new survey of periodical verse, it is vital to consider 'what poetry can do that news reports cannot and vice versa.'[17] Even where their topics seem apolitical and far removed from the 'news' (as in the many poems on domestic life, or on love and courtship), they are part of the wider ideologies disseminated by the press for particular ends. They also helped to create a sense of community, as poets addressed readers, praised each other, and celebrated the *Journal* and *Friend* 'families' of readers and authors. Readers felt that they knew newspaper poets personally, and treated them as minor celebrities, as the many poems in praise of particular authors and poems suggest.

One of the reasons why newspaper verse has seldom been analysed or collected, of course, is that most of it does not meet the aesthetic criteria we (professional literary critics) would apply to 'good' poetry. This is in no way surprising. Newspaper verse was not as ephemeral as we might think (readers often cut out and preserved their favourite poems, pasting them on walls, framing them, or incorporating them into a scrapbook), but much of it was assumed to have been composed rapidly and in response to changing events, with aesthetics as a less primary consideration. No-one could deny that most Victorian newspaper verse is highly conventional, in both form and subject matter. The kind of verse that editors wanted 'their' authors to produce would be smoothly flowing, in a steady rhythm and with regular rhymes, 'correct' in sentiment (i.e. respectable, pious, inspirational and consoling), and on a topic and theme that would not offend readers. Newspaper verse also literally had to conform to a mould because it had to fit within a relatively compressed space: as the poems selected here show, the ur-poem in this genre has four or five four-line stanzas in *abab* rhyme with four iambic beats in each line. Editors discouraged experimentation. The point, as clearly expressed in the *Journal*'s 'To Correspondents', was to come as close to the Tennysonian or Longfellow lyric (or for Scottish poets, Burns's poems) as possible while still retaining a local flavour. Moreover, much newspaper verse is intended, explicitly or implicitly, to be sung, often to traditional and contemporary tunes known to the audience, and is therefore deliberately derivative of existing lyrics.

That many of the poems published in the *Journal* and the *Friend*, as throughout the British press, are very similar to each other, is therefore not because of a failure of ambition or skill on the part of the authors, but because they were aware of the standards they were expected to meet for publication. Poems that did not conform to these standards, either because they were innovative in form, or because they expressed sentiments (especially political, religious or sexual) that were not deemed fit for a family audience, would have been rejected. Yet editors themselves often expressed boredom with the usual set-pieces of Victorian poetry. As the *Friend* editor (probably Andrew Stewart) noted in 1872, for instance, he was fed up with receiving miserable elegiac verse, 'It would seem as if most of our would-be poets had recently returned from the grave of their first, their early, and their only love, and were determined to throw their tear-blotted and heartrending effusions at our inoffensive head' ('To Correspondents', 20 March 1872). This is why editorial staff effectively sponsored a counter-culture of comic 'bad' verse, supposedly printed so that the audience could mock the stupidity of its writers, but often operating instead as a satirical commentary on the expectations of 'good' verse and the role of the humble bard.[18] Readers praised and admired the pious and self-abnegating verse of writers like Elizabeth Campbell, but her success was far eclipsed by the comic and subversive 'poutery' of Poute and his followers, shown in a number of the poems here.

With over a hundred poems published every year in the *Journal*, and many more in the *Friend*, this anthology represents a small percentage of thousands of engaging poems that would repay further study. I have tried to provide examples of the different genres and types of poetry, and poets, who published in the press during these decades. Nonetheless, this selection is overtly biased. If it were truly representative of the overall poetic content of the *People's Journal* and *People's Friend*, then by far the largest subgenres would be courtship and romance; elegy; and sentimental domesticity. Readers – and editors – had a seemingly endless appetite for variations on the theme of 'My Auld Hame', poems on the death of children and loved ones, and courtship poems, modelled on the Scottish song tradition and especially on Burns, usually featuring a fair maiden by the banks of a generic Scottish river. This is particularly true in the *Friend*, which, as a weekly literary paper rather

than a newspaper, and with a larger presumed family
audience of all ages, published far fewer poems on con-
temporary events and many, many more that represent
sentimental domesticity. Although it seemed important to
include a sample of *Friend* poems here, that sample is smaller
because these poems are less representative of newspaper
verse as such than of periodical verse, another huge Victorian
market. Love poems, poems of nostalgic domesticity and
elegiac poems are interesting *en masse*, because of what they
tell us not just about the tastes of the reading public, but
about the ability of working-class poets to produce stan-
dard newspaper verse on these themes to order. But very
few individual poems in this genre stand out, precisely
because the point was that they were not *meant* to stand
out. Those I have included, such as Lisa M. Smith's poem
of lost love, 'Only', David Tasker's 'The Bairnies at Hame'
or G. D.'s 'The Lass o' Broughty Ferry', must therefore
stand for a whole class of poems of this type.

For this anthology, then, I have tried primarily to select
poems that constitute themselves as *newspaper* poems,
usually by directly engaging with political, economic, social
and cultural issues featured in the columns of the press.
This gives the poems historical relevance, as an insight into
the questions that concerned an audience of liberally or
radically inclined working people in the mid-Victorian
period. Such questions include the exploitation of common
land, unemployment, the rise of industry, unions and
strikes, women and children in the workplace, emigration,
electoral reform, and British politics at home and abroad.
The two and a half decades covered here (1859 to 1884)
were exciting times, marked by economic highs and lows,
war and controversial foreign policy, the further expansion
of the franchise, the shift from Tory to Liberal government
and the rivalry of Benjamin Disraeli and William Glad-
stone, and, at home, the rise of Dundee to become 'Jute-
opolis'. Some years, in this collection, are represented more
fully than others (several years had no poems that seemed
worthy of inclusion), but this does not seem indicative of
any overarching trend; it often simply means that exciting
events in particular years attracted more poetic talent. Most
of the poems on contemporary topics are deliberately acti-
vist, in that they seek to inspire their readership to join a

particular cause or agitate for change. Newspapers also
attracted poems that commemorate local causes – usually,
in the *People's Journal*, events in Dundee – such as the open-
ing of Baxter Park, or the building and then collapse of the
Tay Bridge. Such poems help to instill a sense of local pride
and community. Community in a broader sense is also sig-
nificant in the many newspaper poems that take poetry
itself as a theme, and that respond either to editorial dic-
tates about the kind of poetry suitable for publication, or
to other writers published in the same newspaper. These
poems can be aspirational, seeing poetry as a means to self-
improvement, as discussed above, and they can also mock
poetic ambitions through satire. In addressing other writers
and the editor, they serve to create a powerful sense of
a collective of writers and readers linked to the *People's
Journal* and *Friend*.

Of the poets selected, only two, Ellen Johnston and Alex-
ander Anderson, are regularly anthologised and discussed
as leading working-class poets of Victorian Britain, though
recent anthologies do not reprint the poems I have selected
(in Anderson's case, only two out of over twenty which
appeared in these decades).[19] The only poet here whose
poems have as yet been republished for a modern audience
is William McGonagall, and I have included his poem on
the Tay Bridge because it is markedly different in the *Journal*
version. I deliberately did not include two significant poems
by Marion Bernstein, another major working-class woman
poet, that appear in the *Journal* in this period ('The Points-
man' and 'The Highland Laird's Song'), because they are
reprinted, with information on their original appearance, in
the recent edition of Bernstein's works.[20] The one other
poet in this anthology who has attracted positive scholarly
attention is James Young Geddes.[21] Out of one hundred
and four *People's Journal* poems included here, representing
eighty-nine different authors, twenty-seven authors can be
firmly identified – fewer than one-third. The rate is higher
for *People's Friend* poets: six out of the twelve authors repre-
sented are known. This is not surprising, because the
People's Friend quickly attracted a coterie of poets and was
much more prone to publish numerous poems, on an
almost weekly basis, by the same named group of contri-
butors. My selection represents several of the best-known

of these. Most of the identified poets here were anthologised by writer and journalist D. H. Edwards of Brechin, in his monumental seventeen-volume series, *Modern Scottish Poets*, which began in the early 1880s, as this anthology ends. Edwards leant heavily towards anthologising poems on rural Scotland, family life, Christianity and patriotism, and the selection here presents a very different version of 'modern' Victorian Scottish poetry than that he promoted. Nonetheless, it is often thanks to his indefatigable work in tracking down the newspaper poets of his day that we know any biographical details about the poets behind the pseudonyms.

Of the identified poets, all except three women poets (Margaret Wallace, Dorothea Ogilvy and Annie S. Swan) were originally from a working-class background. One, George Bruce, was a wealthy self-made man. Two – Anderson ('Surfaceman' and 'A. A.') and Alexander G. Murdoch – became successful enough to take a step out of manual labour. Anderson was given a post as librarian in Edinburgh, and Murdoch managed to make a career as a writer (McGonagall also arguably managed to do so, though he was constantly on the verge of destitution). For the other poets here, a career in the literary world was well out of reach, though many, including Campbell, Peter Leslie (John Pindar) and Henry Syme ('Grandfather') managed to market their newspaper reputations to gain support in their old age, by publishing a volume that would appeal to those who knew them from the pages of the press. The working lives of the *Journal* and *Friend* poets varied widely, and many moved between different positions. This anthology includes factory workers, field labourers, shopkeepers and shop assistants, engineers and railway workers, miners and musicians, clerks and travellers. Some writers chose to self-identify themselves by profession, such as 'A Missionary' or 'The Factory Muse', though these professions can be fictional and strategic as well as genuine. Others identified themselves by their location. Publishing a newspaper poem in such widely circulated venues was prestigious, and we can safely assume that those poets who deliberately listed their workplace, or gave their initials and home town, expected to be identified by their family and local community. It is clear from jokes about Poute's (Alexander

Burgess's) identity in poems that address him, for instance, that readers knew he was a musician of some repute in Fife, although his alter ego has no such skill.

In some cases, it might be possible to find out further biographical information about these writers through detailed local research, and there are doubtless many more little-known volumes of poetry in local libraries that hold clues to these pseudonyms. Equally, names such as 'E. Lindsay' may themselves be a pseudonym. Although editors did require contributors to submit their real name and address (to discourage plagiarism, a recurring problem), newspaper poets often published under multiple identities, including using pseudonyms that implied differing gendered, class and professional identities and imaginary locations. Robert Ford, for instance, who became one of the leading poetic contributors to the *People's Friend* under his own name, and was well-known in the 1880s and 1890s as a ballad-collector and editor as well as a working-class poet and prose writer, started out by publishing comic verse in the *Journal* under the pseudonyms 'Geordie Lapstane' and 'Matilda Towhead'. It is not impossible, though must remain speculative, that Ford is behind the poems signed 'Mistress Lapstane' and 'Matilda' in this collection. Gendered pseudonyms in newspaper verse are particularly interesting, because they indicate what the author felt would be added to the poem by the stance of female authorship. Political poems signed with female pseudonyms that are comic or generic, for instance, like 'Auld Betty', can be read in terms of solidarity between women engaged in political action, yet would arguably be more likely to be interpreted as satirical rather than supportive if readers suspected that the author was a male comic poet. Conversely, because women poets were generally expected to conform to generic norms, producing poems on love and loss, on nature and family, they had a clear incentive to publish poetry that differed from these norms under gender-neutral pseudonyms. This may be why Jane Duthie, primarily a comic poet, began her poetic career as J. A. Duthie, before switching to 'Mrs Duthie' once her position as a *Journal* poet was secure.

The *Journal* and the *Friend* were generally advocates for women workers – as several of the poems here show – and did support women poets, as did other Scottish newspapers (for example in Ellen Johnston's relationship with the Glasgow *Penny Post* or Bernstein's with the *Weekly Mail*) but the poetry by self-identified women poets that they published is often far more restricted in theme and scope than that by male authors. Male poets were part of the newspapers' social networks in ways that women writers were not: in the comic account of the *Friend*'s Christmas celebrations at Lamb's Temperance Hotel in Dundee, cited below, the Editor makes it clear that the *Friend*'s women contributors were not invited to the party.[22] Sixteen out of one hundred and eighteen poems in this anthology are by writers clearly self-identifying as female, which roughly reflects the overall gendered division of poems in the *Journal*, though whether this bias is due to a greater number of male poets submitting poems for consideration, or a higher rate of acceptance, we do not know.

I have included more than one poem by several authors, but only two authors have more than two poems in this collection: Poute and Will Harrow. This is reflective of their status as top contributors to the *Journal*, and of the high admiration they attracted for their original, comic and satirical verse in Scots. Scots was, as the selection here amply shows, highly respected by the *Journal* and used across all poetic genres. Over one-third of the poems here make significant use of Scots, and some writers deliberately use terms from their local dialect; their variant language would repay more detailed study. No poems in Gaelic were published in the *Journal* or *Friend* in this period, though L. J. Nicolson did contribute a cradle-song to the *Friend* in Shetland dialect, reproduced here. In terms of popular forms, Scottish newspaper poets were drawn to the 'epistle' poem and to the habbie stanza, undoubtedly due to the influence of Burns. Most newspaper poems, however, were simpler in form, usually with alternate rhymes and four-beat lines, or following familiar models of popular songs and lyrics. They also tended to be short. Poems more than fifty lines long are rare, though some do occur. I deliberately excluded two exceptionally long *Journal* poems, G. M.'s 'The Rebels' Route', 28 August 1858 (a satirical anti-Chartist poem recalling the disastrous 1842 march on Forfar, in serial parts) and 'An Aberdeenshire Chiel's "To the Farm Servants of Aberdeenshire"', 25 November 1871 (an emigrant poem, in Scots, in the form of a long discussion about employment conditions for agricultural labourers in Canada) because, despite their interest, their length would have meant excluding a number of other poems.

In his 1936 essay on McGonagall, Hugh MacDiarmid located him within 'the whole debased tradition of popular poetry' associated with Dundee:

> Dundee was then and has since been the great home and fostering centre of the cheapest popular literature in Scotland, and huge fortunes have been built up there on precisely the chief ingredients of McGonagall's art – mindlessness, snobbery, and the inverted snobbery of a false cult of proletarian writers. So far as literature is concerned, the idea of Burns as a 'ploughman poet' has been fatal. Scotland has suffered since from an endless succession of railwaymen poets, policemen poets, and the like.[23]

Although he does not say so openly, MacDiarmid is evidently thinking about the *Journal*, the *Friend*, and the culture they had inspired in other Scottish newspapers. His opinion has all too often been given credibility as a reasonable assessment of Scottish Victorian verse culture. As this anthology suggests, however, to dismiss the *Journal*'s 'cult of proletarian writers' (which certainly did exist) is a profoundly problematic rejection of a milieu that encouraged working men and women to participate in and help to shape a topical, politicised, satirical and self-aware literary culture; one that genuinely offered pleasure, inspiration and a sense of self-worth to writers and readers who were excluded from other forms of cultural participation. What this newspaper culture contributed to Scottish literature and to Victorian literature more broadly is eminently worth serious reconsideration. The writers in this volume would never have expected that their poems would survive into the twenty-first century, nor would they necessarily have wanted to be remembered for verse that they themselves considered light and ephemeral. Nonetheless, they constitute part of a literary heritage that deserves recovery, and their concerns and interests often chime, more than we might expect, with issues still very much current in our time.

Note on sources and text

Since I first began to work on the *People's Journal*, it has been partly digitised in the British Newspaper Archive (which requires a paid subscription to access). While this is enormously valuable for future research into the *Journal*, a number of years are currently missing in the digitised volumes. For this anthology, I used the hard copies of the *Journal* owned by Dundee Central Library, and the hard copies of the *People's Friend* in the British Library. The poems are reproduced unabridged, with the occasional correction where an error was obviously that of the typesetter rather than the poet and was unintentional. I have removed the signature from the end of the poem, except in cases where it clearly forms part of the verse. Signatures are reproduced in the title as in the text, including name or pseudonym, place, and date where given.

In the case of a number of these poems, errors of the author were deliberately printed for comic effect. It is difficult to assess exactly how much of the punctuation and erratic spacing or positioning of words in 'bad' comic verse stemmed from the poet rather than the typesetter. I have assumed that it is important to preserve the appearance of the poem in the original newspaper as much as is feasible. As the notes indicate, comic Scots verse is also often consciously obscure. While I have included basic glosses to assist the reader with Scots terms, glossing every line by a writer like Poute (who has eighty entries of his own in the *Dictionary of the Scots Language*) would undermine the poems' deliberate take on dialect and phonetic English. All glosses of Scots are based on the online *Dictionary of the Scots Language* (DSL): www.dsl.ac.uk.

Notes

[1] *Dundee, Perth and Forfar People's Journal*, 2 January 1858, p. 1. All further references are given in the text by date.

[2] Throughout this anthology, I use 'working-class' in the straightforward definition adopted by Emma Griffin, as indicating 'those who had no income other than that which they earned, those working as manual labourers, and those sufficiently close to the margins of a comfortable existence that a stint of ill health or unemployment posed serious difficulties.' As she notes, this can include a range of circumstances, from 'the reasonably comfortable' to 'the desperately poor' (*Liberty's Dawn: A People's History of the Industrial Revolution* (New Haven: Yale University Press, 2013), p. 64). For a discussion of the complexities of defining a writer as 'working-class' or 'labouring class', see Kirstie Blair, 'Introduction', *Class and the Canon: Constructing Labouring-Class Poetry and Poetics, 1750–1900*, ed. Kirstie Blair and Mina Gorji (Houndsmills: Palgrave, 2013), pp. 1–15, pp. 4–7.

[3] Matthew Rubery, *The Novelty of Newspapers: Victorian Fiction After the Invention of the News* (Oxford: Oxford University Press, 2009), p. 4. On the expansion of the press in Scotland just prior to this period, see R. M. W. Cowan, *The Newspaper in Scotland: A Study of its First Expansion 1815–1860* (Glasgow: George Outram, 1946). Martin Hewitt has recently assessed the 'frenzy' surrounding the repeal of stamp and paper duty, in *The Dawn of the Cheap Press in Victorian Britain: The End of the 'Taxes on Knowledge', 1849–1869* (London: Bloomsbury, 2014), p. 99.

[4] Andrew Murray Scott, *Dundee's Literary Lives, vol 1: Fifteenth to Nineteenth Century* (Dundee: Abertay History Society, 2003), pp. 81, 77.

[5] Ibid., p. 82.

[6] William Donaldson, *Popular Literature in Victorian Scotland: Language, Fiction and the Press* (Aberdeen: Aberdeen University Press, 1986), p. 21.

[7] Ibid., p. 29.

[8] William Lindsay, *Some Notes: Personal and Public* (Aberdeen: W. W. Lindsay, 1898), pp. 297–98.

[9] See 'To Correspondents', 5 March 1870: Mr William Affleck, Gundaroo, New South Wales 'writes to us suggesting that we should announce our next prize competition early in the season, so as to enable our readers in Australia and other remote colonies to enter the lists.'

[10] 'To Correspondents', *People's Friend*, 17 March 1875, p. 175 (*Friend* page numbers refer to those in the collected volume). All further references are given in the text by date.

[11] See Kirstie Blair, ' "Let the Nightingales Alone": Correspondence Columns, the Scottish Press, and the Making of the Working-Class Poet', *Victorian Periodicals Review* 47 (2014), pp. 188–207.

[12] Willie Grahame, 'Among the Poets: A Singular Adventure', *People's Friend*, 9 August 1876, pp. 500–01. The conceit here is that Grahame is an aspiring poet who goes to his friend the editor's office to leave him a poem, and finds a note on the desk about the editor's despair at his task. Comic accounts, by and about editors, about the mass of bad poems received, were very common throughout the Scottish press.

[13] On newspaper verse, see Natalie Houston, 'Newspaper Poems: Material Texts in the Public Sphere', *Victorian Studies* 50 (2008), pp. 233–42; Andrew Hobbs, 'Five Million Poems, or the Local Press as Poetry Publisher, 1800–1900', *Victorian Periodicals Review* 42 (2012), pp. 488–92 and Hobbs and Claire Januszewski, 'How Local Newspapers Came to Dominate Victorian Poetry Publishing', *Victorian Poetry* 52 (2014), pp. 65–87.

[14] See 'To Correspondents', *People's Journal*, 8 December 1860, 'We pass many pieces without altering a syllable; others which are correct in the main, we polish up where there is occasion; and others that are too long or discursive, we abridge to suit our space.'

[15] Olive and Sydney Checkland, *Industry and Ethos: Scotland 1832–1914* 2nd edn (Edinburgh: Edinburgh University Press, 1989), p. 140.

[16] 'Bardic culture' is a phrase drawn from Brian Maidment's important discussion of poetic cultures in Victorian Manchester. See 'Class and Cultural Production in the Industrial City: Poetry in Victorian Manchester', in *City, Class and Culture: Studies of Cultural Production and Social Policy in Victorian Manchester*, ed. A. J. Kidd and K. W. Roberts (Manchester: Manchester University Press, 1985), pp. 148–66. On working-class writers and the newspaper press see also David Vincent, *Literacy and Popular Culture: England 1750–1914* (Cambridge: Cambridge University Press, 1989), especially pp. 214–16. On Dundee's literary cultures, see Aileen Black, *Gilfillan of Dundee, 1813–1878* (Dundee: Dundee University Press, 2006), and on the expansion of Victorian Dundee, see *Victorian Dundee: Images and Realities*, ed. Louise Miskell, Christopher A. Whatley and Bob Harris (East Linton: Tuckwell Press, 2000) and Jim Tomlinson, *Dundee and the Empire: 'Juteopolis' 1850–1939* (Edinburgh: Edinburgh University Press, 2014).

[17] Linda Hughes, 'Poetry', in *The Routledge Handbook to Nineteenth-Century British Periodicals and Newspapers*, ed. Andrew King, Alexis Easley and John Morton (London: Routledge, 2016), pp. 124–37, p. 125.

[18] For a lengthier discussion see Blair, 'McGonagall, "Poute" and the Bad Poets of Victorian Scotland', *The Bottle Imp* 14 (November 2013): asls.arts.gla.ac.uk/SWE/TBI/TBIIssue14/Blair.html

[19] Both Johnston and Anderson, are, for instance, among the twenty-one representative poets included in *Nineteenth-Century English Labouring-Class Poets 1800–1900*, vol III 1860–1900, ed. John Goodridge (London: Pickering & Chatto, 2006).

[20] Marion Bernstein, *A Song of Glasgow Town: The Collected Poems of Marion Bernstein*, ed. Edward H. Cohen, Anne R. Fertig and Linda Fleming (Glasgow: ASLS, 2013), pp. 153, 162.

[21] On Geddes, see Valentina Bold, 'James Young Geddes (1850–1913): A Re-evaluation', *Scottish Literary Journal* 19.1 (1992), pp. 18–27.

[22] See p. 204.

[23] Hugh MacDiarmid, 'The Great McGonagall', in *Scottish Eccentrics*, ed. Alan Riach (Carcanet: Manchester, 1993), pp. 57–75, pp. 65, 64. The fact that MacDiarmid says that 'there are no other writings known to me' which resemble McGonagall and sees him as entirely exceptional (p. 57), suggests that he was not fully familiar with the literature he dismisses: see my notes on the comic poems, especially by Poute, included here.

POETRY FROM THE
PEOPLE'S JOURNAL

1. 'Complaint and Petition of the Muir of Alyth', by The Muir. Published 23 January 1858.

This anonymous poem alerts readers to plans to drain and build on common land near Alyth, a town in Perth and Kinross, using a local bog as a water supply. The focus on curling and winter pursuits also marks this as a seasonal poem appropriate for January. It spurred a response by 'Trebor', followed by another response from 'The Muir'. The author of this poem and the third poem in the sequence, assuming they are by the same writer, has not been identified. 'Will Harrow' (John Campbell) signed one of his early *Journal* poems with the location 'Moor of Alyth', and given his political interests and skill in Scots verse, it is not impossible that he was the author. 'Mr W.' is presumably a local character familiar to Alyth readers.

See also: 2. 'Consolation to the Muir of Alyth', p. 5; 3. 'Eik to Petition of the Muir of Alyth', p. 7; 7. 'Dialogue Between the Auld Brig and the Burn', p. 14.

Ye Alyth gentry hear my plaint,   1
I'm sair ill used it a' was kent,
To drain my bogs some foulk are bent,
     (Foulk aye on watch)
Where mony a blithesome day ye've spent   5
     At Curlin' Match.

But noo, alas! That time has gane,
Nae mair the polished curlin' stane
Shall to my bonny Lochs be taen,
     When Johnny Frost   10
Makes gutters hard as ony stane,
     For a' is lost.

Alake! Nae mair wi' laddie's glee
The youngsters sport aboot on me,
Nae mair the ladies come to see   15
     Bauld Mr W—
Come up an' strike the very T,
     He's sae auld farran'.

Nae mair upon my whinny breast
The bairns gang to seek the nest,   20

Nae mair wi' bonny blooms I'm drest
      In blythesome Spring –
For hooses noo they think I'm best,
      Or some sic thing.

Nae mair, when ends the Autumn days   25
The laddies rin to licht the blaze,
On stane an' lime they noo maun gaze
      Instead o'whins,
An' ower the ance broom covered braes
      The street noo rins.   30

Nae mair my birns shall eldin gie
Tae them wha haena cash tae pay
For sticks to licht their firies wi'
      To stand Cauld's shock;
Nae mair my grass shall pasture gie   35
      To passin' flock.

O! if you'd only hear my prayer,
An' just ae mament wee wad spare,
Tae keep thae men frae layin' bare
      My bosom wide,   40
An' drawin' my water frae me there
      Tae Burnside.

O, then hoo thankfu' I wad be,
An' ilka year that you wad see,
Whene'er John Frost wad visit me   45
      Wi' freezin' hand,
What roarin fun to you I'd gie
      At curlin' grand.

An sae I houp ye winna hain
Nae pains my glory to regain,   50
An' wipe aff me this deadlie stain;
      An' tho' I'm poor,
Yet while I live I'll aye remain,
      Your freend,
        THE MUIR

auld-farrant – old-fashioned   *birns – heather stems/roots*
eldin – fuel   *hain – spare trouble*

2. 'Consolation to the Muir of Alyth', by Trebor.
Published 30 January 1858.

This response poem appeared only a week after 'Complaint and Petition', and uses the same form and language to offer an alternative vision for the Muir's future. The references in the third stanza are to the severe economic downturn of 1857–58, linked to the end of the Crimean War (and Russia's consequent re-entry into the grain market) and the related 'Panic' in the United States. The difficult conditions of unemployed workers in these years and the need to supply material assistance was a constant topic in the *Journal*, as was the lack of good-quality housing for the poor. 'Trebor' is unidentified though 'horny hand' in l. 5 implies a male working-class writer.

*See also: 1. 'Complaint and Petition of the Muir of Alyth', p. 3;
3. 'Eik to Petition of the Muir of Alyth', p. 7; 7. 'Dialogue
Between the Auld Brig and the Burn', p. 14.*

Ye auld respected muirland friend,   1
I've heard yer "plaint" frae end to end,
And a' the comfort I can lend
    I'll here explain –
My horny hand I will extend,   5
    And ease yer pain.

But, friend, I think it's nae disgrace
Upon this toon, or a' the place,
To rouse ye up an' claw yer face
    Wi' heart an' skill   10
For then ye'll aid the human race
    Wi' better will.

And now, when Ruin's ruthless brand
Has sicken'd labour o'er the land,
And made its bluid an' wheels to stand   15
    As dull's a stane,
Ye'll fill the wyme and idle hand
    O mony a' ane.

They'll rid ye o' yer tatter'd claes,
Yer whin an' broom, an' bogs an' braes,   20

An' dress ye up, frae tap to taes,
      In verdure green,
And then ye'll bless the navvies' days –
      That will be seen.

And when yer dress'd and made afield,   25
An' stappit fu' o' seed an' dreel'd,
Ye'll gladden mony a cozie beild
      Wi' milk an' meal,
An' pack the wymes o' mony a chield
      Wi' spuds an' kale!   30

Then what a changed happy spot!
Instead o' curlin' stanes a cot!
Instead o' bogs a boilin' pot!
      An' cows an' kirns!
And here and there a braikit stot!   35
      (Nae blackie birns!)

Yer daisy gems will then be born,
Yer thistle, too, will raise its horn,
An' dockin blades amang yer corn
      Will sprout an' spread,   40
An' theeket stacks, when it is shorn,
      Will mak' ye glad.

On ilka knowe ye'll ha'e a cow!
In ilka crib a gruntin' sow!
An' ducks an' hens, an' whiles a doo!   45
      Will raise their noise,
While draps an' bits for ilka mou'
      Will crown yer joys!

Now, dinna scorn my consolation,
Nor startle at this reformation,   50
But rather crave yer cultivation,
      Bog an' yird,
And ye'll enjoy regeneration –
      Tak' my wird.
          TREBOR

wyme – stomach   *beild – place affording refuge or shelter (home)*
kirns – churns   *braikit stot – speckled/black and white bullock*
blackie birns – blackened heather-roots   *theeket – thatched*
ilka – every   *knowe – hill*
draps an' bits – scones, pieces of bread   *yird – the ground*

3. 'Eik to Petition of the Muir of Alyth', by The Muir. Published 27 February 1858.

This poem is the final of the three, and was the last publication in this sequence. Appearing nearly a month after the first pair, it assumes that readers will recall the exchange, deliberately referencing Trebor's 'Consolation' by citing his phrase 'horny han''. Permission to build a railway line incorporating Alyth was granted in 1858, and a station opened in the town on 12 August 1861. Alyth was thus connected to Dundee (eighteen miles away) as well as Perth, opening the possibility (as the poem notes) that it might become a commuter site or refuge from the industrial town for Dundee inhabitants.

See also: 1. 'Complaint and Petition of the Muir of Alyth', p. 3; 2. 'Consolation to the Muir of Alyth', p. 5; 7. 'Dialogue Between the Auld Brig and the Burn', p. 14.

Ye Alyth gentry! I've again   1
Ta'en up my ever-goin' pen,
Resolved aince mair to lat ye ken
    (You needna start),
What way and for I'd ha'e ye men'   5
    My broken heart!

If ye big hooses on my breast,
An' o' the land make yards the rest,
An' ha'e them a' wi' floories drest,
    An' bush an' tree,   10
Where bonny birds may big their nest
    Sae blythe to see!

Gi'e you these cots to wirkin' men,
Where, livin' quietly, they may ken
Something like bless, when free frae pain   15
    O' warl's care,

That happiness may be their ain
    "Beyond compare!"

An' if ye help the wirkin' man,
Wha honestly tries a' he can   20
Tae win his bread wi' "horny han',"
    Fu' blythe I'd be;
Then as ye like just cut an' plan
    An' big on me!

But I had heard, an' think it's true,   25
A Railway's to be brought tae you;
"An', then," I says, "am thinkin' noo
    'Twill be a case,
They'll hooses big for Dundee crew,
    An' me disgrace!"   30

An', thinkin' sae, I almost grat,
But noo I houp you'll no do that;
An' when ye ha'e some hooses gat
    Upon my soil,
You'll lat the puir man's parritch pat   35
    In them aye boil!

If you do that, O, then, you'll see,
You'll get nae mair complaints frae me;
But I will richt contented be,
    An' quietly rest,   40
While bonny bairns, wi' childish glee,
    Sport on my breast!
            Your freend,
               THE MUIR

eik – addition, supplement   *big – build*
grat – cried

4. 'A Young Rhymester's Address to the Editor', by Apollo, Alyth. Published 1 May 1858.

One of many *Journal* poems about the practice of poetry, this takes a typically exalted view of the poet's role by associating it with love of nature and God, rather than with the pursuit of fame and fortune. Such attitudes are satirised in poems like 'My First Attempt'. The author is unidentified, though he or she published several other poems in the *Journal*, including 'The Dundee Maiden'.

See also: 6. 'The Dundee Maiden', p. 12; 42. 'The Bard of Caldervale', p. 70; 72. 'My First Attempt', p. 122.

Think not I wish to tread the path to fame,   1
    It's not for that intent my lyre I string,
For fame doth rust, and honour's but a name,
    Both vain and fading are the joys they bring.

My harp I'll tune to sing of nature's praise,   5
    Her mountains, valleys, and her seas and lakes.
In every work perfection she displays.
    And beauty dwells in every thing she makes.

In every work of nature we might see
    The working of a great Creator's hand.   10
How beautiful he's formed each flower and tree,
    And given to man a smiling fertile land.

I'll study nature and her works sublime –
    In her deep solitudes I love to stray,
To mark her works untouched by hoary time,   15
    While man's best works fall mouldering in decay.

Of nature only though I wish to sing,
    Yet led by fancy sometimes I will rove,
And all unconscious I will touch a string
    That doth bring forth the thrilling notes of love.   20

Though I have said that nature is my theme,
    Why should my harp to love a stranger be?
Some say that love is an enchanting dram,
    I know not yet, but I will taste and see.

And should I drain the cup of love too deep,   25
    And find it bitter, I will taste no more,
But lay my harp in silence down to sleep,
    In peace to rest, and bid its songs be o'er.

5. [Untitled] 'I sigh not for greatness', by A Son of St Tammas, Arbroath, April, 1858. Published 26 June 1858.

'A Son of St Tammas' was the pseudonym of David Carnegie, who worked in a power-loom factory in Arbroath. Although he does not link his poems to this pseudonym in his pamphlet collection, *Lays and Lyrics from the Factory* (Arbroath: Thomas Buncle, 1879) (which includes this poem, pp. 66–67), he notes he has been so long known to 'fellow-townsmen' as 'an occasional contributor to the local press that the collection of my scattered pieces in a permanent form might have been expected sooner or later.' (Preface) His work appears several times in these years in the *Journal*. This poem is characteristic of many in emphasising the hardships of working life and incorporating radically tinged criticism of societal structures, yet espousing Christian humility and finding apparent redress in the dignity of labour and in happy domestic life.

See also: 8. *'Think For Yourselves', p. 16; 39. 'Hold Up Your Head, p. 67.*

        "As I voyage on life's tide,
        What's my aim, and wha's my guide."

I sigh not for greatness, I pine not for power,   1
Earth's proudest of monarchs may fall in an hour;
Swift, swift from his grasp may his vaunted powers fly,
And he, like a felon, forced to flee or to die;
And the friends of his greatness – the mean-hearted crowd –   5
Will curse him when fallen, as they prais'd him while *proud*,

I strive not for wealth, that the poor I might drive –
By the sweat of another I want not to thrive:
How mean is his soul who, for base sordid gain,
Keeps labour pent up in a dark fetid den!   10
Sad experience doth teach, tho' the charge may seem brave,
That the close-crowded mill is half-way to the grave.

Tho' unknown alike unto fortune and fame,
The wrongs of the suff'ring I'll boldly proclaim;
Tho' feeble my efforts, the *aim* of my mind   15
Is to take for life's *guide* Christ's law to mankind:
Ye mighty of earth, in your pomp and your pride,
Obey ye its dictates, and make it your guide.

Religion is hollow and worthless, I ween,
When only deck'd up for a Sabbath-day scene.   20
If it guides not life's course, it seems useless to me,
And as false as the prayer of the old Pharisee:
True religion consists not in churches and creeds,
Our belief's in our works, and our faith's in our deeds.

As a Scotchman, I love my own native land,   25
And revere the bright deeds of that brave little band
Who fought 'gainst the Prelate, the Peer, and the Crown,
And who bought with their blood that freedom we own;
Yet, I sadly deplore, the proud lords of the soil
Are neglecting to cherish the brave sons of toil.   30

Tho' lowly my lot, I have joys not a few:
Four children to cherish – a wife kind and true –
By the blessing of heav'n, and my toil at the loom,
I'll strive Want's dark shadow to keep from our room;
And may no hungry wand'rer unfed leave my door –   35
He's a brother of mine, tho' he's ragged and poor.

6. 'The Dundee Maiden', by Apollo, Alyth, 1858. Published 3 July 1858.

Deserted maidens are a staple of popular newspaper verse, as are romantic heroines associated with or first encountered in a particular local place. This poem, which begins as a generic poem about a lover's absence, turns to a patriotic commentary on the British Army and the Indian Mutiny of 1858, in which the maiden's lover will be killed. In common with a number of poems in this collection, it thus highlights the contribution that Scots made to the imperial exploits of the British Army and the ways in which Dundee and the Tay were linked to imperial networks of travel, trade and labour. 'Apollo' is also the author of 'A Young Rhymester's Address'.

See also: 4. 'A Young Rhymester's Address to the Editor', p. 9; 16. 'The Lass o' Broughty Ferry', p. 29; 89. 'Isandula', p. 157; 102. 'Victory', p. 180; 103. 'The Battle of Tel-el-Kebir', p. 182.

A maiden sits 'neath a spreading yew   1
    Near the Dundee Ferry Road,
Her eyes are bent on the waters blue,
    And her seat is the grassy sod;
While silent she breathes a prayer anew,   5
    To her own and her father's God.

To that spot she steals to vent her woe
    At morning and evening grey,
To pray that the angels may guard each blow
    Off him that is far away;   10
And to watch the ships move to and fro
    On the breast of the briny Tay.

Her elbow rests on her bended knee,
    And her cheek leans on her hand –
Her thoughts are with him that's across the sea,   15
    Who fights in a distant land;
A tear drops down from her wat'ry e'e,
    And falls in the muddy sand.

Some jealous thoughts rise in her mind,
    Of the maids of the sunny south,   20

And Hope in her bosom is lagging behind,
    While Faith struggles hard for the truth,
She fears he some Indian fair maid may find,
    And forget the betrothed of his youth.

"Away, away! such childish fears,   25
    Let not Fear Hope subdue:
For a British garb my lover wears,
    And each British heart is true;
He'll fight his way through the pointed spears
    Of that Sepoy rebel crew."   30

But the angel of death a round shot bears
    To his warm heart's inmost core;
And alas! who shall dry that maiden's tears
    That waits on our native shore,
When the sad unexpected news she hears   35
    That her love can return no more?

And who shall dry each mother's eyes,
    When she hears that her son is slain?
Or comfort the widow whose husband dies
    In a land across the main?   40
For many's a hero in India lies,
    That we never can see again.

7. 'Dialogue Between the Auld Brig and the Burn, Overheard in a Certain Village Not Twenty Miles from Dundee', by David M. Eli. Published 10 July 1858.

David M. Eli is unidentified, as is the village he mentions in the title. He does not seem to have published other poems in the *Journal* or *Friend* in these decades. Like the 'Muir of Alyth' series, this 'Dialogue' adopts the voice of natural or built objects in order to make a case for (or against) redevelopment and improvement. In this case, the plea is for a village bridge to be repaired in time to help it withstand the winter floods: the poem is also a dialogue between youth (the burn) and old age (the bridge).

See also: 1. 'Complaint and Petition of the Muir of Alyth', p. 3; 2. 'Consolation to the Muir of Alyth', p. 5; 3. 'Eik to Petition of the Muir of Alyth', p. 7.

BRIG   1
Ay, there ye rin wi' constant splash,
An' aye against my ribs ye dash;
Ye've run the lime frae aff my stanes,
An' left me naething but my banes;   5
No even them, for – hang your greed! –
You're rinnin' them awa' wi' speed;
For ilka day my arch is crumblin',
Some awesome hour I'll doon be tumblin';
But that is nought to you ava,   10
You only wish I was awa,
I'm sure you needna wish me doon,
I've been a blessin' to the toon;
An' will be yet for mony a year,
If your mischief you'd just forbear.   15
BURN
I say, you queer auld-fashioned creatur,
Gie me nae mair o' your ill natur –
But I forgi'e you, for I ken
You're getting' auld an' near your en';   20
For me ilka drap I hae's new born,
What I'm the day I'll be the morn,
Except my crystal fountain head
Dries up within its rocky bed

Amang the hills, where springs fu' clear   25
The streamlet pure which ripples here.
I've done my best to save you aye,
I've run a channel doon this wye,
Sae deep and far frae you an' a',
I hardly ever touch ava   30
Your reverend form, and just for fear
I'd do you ill, and bring a tear
Frae ilka toonsman ower your ruins,
An' no be thankit for my doin's.
But when the cheery spring is felt,   35
An' winter snaw begins to melt,
An' ice, that kept me in its jaws,
Begins to yield to Nature's laws
An' torrents frae the hills a' pourin'
Join wi' my luckless waters roarin',   40
Then doon I come, and canna help it,
Altho' your side I firmly skelp it;
For, roarin' wide frae bank to brae,
Sweeps everything within my way,
An' brigs and dams come tumblin' doon,   45
A' sets afloat the half itoon;
An', faith, you'd need to thank the men
Wha biggit you, for this I ken,
They've biggit strong, or else by noo
Your stane an' lime wad baith been throo,   50
An' no ae vestige o' ye seen
To mark the spot where you had been.
But, passin' rain an' snaw an' ice,
I'll gie you noo a gude advice:
You see I canna help your state,   55
Tho' sorry for your backart fate;
You should draw oot a lang petition,
Richt settin' forth your true condition,
An' then I have nae doot you'd find
You wad be mendit to your mind;   60
Ilk chink and crevice wad be filled,
An' youthfu' strength in you instilled.
But first afore you tried ava,
You'd better wait a week or twa –
Somebody's maybe heard oor crack,   65
An' maybe he'll it public mak;

You needna push, at ony rate,
Nor fear e'noo a muckle spate.
BRIG
You've spoken unco weel, I wot,   70
An', troth, I winna say you not;
But, losh, I wish some wanderin' bard,
In passin' bye, has overheard;
An' if there has, O may he prent it –
'Twould do me gude, if he but kent it.   75
June, 1858   Reported by DAVID M. ELI

ava – at all   unco – very, remarkably (intensifying adjective)
skelp – to smack, hit   muckle – great

8. 'Think for Yourselves', by J. M. Published 5 March 1859.

By an unidentified author, this poem exemplifies the *Journal*'s attitude towards self-improvement and the cultivation of reason and thoughtfulness in working men. In supporting 'free-thinking' on all subjects and implying that this will help the poor to recognise their wrongs, it would also have been read as politically radical.

See also: 5. 'I sigh not for greatness', p. 10; 39. 'Hold Up Your Head', p. 67.

Think for yourselves, ye o'er laboured poor –   1
    Think aright on the cause of your wrongs –
So shall ye escape from the ills ye endure:
    Such power to free-thinking belongs.

As the fair fruits of earth are by sunshine and shower   5
    To a healthful maturity brought,
So action, progressive and pregnant with power,
    Is the product of untrammel'd thought.

Then think for yourselves, free and fearlessly think –
    Dive deeply, soar high, scan around;   10
From the fountains for truth be still ready to drink,
    By whoe'er or where'er they are found.

9. 'The Shepherd's Song', by Factorius, Dundee, 1859. Published 10 September 1859.

This song, adopting the classical pastoral trope of an idle shepherd playing his flute and singing, seems positioned in contrast to the labour implied by the pseudonym 'Factorius'. While there are many traditional as well as contemporary songs about the banks of the Tay, this one appeared at the point at which controversy was raging over the railway companies' purchase of the Tay banks and the consequent loss of access for the people of Dundee. John and William Leng of the *Journal* and *Dundee Advertiser* were active in opposing this.

See also: 16. 'The Lass o' Broughty Ferry', p. 29.

The time is noon o' summer's day,	1
The scene the bonny banks o' Tay,	
Where deep o'erhanging woods the stream	
Shade from the noontide's scorching beam.	
Reclined beneath the friendly shade,	5
A shepherd at his ease is laid,	
Who tunes at times the "rustic reed,"	
With dulcet sound the time to speed;	
Or, anon, thus he sweetly sings,	
While Echo with the music rings:	10
And still thou flowest on, bright stream,	
Through forest, glen, and glade;	
Now brightening in the sunny beam,	
Now darkening in the shade.	
And from thy banks sweet infancy	15
Hath gleaned the summer flowers,	
And youthful Love hath spent by thee	
A world of happy hours.	
And Age doth come at evening grey,	
His boyhood haunts to view;	20
Each well-remembered creek and bay	
He views with joy anew.	
And Joy hath sported in the wood	
That skirts thy crystal wave,	
And Misery beneath thy flood	25
Hath sought and found a grave,	
And still thou flowest on, bright stream,	

Through forest, glen, and glade:
Our lives evanish like a dread,
Thy course is never staid.   30

10. 'The Subscription to Garibaldi', by Pro Libertate, Dundee, 18 June 1860. Published 23 June 1860.

In May 1860, Giuseppe Garibaldi led his famous expedition to
Sicily, and achieved a notable victory for the cause of Italian uni-
fication. Like the British press more broadly, the *Journal* was
hugely in support of Garibaldi and the Italian cause and
reported extensively on his campaigns, which were viewed as a
fight for liberty and self-determination, as well as an effort
against the tyranny of the Roman Catholic church. The Scottish
press and people had been particularly active in raising support:
John McAdam of Glasgow led the plea for donations to help
Garibaldi, and eventually a group of Scottish volunteers were
funded to travel to Italy and join the fight. Garibaldi was fre-
quently compared in speeches, poems and editorials to the great
Scottish heroes William Wallace and Robert Bruce (and later
repaid the favour by contributing to the costs of the Wallace
Monument). This poem invites readers to contribute to the
subscription fund and expresses the shared excitement at Gari-
baldi's stirring victories.

*See also: 11. 'Garibaldi's Soliloquy on the Modern Scottish
Muse', p. 20.*

The sceptres of tyrants are falling around us,   1
     Tyranny totters and shakes on its throne;
And say, shall the heroes who battle for freedom,
     Know not a friend, shall they fight it alone?

O, say, shall we coldly and carelessly linger,   5
     Nor offer our aid to the good and the brave –
To those who for freedom and country are fighting,
     Determined to conquer, or win them a grave.

Shall we, who have never 'neath despot's oppression
     Been prostrate, nor known vilest tyranny's pains,   10
Calmly look on, while the slave and the bondman
     Is hurling from off him his thrice hated chains?

Shall we, whose lov'd country in happiest freedom,
    Is free from the dread of the tyrant in state,
While down-trodden hundreds 'gainst tyrants are pitted, 15
    Inactive the issue of battle await?

No, no; we shall pray that the gallant may conquer,
    That they who for honour and liberty fight
May win, and that he who presideth in battle
    May conquer for those who contend for the right.   20

We give them our prayers, and who could deny them?
    But more let us do, we shall tender them aid;
Let us help them to smite down their cowardly foemen,
    Let us put in the hands of each bondman a blade.

And then when we've done what we can in their succour, 25
    Calmly we'll wait till the conflict is o'er,
Till the glad shout ariseth and filleth the Heavens,
    Tyranny's baffled, is conquer'd once more.

And O, should the bonds of the bondslaves be broken,
    The thanks of the freed shall float over the wave,   30
And we'll joy for those words of sweet sympathy spoken,
    The aid that we gave to the strong and the brave.

11. 'Garibaldi's Soliloquy on the Modern Scottish Muse'. Unsigned. Kinghorn, 1860. Published 17 November 1860.

This unsigned poem is a humorous response to the flood of pro-Garibaldi poetry published in the Scottish press in 1860, in which Garibaldi himself speaks to express his dismay at the reams of bad poetry inspired by his exploits. It alludes to poems mentioned and quoted in the 'To Correspondents' column (by 'Queen Moon' and others). The switch to Scots in the final lines emphasises the humorous point that local poets should stick to Scottish subject-matter. 'Bomba' is the nickname of Ferdinand II, King of the Two Sicilies and one of Garibaldi's opponents, who had died in 1859. The reference (line 9) to the 1601 execution of Robert Devereux, 2nd Earl of Essex, by Queen Elizabeth, may refer to Sir Walter Raleigh, who watched the execution, though its rationale here is unclear.

See also: 10. 'The Subscription to Garibaldi', p. 18; 81. 'Burns's Lament', p. 140.

" 'Tis a strange world we live in," some one writes,   1
And I can well believe what he indites;
For instance, 'tis a strange thing, yet how civil,
To find me here, and Bomba at the devil.
But not so strange, that mists produce consumption –   5
Certes, that's well seen in Scotch poetic gumption,
Which lives in gen'ral much like him, but lower,
When hailed that fatal morning in the Tower –
"My lord of Essex dies this very hour."
Oh! never sure could such a muse be found –   10
Seek Pantagon, seek all the world around;
No fall'n Greece, nor Rome, not Italy's self
Could bring forth such incubae, ev'n for pelf,
As at this crisis deluge ev'ry day
The Scottish Press, especially north of Tay.   15
What! can nought serve the driv'llers for their rhyme
Save my poor father's honoured patronyme?
Where shall it end, or what be the next bout?
Will no one rise and snuff these blinkers out?
Like yelping puppies, in their fond caresses   20
They but defame me, as these soil our dresses.
Amongst a host of others, "Queen Moon" comes forth
(Moonstruck, of course – true *nat'ral* of the north),

And lowly christens, nay, actually chimes,
His spawn an ode, in ode-defying rhymes.   25
Not yet content, too dull to feel the nip
Of Monsieur Editor's ironic quip.
He takes it lit'ral, though almost philippic,
And flaming vaunts he'll write, at once, an epic.
An epic – Ha! What – and make me his hero?   30
By Jove! the thought transforms me to a Nero.
I'll have him hanged. But no, the rogue can't dare –
Or, if he does, I hereby vow and swear,
I'll rouse the terra and infernal gods,
Or call for vengeance at the muse of –   35
That wag of Fife, whose mettlesome Pegasus
Delights in funking all such braying asses.
But I must pause, or I shall lose my gravity,
And then the lieges may well doubt my suavity;
Besides, the fools'-heads are grown now so green   40
They'll scarce perceive what my reflections mean.
Wow, wad the creatures min' their single carritch,
Or stint their rhyme to 'postrophise their parritch,
Their brose-cogs, kail, or saucy barley-bannocks –
The first might mend their hearts, the lave their stammaks – 45
An' leave me, an' my spurtle-blade, sae fain,
We'll last the langer that we're lat alane.

single carritch – the Shorter Catechism
brose-cogs – cups/tubs of brose (oatmeal with milk or water)   lave – the rest
spurtle-blade – broadsword (often sardonic, from spurtle = spatula (for stirring
porridge))

12. 'Poem on the Forfar Volunteers'. Unsigned. Published 3 August 1861.

As the poetry columns of the *Journal* became established, the editors took to publishing and satirising extracts from poorly written verses sent to the paper in the 'To Correspondents' column. Occasionally, if a 'bad' poem was deemed amusing enough, they would reproduce it in full with a satirical note. Errors of spelling, punctuation and layout were presumed to have come from the author. This poem is more entertaining to readers because it is one of many celebrating the new Rifle Volunteers movement, in which local militias were formed across Britain as a defence against possible invasion from France. The Volunteer movement was enormously popular in these years, and towns competed for the best showing: a number of patriotic poems on the Volunteers appeared in the Scottish press. Alfred Tennyson's call to join the Volunteers, 'Riflemen, Form!', written for the *Times*, was perhaps the most widely re-printed British newspaper poem of these decades. Because Scottish towns valued their literary reputation (in early years, the *Journal* listed poetic competition entries by town, to show which towns could boast the greatest number of poets), Forfar residents would doubtless have been horrified by this publication.

See also: 14. [Letter to editor], p. 25; 15. 'Odd to a Krokis', p. 27; 18. 'On Top of the Law', p. 32; 26. 'Apostroffe to the Rainbow', p. 46; 30. 'Kale-Wurms', p. 52; 31. 'An Epissel to Poute', p. 54; 80. 'An Address to Thee Tay Bridge', p. 138.

The following effusion is in every way so precious that we grieve to cut it down. We give it with a few slight omissions, nothing doubting that it will be read with absorbing interest, not only by the Forfar Volunteers, but by every one in whose bosom there is the smallest scintilla of patriotism, not to say of poetry:–

O Why the duce should we not go	1
Or have aney douts or Feares	
For we are all come soldiers hight	
We ill go and Join the volunteers	
For we are sworn to Perteck victoria our queen	5
Annd all the rest of her Peers	
And who would not serve where glory to be seen	
Along with the Brave volunteers	

For now we are threatened abroad and at home
But britain is ready so let them come on   10
For we are as well desciplind and every way right
As many Brave vetrans abroad at the fight
likewise ammunition and each warlike store
Which never belongd to Forfar before
Brave Forsyth is captain expert in the law   15
And for its protection his sword he will draw
And tho in a Battle he never has been
he will soon equal many who have the war seen
And the rest of his privates is Blooming young men
that never will stand Back   20
When wars in the Plain
We have sergeants and corporals and drummers
        likewise
and music that Forfar could not despise
and some of those acting as true Private men   25
Are equal to any in Forfar again
Now if any danger should happen to come
From any foren power or rebel at home
Our brave volunteers will then play thear part
And make all our enemies sadly to smart   30
And then they'ill be soldiers not only in name
But acts will perpetuate their warlike fame
And with the rest numbered of so greate renown
Will be the defenders of good Forfar town
And may we be loyal and always at hand   35
and ready to march at the word of command.

13. 'Epistle to Tammas Bodkin', by Hawthorn, Aberdeen. Published 31 August 1861.

'Tammas Bodkin' (pseudonym of author and editor William Latto) was the *Journal*'s most successful creation and features regularly throughout this period. Bodkin, a tailor, was the supposed author of a series of comic Scots prose pieces about his opinions and adventures, and about his life with his wife, Tibbie. Readers adored Bodkin and frequently produced poems, letters and prose pieces both in praise of him and imitating his style, colluding in the shared pretence that he was a real person. From 1864 onwards, Latto published collected editions of his Bodkin pieces. 'Hawthorn' is unidentified, though his Aberdeen signature shows the *Journal*'s increasing popularity beyond Dundee and its environs. The 'Epistle' form, which the *Journal* poets would have been familiar with from Robert Burns and other eighteenth-century writers, was very popular, and often deployed to address other contributors – real and fictional – to the *Journal*.

See also: 31. 'An Epissel to Poute', p. 54; 66. 'Epistle to Tammas Bodkin', p. 112; 97. 'Reminiscences of the People's Journal', p. 171.

Bodkin, my frien', I've never seen   1
    Ye're face, an' yet I lo'e ye dearly,
Wi' a' my heart; tho' far apart,
    I fancy I can see thee clearly.

Ye're country strolls, o'er sunny knolls,   5
    To read them gae me muckle pleasure;
Whate're ye do, we look for't noo,
    As tho' it were for hidden treasure.

Lang may ye write, baith day an' night,
    O' a' ye're deeds, misdeeds, an' doings;   10
An' gin ye've time, gae back langsyne,
    An' tell us o' ye're loves an' wooings.

Atweel, I'm sure ye've been a wooer,
    Whase hinnied words thrilled mony a blossom;
An' mony a maid, I've heard it said,   15
    Wept ye claspt Tibbie to ye're bosom.

She's yours for life, a faithfu' wife,
    Wha maks ye're hame aye blithe an' cheery;
Her sweet smiles cheer, when care sits near,
    Be sure an' loe, till death, ye're deary.   20

But I maun close this rhyming prose,
    I am nae poet, mairs the pity:
If north ye be look out for me,
    The "Hawthorn" o' the Granite City.

14. Untitled [Letter to Editor], by Poute. Published in 'To Correspondents' under sub-heading 'Genuine "Poute-ry"', 5 October 1861.

'Poute', the pseudonym of Alexander 'Sandy' Burgess, a dancing-master and violinist of local fame in Fife, began publication with 'Lines addressed to a Water Lily', extracted to be ridiculed in 'To Correspondents' on 7 September 1861 (mentioned in line 15 below). This inaugurated a relationship with the *Journal* that was to last until Burgess' suicide in 1886, and which led to the publication of a volume of his verse by the Dundee Advertiser Office, *The Book of Nettercaps, Being Genuine Poutery, Poetry and Prose*, in 1875. This untitled poem – an angry letter about his treatment by the editor – marked Poute's second publication in the *Journal*, and at this stage editor and readers had seemingly not realised that rather than simply being amusing examples of 'bad' verse, Poute's poems were clever and sophisticated satires on the level of education and poetic skill that might be expected from a 'natures poet'. He deliberately created a persona of the local poet deluded about his own poetic talent and self-satisfied with his productions. His poems frequently reference news reports from the *Journal*, such as the comment below on its announcement that circulation had reached 33,000, and address editor and readers directly. Poute's poems spawned a host of imitators in the same style in the Dundee press. His longstanding relationship with the *Journal* suggests that in terms of circulation he was one of the best-known comic poets of Victorian Scotland, though the difficulty of reading his verse, especially those poems in phonetic Scots, doubtless limited his circulation across Britain. Poute was associated by contemporaries with popular American prose humorists Artemus Ward and Josh Billings, who used a similar style. All errors, including those of spelling, punctuation and layout, are deliberate and reproduced as closely as possible to the *Journal* copy.

See also: 12. *'Poem on the Forfar Volunteers'*, *p. 22*; 15. *'Odd to a Krokis'*, *p. 27*; 26. *Apostroffe to the Rainbow'*, *p. 46*; 30. *'Kale-Wurms'*, *p. 52*; 31. *'An Epissel to Poute'*, *p. 54*; 60. *'Gouldings Manur'*, *p. 101*; 80. *'An Address to Thee Tay Bridge'*, *p. 138*.

Lundin Mill Oct. one　　　　　　　　　　　1

　　Sir.

Youve surly gotin your stamik cleen.

For you have lately spewed much spleen.

your korispondints all Rank and file.　　　　　　　　　　5

Are like yourself Mighty Spittirs of Bile.

its them and you has much to ansir.

for me. i am above ether your praise or sencir.

I sore aloft in regons high.

beyond the reach of all you small fry.　　　　　　　　　10

I say yet I am self taught. a natures poet.

and well does your poor meen critiks know it.

But tho ive got small edication.

ive raised your Journals circulation.

My lily made your Reedars all to wonder.　　　　　　　15

and caused you to print thirty three thousand hunder.

But like all poets sprung from the ranks.

from you ive only got the divil for my thanks.

For your crew of critiks I care not 1 straw.

if I had Them here I there necks would thraw.　　　　20

With them and you I Wish not to be yokit.

ive wrote this poem cause ive been sair provokit.

Pirhaps youl styld again 1. Of the poute kin'

but sir im nether feard at you nor auld tam Bodkin

Im nether vain conceited nor a foole.　　　　　　　　25

Sir I ance was offered to tech oor skul.

Poute.

15. 'Odd to a Krokis', by Poute. Published under title 'Original Poute–ry', 22 March 1862.

Poute's references to how publication of his poems increased the journal's circulation, and to his resentment that contributors were not paid for poetry, became a running joke in his publications; in part because, by spring of 1862, his poems were already a substantial draw for readers. As his note mentions, a correspondent ('A. M.') had recently requested a new poem by Poute. Poute's notes to the editor were always published with, and as part of, the poem. 'Odd to a Krokis' satirises the genre of seasonal flower poetry and odes on the coming of spring, and sets up a 'moral' about poets who, like the crocus, come out before the time is ripe. The opening references to Apollo, Burns and Alexander Pope are typical of Poute's allusiveness and sly references to the accepted canon and its norms. He also liked to insert footnotes or 'marginal notes' offering his own critical commentary or explanation on his lines, as in the 'good' comment below.

See also: 14. 'Untitled [Letter to Editor]', p. 25; 26. 'Apostroffe to the Rainbow', p. 46; 30. 'Kale-Wurms', p. 52; 31. 'An Epissel to Poute', p. 54; 60. 'Gouldings Manur', p. 101; 80. 'An Address to Thee Tay Bridge', p. 138.

Leven Old Saat Pans

MASTR EDITOR – DEAR CUR, – when i sent you my first peese of peotry on the water lily on the 7 of Sep your circilation was just 30000500 when i sent you my last to wut "largo brig" your reders had increetsed to 34000400 and now you are up to 38000800   .   as it is 3 Months sinse i sent you any skrap and as "a.m." gives me a reminder in your last i beg to in sure you that My silinse has been from no dispeck to you But as you will see from the dat of the enklosed odd that i have changed my residins to soot my bizness i have always been bizy that is one resin.   another is that your circilation is now so inormous that you dont stand much in need of any peotry from me but if you should ever stand in need of my sirvicis or if you want another 8000 reders adit to your list you have no more to do than let me know and i will do my best to lift you up.   with best wishes to you and all your printers. – i remain

poute

P s – i alwas take a pleshure to korispond with those
    which has a taste to kultivate the sublime   .
                ODD TO A KROKIS.   1
                    Febryurry
                        4
                                                    leven saat pans
selestial apoley which Didest inspire.   5
the souls of burns and pop with sackred fir.
kast thy Mantil over me When i shal sing.
the praiz Of A sweat flower who grows in spring.
Which has of late kome under the Fokis
of My eyes.   it is called a krokis.   10
sweat lovly pretty littil sweat Thing.
you bloometh before The lairicks on High sing.
thy lefs art neither Red Nor yelly.
but Just betwixt the two you hardy felly.
i fear you; yet be Nippit with the frost.   15
As Maney a one has known to there kost.
you should have not kome out in such a hurrey.
As this is only the Month of Febrywurrey.
and you may expick yet Much bad wethir,
when all your blads will krunkil up like Burnt leather.   20
alas.   alas.   theres Men which tries to rime.
who have like you kome out befor there time*.
the Moril of My peese depend upon it.
is good so here I End my odd or conit.
                    poute   25
            *good

16. 'The Lass o' Broughty Ferry', by G. D., Dundee Asylum, March 1862. Published 5 April 1862.

This is included as a typical example of poems in praise of a local maiden, which rest heavily on tropes familiar from song and earlier verse. Such poems invariably compare the chosen maiden to women from other locations known to the readers, and celebrate the beauty of the Scottish countryside through which the lovers will wander. The author is probably George Duthie (no relation to poet Jane Duthie, also included in this volume), who was a shoemaker at the Royal Lunatic Asylum, Dundee, for twenty-five years (Edwards, 7, p. 346). Broughty Ferry is four miles east of Dundee city centre, and in these decades was in the process of being transformed into a suburban retreat for the wealthier inhabitants of Dundee.

See also: 6. 'The Dundee Maiden', p. 12; 9. 'The Shepherd's Song', p. 17; 18. 'On Top of the Law', p. 32.

Fair blooms the briar on Dighty's braes;   1
    By winding Dean the broom fu' yellow;
Glen Islay busks in birks and slaes;
    Sweet Earn sings through howms sae mellow.
But sweeter, purer beauty beams   5
    Around my young, my artless Mary;
She's pride o' Scotia's queen o' streams –
    The bonnie lass o' Broughty Ferry.

Though famed St Johnston's dames display
    Their costly charms in scen'ry flowery,   10
Or grandeur deck, in rich array,
    The maidens o' the Carse o' Gowrie;
Though sweet Dundee's fair vestals flare
    In silken sheen, sae cauldly airy,
Their artfu' graces ne'er compare   15
    Wi' her's – the lass o' Broughty Ferry.

Give me the lovely banks o' Tay,
    Or Craigie's gowany glen sae grassy,
In gloamin's gowden hour to stray,
    And fondly press my bonnie lassie.   20
Let false ambition roam the sea,
    The wealth o' ither lands to herry –

Contented I will live an' dee
   Wi' my sweet lass o' Broughty Ferry.

busk – dress   birks and slaes – birch trees and sloes
howm – meadow   gowan – gorse bush
herry – plunder

17. 'To My Husband', by E. J., A Factory Girl. Tay Works, Dundee. Published 9 August 1862.

'E. J.' is Ellen Johnston, 'The Factory Girl', one of Victorian Britain's best-known working-class women poets. Johnston, working in Dundee in this period, had a limited relationship with the Dundee press compared to her imminent celebrity as a poet in the Glasgow *Penny Post*, but did publish several poems in the *Journal* in this period. Her biographer, H. Gustav Klaus, has noted that this poem broke with standard norms by naming the author's husband, and it is an unusually assertive statement of love and desire from a woman newspaper poet (p. 63). It is also, perhaps unintentionally, humorous in describing her husband's lack of beauty. Johnston never married, so the stated relationship here is fictional. Her life, including details of her time in Dundee and her debut as a newspaper poet in 1854, is recounted on her own terms in the well-known 'Autobiography' that prefaces her *Autobiography, Poems and Songs* (Glasgow: William Love, 1867). This poem is included as 'The Absent Husband' (p. 27).

See also: 24. 'The Opening of the Baxter Park', p. 43.

'Tis evening – the sun hath nigh sunk in the West,   1
And its last golden ray gilds the Tay's silver breast,
Whilst its waters flow onward to oceans afar,
I will sing a love song unto thee, Samuel Carr.

'Tis the wife of thy bosom – the loved of thy heart –   5
That doth now call upon thee her love to impart;
And with truth's golden fingers I'll strike love's guitar,
And the theme of my muse shall be thee, Samuel Carr.

I am lonely and languid, my love, without thee,
Like to one that's forsaken I roam by the Dee.   10

But though distance divide us, death only can mar
My heart's deep communion with thee, Samuel Carr.

Ah! the River of Fidoch between us may flow,
And Craigellachie's mountains with heather bells blow,
But no rivers or mountains can ever debar   15
Thy form from memory, my own Samuel Carr.

It is not thy beauty in fancy I see,
For Nature did ne'er give that charm unto thee;
But thy fond faithful heart, it is dearer by far,
Than beauty's impression to me, Samuel Carr.   20

Though the stern breath of fate hath now blasted our
     hopes
Still my heart is unchanged, love's spell yet unbroke;
For that dark 'Retrospect' it can never wage war
With a guide for the future like thee, Samuel Carr.

O'er the Tay's silvery bosom night's curtain is flung,   25
Now my muse it is hush'd, and my love song is sung;
And the young infant moon hails the bright evening star,
Fare-thee-well my beloved one. Adieu, Samuel Carr.

18. 'On Top of the Law', by A. F. M. Published 4 October 1862.

This poem is nicely ambiguous in terms of whether it is deliberate (like Poute) or not (like the 'Forfar Volunteers'). The editor, perhaps mindful of what had happened with Poute, gives no steer to readers. Thus the poem is both a sincere poem about romance in a local setting, and a parody of such poems. The Law hill is very important in the poetic geography of Dundee, and the setting for many songs and poems of courtship; this poem might also hint at the sexual escapades associated with local beauty spots, 'its excusable on top of the law'. The author and stated tune for this song are unidentified.

See also: 12. 'Poem on the Forfar Volunteers', p. 22; 16. 'The Lass o' Broughty Ferry', p. 29.

to the tune of "nothing more"
one day I wandered up a hill   1
over nothing but grass and stone
till on the top I stood quite still
all by myself I thought alone
But as I stood looking around   5
and wondering at what I saw
a lovely maiden appeared from the ground
and said "sir you are on top of the law"

she said "there is the river tay
and see in the distance the vast sea   10
and that is fife you see over the way
and beneath us is Bonny Dundee
and there you see the sibley hills
which has stood since the time of noah
oh such scenery, me with gladness fills   15
whenever I stand on top of the law"

so I shyly smiled upon her
as we then went wandering on,
and assured her upon my honour
that she was a beautiful one   20
then took her hand, looked in her eyes
and kissed her when she said "oh lor!"

but I said "let it not you surprise
for its excusable on top of the law"

then every day I met her   25
in the same place to see
and told her she had better
become a loving wife to me
so one day the parson made us one
and oh how I love her and adore   30
and I allways bless the day I won
the lovely maiden on top of the law

19. 'Nan Tamson's Wean', by J. E. Watt, Montrose. Published 22 November 1862.

James E. Watt was a self-taught working man (employed in brass-finishing and then as a weaver in a flax mill in Montrose) and a relatively well-known newspaper poet, who specialised in narrative Scots verse about contemporary life (Edwards, 1, p. 73). His 1880 collection, *Poetical Sketches of Scottish Life and Character*, was published from John Leng's newspaper office in Dundee ('Nan Tamson's Wean' is reprinted pp. 123–24). Watt published more extensively in the *People's Friend* (appearing in its first issue in 1869) than in the *Journal*. This poem features a characteristic narrative of the mid-Victorian period in inciting support for the temperance movement by depicting the suffering child of a drunken mother. Like most newspapers, the *Journal* supported temperance; a note from 10 January 1863 rejecting a poem in praise of whisky stated, 'Our desire is to discourage the drinking customs of the present age, and we should like our correspondents in their contributions to do the same.' Sentimental poems about suffering, homeless, mistreated children were also enormously popular in newspaper poetry columns, and were central in arguments about the need for social and political reform in various causes. Typically, the dying child's hard life on earth is here redeemed in death, when angels take him to heaven.

See also: 27. 'The Chappin' Laddie', p. 48; 50. 'The Herd Laddie', p. 83; 77. 'Rapidly, Rapidly', p. 132.

At the edge o' the e'en when keen was the air,   1
An' Winter-wrapt forests look'd dowie an' bare;
The bleak norlin' win' cam' sae piercin' an' chill,
Owre cauld wreaths o' snaw that lay thick on the hill;
Yet though the win' fra a cauld airt was blawin,   5
An' dark shades o' e'enin sae fastly were fa'in
Alane on the road a bit laddie was seen
'Twas drucken Nan Tamson's puir wanderin' Wean.

A' day he'd been ca'in the hail Parish through,
For a dud to his back, or a bit to his mou';   10
An' wae were his looks, for his heartie was sair,
As he hirpl'd alang i' the cauld e'enin' air.
Sma' comfort at hame did the puir laddie hae.
A bed in a neuk 'mang a picklie o' strae,
While his Mither was drunk aye frae morn till e'en,   15
Nor car'd for the wants o' her wanderin' Wean.

Tir'd now wi' wanderin', an' stiff wi' the cauld,
His wee bits o' leggies they scarcely wad fauld,
His headie was bare, too, an' smartin' wi' pain,
Frae greetin' the laddie cou'd hardly refrain: 20
He thocht o' his hame, but he cou'dna' gae there,
An' wearied, he amaist had sunk in despair,
For hope's feeble ray its last blink had gi'en
To urge on the feet o' the wanderin' Wean.

At a house on the roadside, when o'ercome wi' pain,   25
He pleadit for shelter, but pleadit in vain;
An auld hoary Carlin, to eild a disgrace,
Sae heartlessly dash'd the cot-door in his face;
Her heart micht hae meltit, if heart she had hain,
For ony wild Savage frae Africa's clain   30
Wi' a heart as hard as the grey granite stane,
His bield wad hae shar'd wi' the wanderin' Wean.

He totter'd awa frae the door in a swoon,
An' helpless an' hopeless he laid himsel' doon,
Upon the cauld road, there sae lanely to lie,   35
Wi' nae kindly frien' near, to hear his faint cry:
At length a kind message o' sweet love to bring,
An angel approach'd him on seraphic wing,

Sae ayont the bricht starns to glory was ta'en,
The soul of Nan Tamson's puir wanderin' Wean.   40

At the first glint o' morn sae dowie an' gray,
Ere Sol ting'd the sea wi' his faint glimm'ring ray,
Cauld, stiff an' streekit, by the roadside was seen,
The corse o' Nan Tamson's puir wanderin' Wean.
To a lonely kirk-yard they bore him awa',   45
An' made his last bed neath a cauld wreath o' snaw,
But now in sweet summer, the wild grass grows green,
O'er the grave o' Nan Tamson's puir wanderin' Wean.

dowie – melancholy, dreary	*airt – direction*
hirple – to limp or hobble	*neuk – corner, recess*
picklie – a small amount, a few bits	*fauld – bend*
carlin – old woman, in a disparaging sense, crone	*eild – old age*
streekit – stretched out	

20. 'The Bairnies at Hame', by D. Tasker, Dundee, 1863. Published 6 June 1863.

David Tasker was a Dundee factory worker and one of Rev. George Gilfillan's poetic protégés, who published extensively in the local press. 'To the readers of the local newspapers many of these rhymes will be familiar', he notes in the opening of his preface to *Musings of Leisure Hours* (Dundee: James P. Mathew, 1865). 'The Bairnies at Hame' is included in this collection (p. 92). It presents a fantasy of happy rustic life in the Scottish country-side, with the cheerful ploughman returning home to his loving wife and children and their domestic comforts – and then engaging in self-improvement through reading or studying – that was an extremely powerful ideal in popular Victorian poetry. For Scottish writers, it was exemplified by Burns's 'The Cottar's Saturday Night', a major influence on this genre. Such visions of a rural and domestic idyll, especially when voiced by a working man presenting himself as a devoted husband and father, are ubiquitous throughout the Scottish press in this period.

See also: 22. *'Home Recollections', p. 40;* 64. *'A Homely Rhyme', p. 109.*

The bricht sun o' simmer sinks grandly to rest,   1
Mid calm rosy cluds doon the fair gowden west;
Th' blue hills are smilin', wi' glory arrayed,
Th' bonnie wee birds i' th' hawthorn glade
Are carollin' sweetly on ilka green spray,   5
As hameward I trudge frae th' toils o' th' day.

Far awa doon i' yon sweet mossy dell,
Whaur blossom th' craw-pea an' wavin' bluebell,
An' whaur th' lang fern creeps th' grey rocks amang,
A clear siller burnie rows wimplin' alang;   10
In a green shady neuk, by its water sae bricht,
Stands th' snug cosy biggin' sae dear tae my sicht.

Juist noo its low rooftree, close theekit wi' straw,
Tae keep us a' warm when the winter winds blaw,
Keeks thro' th' thick foliage, sae welcome tae view.   15
While frae the lum head th' reek curls up sae blue;
Ha ! th' wee tots are crossin' the brig ower the stream,
Tae welcome their dad tae his luve-lichtit hame.

O sweet are th' joys that th' gloamin' time brings,
Then luve roond oor dwellin' a bricht halo flings;   20
We a' are sae happy, tho' frugal oor fare –
We aye are contented, then what need we mair:
Ony pleasures that wealth gies are no worth th' name,
Compared wi' the joys 'mang the bairnies at hame.

Hoo cosy we sit roon th' warm ingle neuk,   25
Th' totums a' daffin', while I'm at my beuk:
My dear wifie sits wi' th' wean on her knee,
An' croons it tae sleep wi' a sweet lullaby;
Or's darnin' a stockin' or steekin' th' seam
O' a duddie o' claes for the bairnies at hame.   30

Tho' sair I maun toil frae the dawin' tae nicht,
My heart is aye cheery, my spirits are licht;
I think o th' weans that ilk turn o' the pleugh
Helps tae bring a sma' dud or a bit to th' mou';
I envy nae riches, I covet nae fame,   35
But strength tae provide for the bairnies at hame.

Nae doot we hae haen cares an' sorrows eneugh,
But if life was a' sunshine oor joys wad be few;
For if winter ne'er cam', wi' its cauld gloomy skies,
We wadna sae dearly th' summer time prize;   40
Sae oor joys hae been purer, sin' tearfu' we saw
Oor dear little Archie laid deep 'neath th' snaw.

Sae adoon life's dark stream may we peacefully glide,
My wifie, an' angel o' luve, by my side;
An' th' totums, God bless their wee hearties, I ken   45
Will grow tae be braw bonny lasses an' men;
But altho' I sud leeve till I'm donnart an' lame,
I'll aye mind the joys 'mang the bairnies at hame.

biggin – cottage   lum – chimney
daff – to jest, play   steekin' – sewing
dud, duddies – clothes   donnart – dazed, stupid (often of old age)

21. 'The Author of "Bonny Strathtay's" Apology to the People's Journal', by Iain Ban, Blair Athole, 21 July 1863. Published 1 August 1863.

Iain Ban, pseudonym of an unidentified author, apologises here for accidentally breaking the *Journal* rule that only new poems, which had not appeared elsewhere in the press, could be accepted for publication. The editor's note of 18 July 1863 in the correspondents' column read 'Bonny Strathtay, having already appeared elsewhere, cannot be admitted into our columns.' The author, with deliberate comic effect, uses this apology poem to puff his own work by noting that although 'Bonny Strathtay' was his first effort, it was accepted by two other papers. He also attributes noble motives to an editor who reprints his poem – readers may suspect further satire here – and praises the 'journal family', including the famous Tammas Bodkin. Ban's poem provides insight into a poem's circulation in other newspapers, and shows how astutely the editor kept up with poetry columns across the press. It is one of many poems reflecting on the *Journal*'s editorial processes.

See also: 29. 'A Voice from Parnassus', p. 51; 52. 'Charge of the Light Brigade', p. 86; 61. 'Defeatit', p. 104; 85. 'The Poets' Wail', p. 148.

I greet to think, Sir Editor, I hae sic trouble gi'en,   1
To ane whase precious hours are spent "frae morning light
    till e'en,"
In teachin' lessons to mankind in virtue, love, an' truth –
But I'm but young, an' you'll forgie the shortcomin's o'
    youth.
I was a stranger to your rule, an' thocht nae faut 'twad be,   5
Altho' to ithers I should sen' the sang I sent to thee;
But noo' that ye hae tauld me what I should hae kent
    afore –
Forgie, forgie my first offence, an' I will "sin no more."
But wi' your leave, Sir Editor, I'd here a tribute pay
To those wha kindly deigned to print my humble
    mountain lay;   10
Yon chiel in Crieff has kindly gi'en a corner to my sang,
For whilk I thank him as I should – Lord spare his vigour
    lang.
The *Constitutional* likewise his kindness did extend,
An' gave my sang a neuk, for whilk I thank him as a
    friend.
Tho' *Snowdon's Journal* gave it room, I never sent it there,   15
But for that very reason, Sir, I thank him still the mair.
He aiblins guess'd – for Editors can guess wi' great
    precision –
It was my first attempt in print, an' for that verra reason
Thocht that an' act o' kindness might produce a good
    effect,
An' raise the soul that else wad sink if treated wi' neglect.   20
If sae, I vow gif e'er in life yon chap an' I should meet,
Tho' I should pawn my *Cota Mor*, his whistle I shall weet.
An' as for you, Sir Editor, think not I bear you spite,
'Cause ye refused my stuff to print – ye did but what was
    right.
Ye walk accordin' to your rule, for whilk I gi'e ye credit –
That rule before I never knew till yesterday I read it.
Ance mair your pardon, then, I crave, an' I am sure ye'll
    grant it,
An' I will never fash ye mair, tho' I should dee dementit.
Whare'er ye gang, Sir Editor, I'm sure I wish ye weel,
An' dootless sae, thro' Scotland wide, does every rhyming
    chiel'.   30
Whare'er ye gang, whare'er ye be, ye hae my best regards –

Prosperity be yours, an' peace, unfashed by Hielan' bards.
Gi'e my respects to a' yer staff – Tam Bodkin wi' the rest;
An' Tammas, by the way, 's a chiel o' chiel's the verra
    best.
I owe him much, for much 've laughed o'er baith his verse
    an' prose –   35
Gif e'er we meet I'll treat him till a waught o' Athole
    Brose.
Fareweel, fareweel, Sir Editor, for I am growing funny,
An' ye may tak' my jokes amiss – fareweel, an' blessin's
    on ye;
Lord grant ye rowth o' every thing that glads the heart o'
    man,
In wit an' learnin' still to shine – so prays your   40
            IAIN BAN.

chiel – a young man (equivalent of 'fellow') or woman
aiblins – perhaps   cota mor – greatcoat (Gaelic)
fash – to trouble, annoy   waught – draught, long drink
athole brose – honey and whisky drink   rowth – plenty

22. 'Home Recollections', by James Watson, East Indies. Published 29 August 1863.

This is an instance of an emigrant poem, presumed to be sent home to the *Journal* from overseas. In this example, the author suggests that due to hard times and the need for work, he has left his family in Dundee to seek better employment. As in Tasker's 'The Bairnies at Hame', the poem again presents the working man's ideal as domesticity and a happy family circle. Watson is unidentified.

See also: 20. 'The Bairnies at Hame', p. 35; 66. 'Epistle to Tammas Bodkin', p. 112.

Four years ha'e gane by sin' I sat at the ingle   1
    Wi' my cantie wee wife o'er a wee drappie tea;
It's four years an' mair I've kind o' lived single,
    And lost the sweet joys o' my hame in Dundee.

I miss my bit laddie that ca'd me his daddie,   5
    And played wi' his boolies and stottet his ba';
The nichts are noo eerie that used to be cheerie,
    Wi' my laddie an' dearie 'fore I gaed awa.

Yet what could I do when my work I but follow;
    Puir fouk maun just do as they best can get dune;   10
And it's weel enough kent that Jamie, puir fellow,
    Came into the warld without the braw spune.

Sae what need I growl? it was dune for the best,
    An' we canna frae trouble entirely be free;
The time may yet come when in pleasure I'll rest   15
    Wi' my bonnie wee wife in my hame in Dundee.

cantie – lively, cheerful   *boolies – marbles*
stottet – bounced

23. 'Rouse, Brothers, Rouse' [A new version – Adapted for Singing at the Opening of the Baxter Park]. Unsigned. Published 5 September 1863.

'Rouse, Brothers, Rouse', did not appear as original poetry, but in a column recounting plans for the procession on the opening of Baxter Park in Dundee: the song was designed to be sung as part of the celebrations. The gift of Sir David Baxter, of the wealthy Baxter family of millowners, Baxter Park, designed by Sir Joseph Paxton, was the focus of considerable civic pride. In emphasising that the park provides freedom and access to green space for city workers, and in assuming the voice of working men, these song lyrics follow a standard line on the benefits of the park to the working classes. 'Rouse, Brothers, Rouse' was an emigrant or pioneer song by Charles Mackay, urging men to flee the industrial cities and 'ply the hatchet and the spade' in new lands. It was widely circulated in anonymous broadside form. The lyrics here closely follow the original, though they suggest that escape from the city is possible while still remaining within it, through the new civic parks.

See also: 24. 'The Opening of the Baxter Park', p. 43.

    [Chorus]
    Rouse, brothers, rouse, the day beams brightly o'er
       us,   1
        Free and unfettered here we may roam;
    Swell the glad chorus over the meadows,
        Carry the tidings to every home.

Still must we breathe in crowded alleys,   5
    Still must we toil in haunts of trade;
But here we may feel the green sward beneath us,
    And woo the sunshine or the shade.
    Rouse, brothers, rouse, the day beams brightly o'er us
        Free and unfettered here we may roam;   10
    Swell the glad chorus over the meadows,
        Carry the tidings to every home.

Here in the morn the youthful may gambol,
    Here at high noon the aged may rest,
Here in the twilight lovers may wander,   15
    And mark the sunset's glow in the west.

Rouse, brothers, rouse, the day beams brightly o'er us
    Free and unfettered here we may roam;
Swell the glad chorus over the meadows,
    Carry the tidings to every home.   20

Gladly we hail the bounteous givers,
    Fondly we'll cherish their memories dear;
Long may our prayers like angels attend them,
    And guard their footsteps from year to year.
    Rouse, brothers, rouse, the day beams brightly o'er us
        Free and unfettered here we may roam;
    Swell the glad chorus over the meadows,
        Carry the tidings to every home.

Time cannot chill the loving remembrance,
    Nor from our hearts can it e'er pass away,   30
And from the lips of future generations
    Shall rise the anthem of this day.
    Rouse, brothers, rouse, the day beams brightly o'er us
        Free and unfettered here we may roam;
    Swell the glad chorus over the meadows,   35
        Carry the tidings to every home.

Now let us all, with voices united,
    Make every hill and valley to ring;
And may the hearts of our benefactors
    Beat to the notes of the song that we sing.   40
    Rouse, brothers, rouse, the day beams brightly o'er us
        Free and unfettered here we may roam;
    Swell the glad chorus over the meadows,
        Carry the tidings to every home.

24. 'The Opening of the Baxter Park', by E. J., The Factory Girl, Verdant Works, Dundee. Published 12 September 1863.

Ellen Johnston's Baxter Park poem was republished in her *Autobiography, Poems and Songs*, p. 102. It describes the procession and celebrations on the day of the opening, 9 September 1863, particularly emphasising the role of the Rifle Volunteers and the trades' procession. Her final stanza refers to the statue of Baxter placed in the park, funded by the people of Dundee. Johnston's reference to *'our park'* echoes the sentiments of the editorial of 12 September, which comments, 'To-day the mechanic may put on his walking face and his walking coat, and stroll through *his* grounds; and, when he is weary of wandering between banks of flowers, he may rest himself in *his* "pavilion", which will be none the less for being enjoyed in common by his fellows' (p. 2). Johnston frequently published poems in honour of wealthy patrons and on special occasions and events. Her signature is interesting in context, since in this issue her poem appears next to an instalment of David Pae's serial novel, *The Factory Girl; or the Dark Places of Glasgow*.

See also: 17. 'To My Husband', p. 30; 23. 'Rouse, Brothers, Rouse', p. 41.

The ninth day of September	1
The sun arose in splendour,	
His glory to surrender	
To Sir David of Dundee.	
The Trades came forth in grandeur,	5
Each led by its commander,	
Bold as an Alexander	
Of eighteen sixty-three.	
Rosettes and ribbons flowing,	
A radiant hue bestowing	10
On bosoms warmly glowing,	
Where freedom's fire ran through;	
Their banners gaily swelling	
Hailed from each hall and dwelling,	
Their mottoes proudly telling,	15
"Give honour where it's due."	

They, with their drums a-beating,
The Barrack Park did meet in,
Hailed with a hearty greeting,
    Saluted with three cheers;   20
With eyes like star-lights dancing,
With drawn swords brightly glancing,
So warlike and entrancing
    Were our brave Volunteers.

God bless our gallant sailors,   25
Our shoemakers and tailors,
Our engineers and nailers,
    With all their kith and kin!
May our gardeners gather honey,
Our bakers still have money,   30
Our autumn still be sunny
    Till our crops are gathered in.

Our Queen, peace rest upon her!
Her noble Lord of honour
Came here to greet the Donor   35
    Of *our* Park, and get the key
To open for our pleasure
That lovely flower-gemmed treasure,
Where we may sport at leisure,
    When from our toil set free.   40

May the brightest boon of heaven
To the Baxter race be given!
When from us they are riven
    Their loss we will deplore.
The statue of their glory,   45
Immortalised in story,
Shall stand through ages hoary,
    Till time shall be no more.

25. 'A Voice from Stanley Mills', by Will Harrow.
Published 19 December 1863.

'Will Harrow' was the pseudonym of John Campbell of Stanley, known locally as 'Chartist John' for his radical and anti-clerical sentiments; he worked in a number of professions in Glasgow, Dundee, South Africa and rural locations but was primarily involved in digging, draining, trenching and other work with the spade, at which he was considered expert. Robert Menzies Fergusson collected some of his poems, with a short autobiography, in 1897. Notable 'Dundee worthies' in this period included carter 'Willie Harrow' (whose nickname was said to come from his wide-spaced teeth) and a 'Wull Harrow' who sold sawdust and firewood (see Martin, pp. 137, 147). Whether Campbell would have known of these characters, or whether 'Will Harrow' worked as a generic comic pseudonym in this period, perhaps related to the varying uses of 'harrow' in Scots phrases, is unclear. As Harrow, Campbell contributed to the *Journal* during the whole period represented here and was one of its best-known poets. His other poems included in this anthology are 'The Tory Lords' and 'Epistle to Tammas Bodkin'. He evidently published in other newspapers too – the editor reproves him on 5 December 1863 for sending the *Journal* a poem that had already appeared in print elsewhere. Stanley Mills, located on the Tay seven miles outside Perth, were built in 1786 and remain a major landmark of the late eighteenth-century industrial revolution. From the 1820s to the 1840s, the Mills thrived as the cotton-trade grew, and housing and other amenities were built on the site. In 1863, during the Cotton Famine, the owner Samuel Howard closed the Mills, leading to mass unemployment in Stanley. Harrow's poem fits into the popular genre of verses lamenting a lost and neglected village community, but the fact that the closure of Stanley Mills was current news lends an edge of protest to this seemingly regretful and nostalgic piece. 'St Mungo' refers to Glasgow, 'Blair' probably to Blairgowrie in Perthshire, which had a thriving textile industry in this period.

See also: 43. 'Hard Times', p. 72; 49. 'The Tory Lords', p. 81; 66. 'Epistle to Tammas Bodkin', p. 112.

The traffic on our grass-grown streets is thinning,   1
    (A donkey on the verdure fondly browses),
And none are left, alas! to do the spinning,
    Except the spiders in the empty houses.

Here merry maids the smooth footpaths have trod,   5
    Like blooming rosebuds linked by twos and threes,
With swift feet tripping o'er the sylvan road –
    Their snowy kirtles waving in the breeze.

"It was a merry place in days of yore;
    But something ails it now – the place is curst;"   10
For long the wolf's been howling at our door,
    And now into our midst the brute has burst.

And from its hungry glare the fleet did flee,
    Some to St Mungo – others hied to Blair –
But most have winged their flight to sweet Dundee,   15
    Hoping to find a crust and welcome there.

26. 'Apostroffe to the Rainbow', by Poute. Published 30 January 1864

Like Poute's 'Odd to a Krokis', this poem satirises the tradition of pastoral poems on nature, particularly as practiced by working-class writers. In its final line, it references one of the most important and widely read eighteenth-century pastoral poems, James Thomson's *The Seasons* (1730), in which Thomson alludes to Isaac Newton's theories in his description of a rainbow. Poute emphasises the extent to which nature is mediated by the poet in viewing the rainbow in terms of the new Victorian visual technologies of photography and magic lanterns, and in considering how a painting of the rainbow (unlike a poem) could be marketed to profit the artist. The opening note refers to the standard requirement that authors sending works for publication write on one side of the paper only, marking Poute as no longer an amateur at newspaper publication.

See also: 14. '[Letter to Editor]', p. 25; 15. 'Odd to a Krokis', p. 27; 30. 'Kale-Wurms', p. 52; 60. 'Gouldings Manur', p. 101.

    i hav wrote this on   1
    one sid of the papir

                                levin saat pans
Sun when Thou shines In The West at The fal of the day
my shadey Is Fifty Yards long And Mor i daarsay   5

Then a Dismil cloud rising in the est one would think
insted of Rain That it was filled with soot or Ink
And yet on the fase of this cloud Anyhow
is Foty graft A truly pretty and Admirable rainbow
To sing its praises is above my potek comprinshin   10
as It posesess Mor coulirs than i can ever mention
Blue red and green and gud kens how Many
You are there im Told for A Sign when it Is rainy
You're the Best specimen of your kind i evir Saw
One of your ends is at the bass and one right over largy
    law   15
To pent you by estimate. Lo what a money it would take
For pentirs:* Let them alone:* know what charges for to
    Make
Im pretty sure you would been beter had the cloud been
    white
Im sure some of the coullers would have come out mor
    bright   20
Them that use majeklantrns hing up a white shroud
But it mabey wudna be very easy to Make it White cloud
But I shal Drop the subjek For varios resins
If any wishes Mor he can go to tamsons seasons
                   poute   25
p s If i got a peny the line the Above would come to 20 pense
    *dont dot it   p—
                                  Janwry 20
                                   1864

27. 'The Chappin' Laddie', by A Missionary. Published 30 January 1864.

This poem, its Christian and charitable message signaled by the author's chosen pseudonym and the Biblical reference to the Sermon on the Mount in line 21, is also concerned with sympathy for working-class children. Although it has strong associations with many other mid-Victorian poems focused on the exploitation of child workers, here the child makes a positive and necessary contribution to the household finances and works with 'cheerfu'' heart, not only as a 'chappin' laddie' (waking up workers in the morning), but in the factory. The poem also gives us a brief vignette of the working women of Dundee, in the second and third stanzas. The fact that no adult men appear as wage-earners in this piece shows the extent to which the factory economy was dependent on women's and child labour.

See also: 19. 'Nan Tamson's Wean', p. 33; 28. 'The Working Lasses', p. 49; 50. 'The Herd Laddie', p. 83; 86. 'The Sack-Sewers of Dundee', p. 149.

The wee chappin' laddie is rinnin' doon the street,   1
Wi' his lantern in his han', amidst the cauld sleet;
He's up at early mornin', ere the crawin' o' the cock,
Wi' his chapper in his pouch, to waken sleepin' folk.

He tirls at the window, he chaps at the door,   5
The auld wife rubs her sleepy een, an' waukens wi' a snore –
"There's the chappin' laddie, lassies rise an' rin,
Yer mornin' piece is in the press, yer claes are on the pin."

"Mither, whaur's my crinoline, whaur's my apron clean?"
"Mither, whaur's my wrapper? mither, gies a preen?"   10
"Stop yer clatter, Kirsty, the whistle's blawin' in –
Rin wi' a yer feet, ye jades, for fear ye be ahin'."

An' this way every mornin' he gangs his eerie roon',
When ither folks are in their beds sleepin' safe an' soon';
And in the mill through the long day, midst a' its stoor an'
    din,   15
He toils, wi' cheefu' happy heart, his honest bread to win.

Then dinna grudge the laddie his hard-won penny fee;
His widow mither is at hame wi' helpless bairnies three;
She's workin' hard at sewin' sacks, their wee bit mou's to
  fill,
An' lookin' up to God aboon to keep them frae all ill.   20

May He wha feeds the sparrows sma', an cleeds the lilies
  fair,
Guide the chappin' laddie through a' this warld o' care;
Whilst he's up at early mornin' ere the crawin' o' the
  cock,
Wi' his chapper in his pouch, to wauken sleepin' folk.

chapper – a knocker   tirls – taps, rattles
piece – a snack, usually bread, oatcake or scone   preen – pin
stoor – struggle, stress, commotion   cleed – to clothe

28. 'The Working Lasses'. Unsigned. Published 16 July 1864.

Dundee was known for its culture of working women, who were
often perceived as dominating street life and entertainment in
the city. Given widespread Victorian anxiety about women
working outside the domestic sphere, especially in factories, and
the effect this might have on their morals and behaviour and on
family life more broadly, it is important that the *Journal* was
generally supportive of women workers and published poems,
like this, that defended their character against detractors.

*See also: 62. 'To the Domestic Servants', p. 105; 74. 'The Lassies
o' Bonnie Dundee', p. 127.*

Where will ye find in Scotland wide,   1
    In city or in borough,
Or in the halls of lordly pride,
    That ne'er ken poortith's sorrows
Or even in kingly palaces,   5
    Where gowd in gowpins passes,
Maidens mair rich in loveliness
    Than the fair working lasses?

Braw dames, wha hae nor care nor wark,
    They are like poor caged linties;   10
The working lass is a blithe lark,
    And modesty ne'er tint is;
She eident works and blithesome sings,
    She knows nor wile nor cunning –
Her thoughts like blooms by crystal springs   15
    O'er pearls and pebbles running.

And in her balmy, cozy breast,
    A thousand beauties nestle;
And there with the young Love, sae blest,
    They kiss, and daff, and wrestle.   20
The tochered maiden may be fair,
    But unco proud and saucy;
She wha has than hersel' nae mair –
    O she's the frank kind lassie.

Health to the working lasses a',   25
    To each a lover dainty;
And may they aye be blithe as braw,
    Of maidhood ever tentie.
What would the world without them be?
    Dark as the caves of ocean;   30
The flowers of love would fade and dee,
    And every brave emotion.

poortith – poverty, destitution
gowd in gowpins – handfuls of gold (fig. expression)
tint – lost, destroyed   eident – industrious, busy
tocher – dowry   unco – remarkably, extraordinarily
tentie – careful

29. 'A Voice From Parnassus', by J. F., Dundee. Published 1 October 1864.

The dedication refers to the reviews, usually scathing, included in the 'To Correspondents' column. The unidentified 'J. F.' stands with the editor in critiquing and patronising the work of his fellows, and adopts the comically arrogant persona of a poet who has nearly made it to the top of Parnassus.

See also: 4. *'A Young Rhymester's Address to the Editor'*, *p. 9*; 21. *'Apology to the People's Journal'*, *p. 37*; 85. *'The Poets' Wail'*, *p. 148.*

Respectfully inscribed to the poets whose works are weekly reviewed in the *People's Journal.*

Gie heed to me ilk poet chap   1
Wha fain wad reach Parnassus tap,
While I cry to you frae a knap
       Fu' far aboon –
"Tak' tent, or else you'll clour your scaup   5
       Again' the Mune."

For I, wha am sae high already –
To look doon moistly maks me giddy –
Can tell you weel you'd be unsteady
       Gin ye were here –   10
An' stot an' reel like's ye were heady
       Wi' tippeny beer.

O, laddies, (for fu' weel I ken
Sic verses ne'er were made by men) –
Juist gang back to the schule again   15
       An' learn to spell,
And hoo to gar a doitit pen
       Behave itsel!

knap – *hill or mound*   *tent* – *care*
clour – *batter*   *scaup* – *scalp*
stot – *to stagger*   *doitit* – *foolish*

30. 'Kale Wurms. A Dairgy', by Poute. Published under heading 'Original Poute-ry', 26 August 1865.

By 1865 Poute merited his own section in the *Journal*, and the appearance of a new poem by him was trailed in advance in the paper. This poem appeared directly under a letter from a reader who claimed to have visited Poute in his Fife home and been 'very much pleased' with him, another sign of the interest which readers took in Poute and his persona (p. 2). 'Kale Wurms' recounts, in mock-epic heroic couplets (and one marked triplet), how a plague of caterpillars consumed Poute's kale and infiltrated his house, despite the efforts of himself and his wife. 'Ceres', invoked in the opening line, is the goddess of the harvest. As befits the subject matter, 'Kale Wurms' uses more Scots terms than 'Odd to a Krokis' and 'Apostroffe to the Rainbow' (I have not glossed these in full: the difficulty of Poute's language is deliberate). The age in the header does not correspond to Alexander Burgess' actual age, and the location in the 'saat pans' alludes to the imagined occupation of his poetic alter ego, in the salt industry in Leven, Fife. As in his other works, misspellings and obscure references to local characters and relations are deliberate, and his instructions to the typesetter to add punctuation ('dot it'), plus his own 'marginal notes', interjections and postscript, are part of the comic effect. The final footnote references the *Journal*'s charity drive of 1865, spurred by readers' enthusiasm and productive of a number of exhortative poems, to raise money for a 'People's Journal' lifeboat. By May 1865 enough money had been raised for two lifeboats, installed at Peterhead and Arbroath.

See also: 14. [Letter to Editor], p. 25; 15. 'Odd to a Krokis', p. 27; 26. 'Apostroffe to the Rainbow', p. 46; 31. 'An Epissel to Poute', p. 54; 60. 'Gouldings Manur', p. 101.

levin saat pans 1856 agest 23
     dot it if you plese

Ceres desend o help me to Bewale	1
the qwik despatch of my Most Splinded kale	
onse Lairg as Johnys Gurde wi Bledes lyk lethir	
Now pykit to the Benes as bairs the hethir	
it was their Bulk aliss! & Monstriss Syse	5
which drew furth Rejmints of whyt butrflys	
To sitt on them lyk Teylyers on Their furms	

& klekk their Skore and Mulyins of kale wurms
im sure maist a The butrflys in fyf
were on my kale in Drovs & lejins ryfe   10
klekkin a Rece o kraalin ugli dee—ls [an il wurd]
to et my krops among The wurst of Evils
That they are Nyaad and tshaad to kaff & lost
My Swyn as weels Mycell kens to oor kost
had They got Leev to Looke for this kurst Grubb   15
By this tyme Evry hert wud fild a tubb
& now that they are pykit to the Lingins
im ferd the bruts yok nickst to et my ingins
The swyn pure Brut! may now gee owr its Grunts
for nethings left But synnins & the runts (1)   20
Nor is this al the bruts so pert & kruse
kraals in to take poceshion of my huse
My wyf stands with a Bizim at the dore
onse she kild 30 dizen in the hour (2)
its of no uss for hir to wats and singe Hey hum   25
For spyt of Al her efurts in they kum
As they sklim up the Wa & then gump doon the lum
if im but spaird till Wuntir evry brut
May kalkulat upon a Dozz of Saat or Sute (that's Al)
        mairijen nots   30
(1) Deed wuly reedys is no mukil beter
(2) She kils them wi her fit
POUTE
Ps mr editer Did the folk of petirhed not hav The Sens to
gi me a vott of thanks for my jenires ofir of the girnal to
hud the lyfbot – i supos not

gurde – belt or hoop   klekk (claik) – to hatch
nyaad and tshaad – gnawed and chewed
lingins – stripped heather stalks   yok – to set to, engage in
ingins – onions   synnins – sinews
kruse (crouse) – confident, self-satisfied   gump – grope
lum – chimney

31. 'An Epissel to Poute', by Moses Daylite. Published on 10 March 1866.

Poute's work attracted numerous admirers and imitators, among which 'Moses Daylite' (sometimes 'Dalite') was one of the most prominent; this poem occurs after others featuring mutual praise between Daylite and Poute, as referenced in lines 27–30. Several comic poems in phonetic English or Scots by Daylite appear in the *Journal* in these years: the poet behind the pseudonym is unidentified. As in Poute's poems, difficulties of interpretation here are deliberate and are not glossed. Daylite also references the pseudonymous comic *Journal* writers Tammas Bodkin and Bill Stumps. Epistle poems to fellow poets and contributors to the *Journal* were very common, as the other examples of this form collected here show.

See also: 13. 'Epistle to Tammas Bodkin', p. 24; 14. [Letter to Editor], p. 25; 30. 'Kale Wurms', p. 52; 66. 'Epistle to Tammas Bodkin', p. 112.

Awaik! are eyes! kum 4th ye tuenfil 9,   1
End rows to life this drowsie mews of mine.
Kum, strik my sounding lire with magik pours,
Till eye do weeve a garlind of wild flours,
To plais upon the klasik brow of wan   5
An aktif, smart, onkomin kliver man.

Hale leven saut pans bard! this long time bak
I've yernd with yew tue hav a soshil krak
Butt posibly we to mite niver meat
To feest on sutch an intillektewl treet   10
Thairfor I've tuke it in mi hed to rite
Sum centymints in prays of yew to nite
Eye do not meen to flatir but to sho yew
That I add myre suppose I do nut no yew.

Grate poute, when 1st ure famis water lilly   15
Did spring to vue vast numbers thote it sily
Butt only senslis, blind, benited fools
That did nut no the komin gramir rools
End shood nut nair hav left the infint skools
Eye saw when air I skand it with my ize   20
A star had roes to gem the poutik skize

For marvlis wit & sens threw every line
Kwite kleer as day konspeakusly did shine,
"A 2nd shapeskeer's kum to lite'!" eye shoutid.
Buy what yuve rot sins then I do nut dout it.   25

Eye notis in the last to poims yew prentid
Ewer humbil friend is hily komplimentid
In wan of them partiklerly i sea
Yew stait ure shure to be iklipsd buy me
Fals feer; ure jeanis mine buy far outstrips   30
Yew are a star that daylite kant eklips,
But tho' that eye bee taim kumpaird with yew
I'll do my best, what morer kan I do?
Our aim is wan – to elyvait the naishon,
End to inkreas the *Jurnil's* circkilayshun.   35

Then far faimd bodkin well noan man of mirth
Dra frum yewr goose a kwill, kum kwikly 4th
Ikspose ure fertile jeanis to the vue
Of kountlis ize that wait to welkim yew
Kum frum yure shel my pawky frind Bil Stumps   40
End tune ewer pipes ure shurely in the dumps
Or have yew seteld down & tuke a wife
That now so celdim yew give sines of life.
Let eatch & wan end awl with mite & zeel
Poosh bravely with our sholdirs to the wheal   45
End air the ear is out eye wood nut wundir
To sea the *Jurnil* at 2 thowsind hunder.

But hear my mews does fale; eye must kunklood
Hopin ure ginral helth is keapin good
End long on erth may yew be spaird to sing   50
When yewr prolific mews dose taik the wing.
Eye trust the present most disastris storms
Has starvd to deth ewer fose – the grubs & worms
That sneak end krawl threw out ure garden ground
Devourin ivery grean thing to bee found.   55
I paws! deer frind fair well! adew! good nite!
Beleeve me trooly ewers   MOSES DAYLITE
Kats Klose Dundee.

32. 'The Scottish Servant Maid', by J. C., Elie. Published 17 March 1866.

Disputes over the difficult conditions of employment for female servants had featured in the poems and prose of the Scottish press since at least 1860, when A. M. B.'s stirring 'Song of the Servant Maid', was reprinted in several papers, including the *Dundee Advertiser*. In spring 1866, the *Journal* hosted a revived debate about servants' rights in its letters columns, featuring the views of both servant maids and their employers. This poem refers specifically to a letter published on 3 March from 'A Servant Lassie' ('your Denhead female correspondent'). J. C. makes a common comparison between maidservants and slaves, and suggests that men fighting for a nine-hour working day need to turn their attention to the rights of female workers. This is his first poem on the subject: a second appears below. On 19 May 1866, a correspondent signing herself 'A Scottish Servant Maid' concluded her letter to the *Journal* in support of the maids with a stanza from this poem, describing 'Elie' as 'one whose name is immortalised in the memory of thousands of us' and 'our noble poetic friend' (p. 2).

See also: 33. 'A Scottish Servant Maid', p. 57; 36. 'Song. (Dedicated to the Scottish Servant Maids)', p. 62; 62. 'To the Domestic Servants', p. 105.

SIR. – Your Denhead female correspondent calls on some kind friend of the male sex to come forward in vindication of female rights. Old as I am, I cannot resist her earnest request. I only wish I had power to rouse up every manly heart in their behalf.

At meetings for the India girls   1
    What tender things are said;
But sounds of pity never greet
    The Scottish Servant Maid.

Long hours of labour, few of rest   5
    (Exceptions must be made);
And if they murmur, woe betide
    The Scottish Servant Maid.

Their ceaseless toil, their paltry fee,
    With other ills arrayed,   10
And oft a haughty mistress scolds
    The Scottish Servant Maid.

We pity sore the sable race,
    Denounce the slaving trade,
But not a word of comfort cheers   15
    The Scottish Servant Maid.

Ye fathers, brothers, lovers all,
    Oh! hasten to their aid,
And brave the system that enthralls
    The Scottish Servant Maid.   20

And when we have our nine hours gain'd,
    It never shall be said
That we have left in slavery
    The Scottish Servant Maid.

33. 'A Scottish Servant Maid', by A. L. B., Craigellachie. Published 19 May 1866.

This poem addresses the pseudonymous 'Scottish Servant Maid' who had been supplying letters to the *Journal*, including one thanking J. C., Elie, for his poetic support (see 32., above). Like J. C.'s earlier poem, this offers support to female servants from working men, suggesting that women fighting for their rights as workers is a welcome development. On 6 June 1866, the *Journal* published a letter from 'An Aberdeenshire Lassie', which stated, 'Cheer up, my sisters, and let us all unite hands and hearts together. We are no longer to be mere walking machines, with no higher aim than to eat and sleep, that we may be able for our work', and continued, 'I am much obliged to the Craigellachie Bard, who last week cheered our hearts with his beautiful lines.' (p. 2).

See also: 32. 'The Scottish Servant Maid', p. 56; 36. 'Song. (Dedicated to the Scottish Servant Maids)', p. 62.

Hail, daughter of the old Cake Isle,   1
    We welcome thee, and shall prove true

To every cause where freedom's smile
    Is justified by you.

Harbinger of a better day,   5
    That is not, but shall surely be,
Since thou hast shone a spreading ray
    To all futurity.

Come – for we thought that thou hadst slept
    In ignorance, nor wished to raise   10
Thy voice o'er slavery, and protect
    Sweet freedom's sunny days.

But no, it is not so, for we
    A Scottish Servant Maid can find
To bear the palm of liberty,   15
    And lead fair womankind.

On, on; and may thy future be
    In health and happiness enshrined;
And love, faith and sincerity
    Be standards of thy mind.   20

34. 'The Navvies', by John Taylor. Published 7 July 1866.

Navvy work on the railway lines was a very common form of employment in this great age of railway development, and navvies were popularly regarded as rough and uncivilised. Taylor's poem appears only a few years before Alexander Anderson would use these presumptions to build his reputation as a 'surfaceman' poet. Like Anderson's poetry, it makes the point that working men may be sensitive, intelligent, and devout. John Taylor is almost certainly the Ross-shire working-class poet who worked as a navvy on the railways in the early 1860s. His autobiography, which prefaces *Poems, Chiefly on Themes of Scottish Interest* (1875), suggests that at the time of writing this poem, he would have been unhappily employed as a labourer on the Caledonian Railway at West Calder, near Edinburgh (pp. 41–42). Several of his other poems also appeared in the *Journal*, and his collection was favourably reviewed on 27 February 1875. 'The Navvies' is not included in his *Poems*.

See also: 48. *'John Keats'*, p. 79.

Good people of our native land,   1
    Where peace and freedom shine,
Oh! think of those brave men who toil
    Along the railway line –

Whose noble hearts are ever true,   5
    In danger's awful hour;
Who stoutly bear the boisterous blast
    Of winter's dismal shower.

Think not, because their hands are rough,
    Their faces brown and hard,   10
Their souls must evermore remain
    Unworthy of regard.

Think not, because the railway life
    Is wild along the line,
That none among the navvie boys   15
    Have hopes of joy divine.

Oh! ye who look with proud disdain,
    Cold and unlovingly,
On those who tread the weary paths
    Of mean obscurity.   20

Ye know not of the sympathies,
    The feelings soft and fine,
That warm the breasts of those who toil
    Along the railway line.

35. 'A Lay of Reform', by William Donaldson, Keith, 1866. Published 11 August 1866.

William Donaldson was a shoemaker from Keith in Moray, north-east Scotland (formerly Banffshire) and the author of *The Queen Martyr, and Other Poems* (Elgin: J. McGillivray and Son, 1867): the *Journal* noted this book on 1 June 1867 as by 'a young man whose poetical effusions have occasionally appeared in our columns' (p. 2). 'A Lay of Reform' was not included in this collection, probably because of its political content. In spring and summer 1866, agitation over the Second Reform Act, eventually passed in 1867, was gaining pace. The *Journal* was fervently pro-Reform and had assisted with Dundee's petition in support of the bill in March 1866. In June 1866, the government collapsed when it could not get Lord John Russell's reform bill through parliament: Russell was replaced as leader of the Liberal party by William Gladstone, and the Conservative Lord Derby became Prime Minister. Donaldson's poem refers to the dispute over the London 'Hyde Park Riots' in July 1866, when soldiers cleared protestors from the park, and appeared the week after the *Journal* published a special supplement reporting on Dundee's massive Reform meeting on the Magdalen Green, described as 'perhaps the largest which has ever been seen in Dundee – rivaling and even excelling those of the great Chartist agitation' (4 August 1866). William Latto, *Journal* editor, was on the stage at this meeting. Directly below Donaldson's poem in the 'People's Opinions' letters section, a correspondent wrote that the *Journal*, 'by its advocacy of the cause of Reform, both political and social, has proved that its name is not an empty title, but is the *People's Journal* indeed' (p. 2). Besides Russell and Gladstone, Donaldson's poem celebrates John Stuart Mill (who had proposed an amendment to the bill to enfranchise all householders, both men and women) and John Bright, radical MP and leading reform campaigner. It also references the participation of working men in the Rifle Volunteer movement.

See also: 37. 'Reform', p. 64; 49. 'The Tory Lords', p. 81.

Hurrah! hurrah! for the dawning streaks of freedom's
    glorious day;   1
Hurrah! hurrah! for the daring hearts that will level the
    Tory sway.
O toiling sons of our Fatherland! O men, with the sinews
    strong,

Break, break, the shackles that have bound the strength of
   your wills so long.
Nor gift we seek, nor boon we crave – for plunder we
   scorn to fight;   5
But each of us all eagerly shall demand our legal right,
As each of us would stand or fall a hostile line before,
Defending the land that gave us birth, and the Queen
   whom we adore.

We earn the bread we eat – can that be said of the rich
   and great?
Ours are the hearts that guard the Crown, and the limbs
   that pillar the State;   10
We want a voice in the senate, and though the
   Conservatives haughtily frown,
We know our power, and we know that they are unable
   to bully us down.
The opening strokes of the Tory dirge on the bell of
   Reform have rung,
Our foes can never put thought in chains, but they try to
   fetter the tongue;
We will not shout with the rabble rout, whose motives
   and deeds we despise,   15
But, brethren, hark, in square and park let the voice of the
   nation rise.

We patiently waited for liberty – we waited and earnestly
   prayed;
Through the pages broad of the British press we quietly
   gave patriots aid;
But tyrants sneer'd at the efforts we made, and traitors
   betrayed our cause –
Declaring our utter indifference to change because we kept
   the laws.   20
When, stung by the taunts of treason and guilt, we rose to
   discuss our wrong,
They styled us a lawless, reckless mob, for they saw that
   we were strong;
The gleaming blades, swung o'er our heads, brought fear
   to no heart that day,
But the Tory Lord put the edge on a sword that will his
   own Government slay!

O working men of the British Isles, by the memories of
    old,   25
I charge ye all, as ye love and revere the names of our
    martyrs bold,
By those who pined on a distant shore, or died 'mid the
    faggot's flame –
I charge ye all to zealously strive and burst the shackles of
    shame.
They gave us rifles to guard the land, which they say we
    are willing to do,
Then why not trust us with a vote if they think our souls
    so true?   30
We seek no boon – we crave no gift – we claim but our
    simple right!
Hurrah! for Russell and Gladstone! Hurrah! for Mill and
    Bright!

36. 'Song. (Dedicated to the Scottish Servant Maids.)', J. C., Elie. Published 18 August 1866.

J. C.'s second poem draws together the August 1866 agitation
over Reform and the maidservants' debate, arguing that working
men who ignore the plight of these working women are not
worthy of the vote. In a 16 June 1866 letter, he reminded male
readers that women had helped them to gain Reform in 1832: 'In
1832, during the great struggle for Reform, the women of Elie
cheered us on. They united and made our Reform flag, on which
was inscribed the beautiful motto, "Union, Liberty and Peace"'
(p. 2). He also links the maidservants' cause to the temperance
movement, and strongly implies that the maids ought to form a
union.

See also: 32. 'The Scottish Servant Maid', p. 56; 33. 'A Scottish
Servant Maid', p. 57.

    Air – My Mary and Me

Cheer up, Scottish maidens, your cause cannot fail,   1
'Tis founded on justice, and truth must prevail;
Against honest service you set not your face –
'Tis the system of bondage you wish to efface.

The horse and the ass are protected, you know –   5
No rude cruel driver dares give them a blow,
And when overladen law comes to their aid –
Alas! law protects not the overwrought maid.

Then do for yourselves what the law fails to do;
Unite for protection – demand what is due –   10
Hours shorter, less labour, are what you must have,
And not to be used like the poor galley slave.

Ye lads cease your song o'er the brain-stirring glass,
Arouse at the call of the poor toiling lass;
Love-songs are cold things in a rough drinking den –   15
Come soberly forward and prove yourselves men,

Ye workmen who favour the temperance plan,
In defence of the fair sex stand up every man;
So long as our females in bondage remain,
So long we will look for the franchise in vain.   20

Without woman's service man would be forlorn –
A poor helpless creature, "all tatter'd and torn;"
Then let us be grateful, and render our aid
To lessen the toil of the dear Scottish maid.

37. 'Reform', by A. W., 7 October 1866. Published 13 October 1866.

As in Donaldson's 'Lay of Reform', A. W. addresses working-class pro-reformers and references Gladstone, Bright, and Russell. He also alludes to Edward Stanley (son of Lord Derby), Conservative Secretary of State for Foreign Affairs; Spencer Walpole, Conservative Home Secretary; Lord Derby, Conservative Prime Minister; Benjamin Disraeli, Conservative Chancellor of the Exchequer, and Robert Lowe, a passionately anti-Reform Liberal MP who was strongly opposed to trades unions and dangerous principles of equality, hence a 'traitor' (line 10). Disraeli ('Dizzy') had attempted to turn the Tory party towards Reform. He introduced his bill in March 1867, and after many amendments it was eventually passed and became the Second Reform Act in July 1867. Lancaster, Totnes and Yarmouth were all boroughs under investigation for electoral corruption in autumn 1866.

See also: 35. 'A Lay of Reform', p. 60; 49. 'The Tory Lords', p. 81.

Reform! Reform! Be our cry, my boys,   1
    As united and firm we stand.
Not from Stanley the sleek, nor Walpole the meek,
    Nor the haughty Derby's hand.
Nor the haughty Derby's hand, my boys –   5
    We can wring it from that if we will;
But we want Reform from Reformers, boys –
    Not a Dizzy's swindling Bill.

Venal and drunken and violent, boys,
    We are called by the traitor Lowe.   10
Lancaster, Totnes, and Yarmouth, boys,
    Show you things as they're managed now.
Show you things as they're managed now, my boys –
    How electors are bought and sold.
But we'll clear that scum away, my boys –   15
    Skim the upper dross from the gold.

Venality, drunkenness, violence, boys –
    Let the words on their heads recoil
Who meet thus the just demands, my boys,
    Of the strong-armed sons of toil.   20

Of the strong-armed sons of toil, my boys,
    Who are marching along to their right,
With the wisdom of Russell, with Gladstone's zeal,
    And the fire of intrepid Bright.

For the land we live in is *ours*, my boys;   25
    We will see her safe through this storm.
Our brothers for her have bled, my boys;
    For her sake we fight for Reform!
For her sake we fight for Reform, my boys,
    We ask and will have our own.   30
We have reason and right and might on our side –
    We have Gladstone and Bright and the Throne!

38. 'The Plague-Stricken Village', by Justitia, Methilhill. Published 8 December 1866.

This is a cholera poem, focused on an outbreak in Methilhill, Fife. 1866 saw the fourth and final cholera epidemic of the century in Britain: several editorials dealt with the cholera epidemic in Dundee (e.g. 3 November 1866, p. 2). The statistics given by 'Justitia' at the end of the poem indicate the heartfelt immediacy of her plea. No other poems under this pseudonym appear in this period.

Can any stay this mighty plague,   1
    Or say from whence it springs,
Or wipe away the sad result –
    The misery it brings?

The father here is left to mourn,   5
    The mother's heart to grieve,
And children orphans here are left –
    A loss they can't retrieve.

Oh God! Who in thy providence
    Didst see it meet to chide,   10
Remove the plague, and let thy love
    With stricken hearts abide.

Wipe thou the tear, assuage the grief.
    And cheer the drooping heart.
May all from this the lesson take   15
    To choose the "better part."

And then though plague and pestilence
    With sudden pain assail,
Thou'lt be our rock and confidence –
    In thee we will prevail.   20

And ye who have no loss sustained
    Yield thanks to God most high.
Relief send those who are bereft –
    Oh! hear the infant's cry.

Note – The census of the population of Methilhill having been taken to ascertain the number of inhabitants before cholera broke out and the number of deaths, the following is the result:–
    Before cholera broke out................403
    Number of deaths up to this time 67
          Being 16.4% of the population.

39. 'Hold Up Your Head', by Fernogus, Perth. Published 9 February 1867.

While this does not present itself as a Reform poem, the emphasis on working-class pride and self-respect clearly relates to the reform debates of spring 1867, and consequent heated discussions in Parliament about the fitness of working men for the franchise. The emphasis on being mentally and physically 'upright' also speaks to the *Journal*'s general project of improving and inspiring working-class readers. 'Fernogus' is unidentified.

See also: 5. *'I sigh not'*, p. 10, 8. *'Think For Yourselves'*, p. 16.

Hold up your head, be a man as you ought;   1
    If honest, why frighten'd the world should know it;
Be free and be fearless, why crouch to a coat?
You'd pass it by proudly enough, would you not?
Were fustian its texture: nor value a groat   5
    The thoughts of the sinner who swaggers below it.

Your clothes are well worn – Why, what though they be?
    I take it for granted you've honestly paid them;
Your hat – Yes – it might have been newer, I see;
Your trousers – Well, well! – there's a patch on the knee; 10
Be thankful, and think yourself better than he
    Who may own all he wears to the tailor who made
      them.
Be true to yourself, and be true to your kind;
    What, afraid of your fellows? – Shame! – should it be
      said?
Be upright in bearing. If upright in mind,   15
No matter how thinly your purse may be lined;
Have respect for yourself, and the consequence find
    That others respect you. Hold up your head.

40. 'Despondency', by James Gow, Weaver. Seafield Road Works, Perth Road, Dundee, 8 July 1867. Published 13 July 1867.

James Gow (1814–1872) was a well known Dundee weaver-poet and an ardent Chartist, who had published widely in British periodicals and newspapers, producing one volume in 1845, *Lays of the Loom*, that is now extremely rare. On his death in 1872, the *Journal* published a detailed obituary recalling his participation in the literary and radical cultures of Dundee: 'All the humble sons of muses in Dundee would be found at the back of the poet's loom.' ('History of James Gow, the Weaver Poet', 10 February 1872, p. 2). As 'Despondency' suggests, his later years were reportedly unhappy. By publishing his work address with the poem, Gow invited supportive correspondence.

See also: 41. 'Lines Addressed to James Gow, Weaver', p. 69; 73. 'Three Score and Ten', p. 126.

My weary life-clockie is gaun to stand still,   1
For the sma' broo o' age through my bosom rins chill,
While my limbs are sae frozen nae simmer can thaw,
An' the sunshine o' my day is langsyne awa.

Sae craz'd is my auld heart, an' dim is my e'e,   5
That a' thing looks changed an' eerie to me;
Like a sna'-bodin' mune looks the sun to my sicht,
An' mid-day's like gloamin' an' gloamin' midnicht.

An' aften I tak', when I'm lanely an' wae,
The mornin' for nicht, an' the nicht for the day;   10
Syne the thochtless will jeer me, an' tell me an' mine
I'm just like an auld clock that's past keepin' time.

I'm like yonder hawthorn, wrinkled an' bare,
That's destined by nature to blossom nae mair;
For sin' the gay simmer cam' dancin' wi' mirth,   15
I'm weaker, an' sicker, an' liker the earth.

How I'll welcome the hour when, ascendin' on high,
I'll meet the Great King, frae His throne i' the sky,
To welcome me hame to a warld o' bliss –
To a lang simmer day frae a winter i' this.   20

When neist the green meadows are speckled wi' flowers,
An' auld hearts like mine seek the sun-warm'd bowers,
Some time-worn pilgrim may covet a rest
'Mang the gowd-gilded gowans on my clay-shrouded
    breast.

41. 'Lines Addressed to James Gow, Weaver, Seafield Road, Dundee', by W. R. Mainds, Painter. 20 Constitution Street, Dundee, 15 July 1867. Published 20 July 1867.

This is an immediate response poem to James Gow's 'Despondency', dated two days after its publication. Such sympathetic exchanges between poets, offering support and friendship, were common in provincial newspaper poetry columns. The author puns on Gow's profession as a weaver in the final stanza. Mainds is not known to have published any further poems.

See also: 40. 'Despondency', p. 68.

In the *Journal* last week I read wi' great care	1
Your sweet little dittie, an' fan' my heart sair,	
To think that "despondency" clouded the brow,	
Or enter'd a kind heart like yours, Jamie Gow.	
What though the thochtless may tell you an' yours	5
Ye're like to an auld clock that strikes na' th' hours?	
Ne'er heed, while your boat on life's ocean doth row –	
There's a licht i' yer maintop, my friend, Jamie Gow.	
A licht i' yer riggin', which they on the land	
May see ere it's ower late, and lend ye a hand;	10
For a body's aye better o' gettin' a tow	
When stemming life's spring-tide, like you, Jamie Gow.	
So never repine, Jamie, never despair,	
Sweet is your rhyme, Jamie, haste ye wi' mair;	
For the *People's* ain *Journal* is ready, I trow,	15
Wi' a nook for sic pieces as yours, Jamie Gow.	

When your last shot is ca'd, and your shuttle is toom,
And the speeders hae started to weave on your loom,
The spark o' your licht will get up wi' a low,
And show to the warld yer worth, Jamie Gow. 20

toom – empty   *low – a flame*

42. 'The Bard of Caldervale', by David Morrison, Night Watchman. Caldervale, by Airdrie, July, 1867. Published 10 August 1867.

Morrison, born in 1824, had no formal education and worked as a miner, then in Moffat Paper Mill, before moving to Calder-vale Printfield, as the sketch of his life attached to his *Poems and Songs* (published by the *Airdrie Advertiser* office) indicates. His preface to that volume states that he was persuaded to publish due to the success of his newspaper verse, which appeared widely in the local Scottish press; he engaged in poetic exchanges in the Glasgow papers with poets including R. H. P. (John Pettigrew) and Ellen Johnston. 'The Bard of Caldervale' is a typical 'lowly poet' poem, emphasising the solitary pleasures of poetry and the poet's modest desires, while also seeking recognition – and inviting readers to get in touch. It is republished in David H. Morrison, *Poems and Songs* (Airdrie: Baird and Hamilton, 1870), p. 20.

See also: 4. 'A Young Rhymester's Address to the Editor', p. 9; 72. 'My First Attempt', p. 122.

Will none appear to recognize 1
    The humble bard of Caldervale?
Who toils beneath the midnight skies
    Tho' tempests sweep adown the dale.

The rich repose on beds of down, 5
    Free from each care of want or storm;
When I, beneath misfortune's frown,
    My arduous task must still perform.

Yet pleasures dwell within my breast
    Which richer men can seldom know, 10

For, when they on soft couches rest,
    Upon my mind bright fancies flow.

And earthly cares are all forgot
    Whilst golden feelings fire my mind,
And give the ever-pleasing thought   15
    "That darkest clouds with light are lin'd."

'Tis then I feel hope's pleasing glow,
    And hail with joy the future times,
When Scotland's gen'rous sons will show
    Their love for David and his rhymes.   20

I seek not joys from wealth that spring –
    The gaudy dress, the dwelling grand;
My highest wish is but to sing
    The praises of my native land.

And should I meet a comrade dear   25
    Who every sinful system spurns,
I'll happy be to let him hear
    My songs of Wallace, Bruce and Burns.

43. 'Hard Times', by J. G., Markinch. Published 16 November 1867.

Britain was going through a period of recession in 1867–69, largely due to knock-on effects from the recession in the U. S. after the end of the American Civil War. The unidentified 'J. G.' attempts to find a cheerful resolution, looking forward to 1868, in the closing lines, but the primary focus of the poem is on the woes of unemployment. The song tune may be ironic, given that the lyrics of the traditional song 'Paddle Your Own Canoe' celebrate the joys of being single, carefree and self-reliant.

See also: 25. 'A Voice from Stanley Mills', p. 45; 45. 'Woe', p. 74.

Tune – "Paddle your own canoe."

Hard times have come, and now I must   1
    An idle life pursue:
My wife will sigh and children cry,
    For I have no work to do.

When toiling on in days gone by,   5
    What little cares we knew;
But now, alas! what days I pass
    In having no work to do.

I weary all the live-long day,
    And fain would travel through;   10
But where to go I do not know,
    For there is no work to do.

Hard times have come, and winter nigh,
    And now my rent is due;
But this we say, How can we pay,   15
    If there is no work to do?

How will my wife and children dear
    Be fed and clothed too;
Provisions high and winter nigh,
    And having no work to do.   20

Hard times have come, but let us trust
    For brighter days anew,
When we will cheer a glad New Year,
    With plenty of work to do.

44. 'Lines on Receiving a *People's Journal*', by J. S. M., Oldham. Published 30 May 1868.

One of many poems celebrating the *Journal*, J. S. M.'s location in Oldham marks him as an expatriate Scot in England keen for news of his native land. It is notable that he particularly celebrates the *Journal's* focus on Scots, and that the primary contributor named and praised here is Poute. 'Pitman' refers to Isaac Pitman's famous phonetic system of shorthand (invented 1837).

See also: 97. 'Reminiscences of the People's Journal', p. 171; 109. 'I'll Hae My Freen', p. 197.

Hail! Welcome news, from Scotia's heath'ry hills,   1
    And scented glens, and woods, and crystal streams,
Your every page some tale my mem'ry fills
    With recollections of my boyhood's dreams.

Your oft-read pages place before my mind   5
    Some happy scene – some well-remembered spot,
Where lightsome days I spent: all left behind,
    With cronies dear, but ne'er to be forgot.

Oh! could my humble pen in truth pourtray
    The pride I have in thee, my native tongue: 10
No lintie to his mate upon the spray
    In sweeter, purer strains has ever sung.

Your local news, Scots Worthies, tales, and lays,
    All feed and cheer the literary mind;
Good words they are, that call forth higher praise   15
    Than those which claim to be far more refined.

Here "Poute" in all his glory dazzling shines,
    But ruthlessly he kills orthography,

And dims the brilliant lustre of his lines –
    Ah! pardon, "Poute," you write Phonography.   20

Like Pitman, Poet "Poute" can spell by sound,
    Then where's the fault? Too well 'tis understood
There's one for writing *bosh* gets many a pound,
    And "Poute" for one must help to make it good.

Long may the *Journal* live, far may it spread,   25
    And may its circulation ne'er grow less;
"From Maidenkirk to John o' Groat's" be read,
    From Ardnamurchan Point to Buchan Ness.

45. 'Woe', by James Winthrope, Mill Worker, Weensland, Hawick. [Prize – Ten Shillings]. Published in the Christmas supplement for 1868.

Winthrope's 'Woe' was an entry in the 1868 Christmas poetry competition (one of 420 entrants) and was awarded one of the ten-shilling runner-up prizes: winning stories, letters and poems were published in a special supplement each year. 'Woe' deals with unemployment (again, probably due to the 1867–69 recession), and with the terrible absence of the comforting domesticity held up as an ideal to workers. Given that Winthrope identified himself as a worker in his signature, we might presume that the circumstances here are imagined rather than autobiographical. This is an unusual poem in the context of the Christmas prize competition, which strongly favoured generic sentimental works on nature, religion, family and related themes. The first-person perspective, lack of any happy ending or Christian consolation, and the relatively unstable pattern of line-lengths and stresses, also mark this poem as different and more innovative than the standard piece on this subject. 'Woe' was republished in the collection of *People's Journal* competition pieces, *Poems for the People* (Edinburgh: John Menzies, 1869), pp. 6–7. Winthrope, born 1832 in Hawick, later emigrated to Canada. He published one book of poems but no surviving copy has been traced.

See also: 25. 'A Voice from Stanley Mills', p. 45, 43. 'Hard Times', p. 72; 87. 'Died on the Street', p. 151.

Tramp, ever tramp,   1
    In the snow, the sleet, and the rain,
In the stinging frost and the chilling damp,
    In poverty and pain,
O'er the hill, the morass, and the moor,   5
    With hunger to drive us on,
With his knotted scourge, to the poor man's door,
    And the gates of the lofty one –
To be wetted and chill'd to the bone,
    Exposed to the pitiless blast,   10
Till even the light of hope is gone –
    Oh, God, how long can it last?

Not for myself care I –
    I could suffer and die alone,
But those hungry bairns, and that poor wife's cry,   15
    Would melt the heart of a stone.
Their faces all pinch'd and blue
    With the sufferings of many a day,
And their little shoes with the feet coming through
    In the mire upon the way.   20
With scarcely a rag to wear,
    To shelter them from the cold,
Till the icy stare of dull despair
    Makes their faces look worn and old.
Yet they are but bairns in years,   25
    Tho' old in sorrow and woe.
What wonder, then, that I melt in tears
    As I see them come and go,
Begging a crust of bread?
    My children, the light of my eye!   30
With no fireside, and no cosy bed,
    Not even a grave, if they die.

Tramp, ever tramp!
    And all through no fault of my own,
Did they quench the light of my household lamp,   35
    And bid me make haste and begone;
Though the winter was swelling and wild,
    And food was scarce to be had,
An ailing wife and an infant child,
    And all because trade was bad.   40

So we have no roof but the sky,
    And we tramp back and forwards again –
Four little bairns, a wife and I,
    Begging for work in vain.
Oh! for a home again!   45
    For a fireside of my own,
Where my little children may have bread,
    And there fear no one's frown.

46. 'What is Sweet', by J. Pettigre [Pettigrew], Parkhead. Published 27 March 1869.

The author here is signed 'Pettigre', which is almost certainly a typesetter's error for newspaper poet John Pettigrew, the 'Parkhead Minstrel', who often published as 'R. H. P., Parkhead'. Pettigrew's brief poem is entertaining because of its subversion of a set of standard clichés in the final line. He was a gardener living in Parkhead, a suburb in Glasgow's East End, in the 1860s, who primarily featured in the Glasgow press, particularly the *Penny Post* (see Edwards, 5, pp. 35–36). This is his only *Journal* poem in this period.

See also: 98. 'A Year Ago', p. 173.

Sweet is the breeze which blows o'er the mountain   1
    Sweet are the notes of the wild cushet dove;
Sweet is the water that falls from a fountain;
    Sweet is the sight of one's own true love;
Sweet it must be when a beautiful maiden   5
    Sweetly says "Yes, I will share your poor lot."
Sweet are the orchards with mellow fruit laden –
    Sweeter to me is a *one pound note.*

47. 'Co-operation' Air – Tullochgorum, by David Johnson, F—, by Brechin. Published 3 April 1869.

The co-operative movement, with its strong roots in Scotland and the North of England, was gaining national momentum in these decades, and Johnson's song probably responds to the first national Co-operative Congress, held in London in 1869. He argues that the co-operative movement provides a solution to the strikes and industrial unrest of this period. Brechin United Co-operative Society operated from the early 1860s, but the town's longer history of co-operative movements is commemorated by a centenary plaque, which dates their origins to 1833. The repetition fits the tune for 'Tullochgorum'. The lyrics of this lively traditional song about drinking and dancing invite 'Whig and Tory' to drop their enmity and join 'in mirth and glee.' Johnson is unidentified. This seems to be his only poem in the *Journal* from these decades.

See also: 62. 'To the Domestic Servants', p. 105; 84. 'The Millennium of Capital', p. 146.

Come ye who cry in doubting mood,   1
"O, who will show us any good?"
Come all ye toiling multitude –
    Your strikes are ruination;
They're doubtful triumphs at the best,   5
Doubtful triumphs, doubtful triumphs,
Doubtful triumphs at the best –
    How trite the observation!
They're doubtful triumphs at the best;
But there's a plan by a' confest –   10
The only one will stand the test –
    It's just Co-operation.

Co-operation's just and right,
It makes us a' in ane unite,
No more to madly waste our might   15
    In strikes or agitation:
But wise and prudent to achieve,
Wise and prudent, wise and prudent,
Wise and prudent to achieve
    Our social elevation;   20
But wise and prudent to achieve –

All – all our proudest hopes conceive,
And all the blessings we believe
    Lie in Co-operation.

Let lazy drones – who dread the hour   25
When they'll no longer have the power
The sweets of labour to devour –
    Sneer at our aspiration;
Shall we then fooled and frightened be?
Fooled and frightened, fooled and frightened?   30
Shall we then fooled and frightened be
    By their prognostication?
Shall we then fooled and frightened be,
And never seek to use the key
Will set at length poor Labour free –   35
    Our own Co-operation?

Then let us all go join the Store,
The boat that waits to waft us o'er
The gulf between us and the shore,
    Of our emancipation.   40
Now wise and saving we'll be a'
Wise and saving, wise and saving,
Wise and saving we'll be a',
Our profits, like a big snawba',
Will grow, till they employ us a' –   45
    That's true Co-operation.

A brighter day is drawing near,
When sovereign justice shall appear
To watch o'er labour's glad career,
    Freed from its long probation;   50
Then peace and plenty shall displace,
Peace and plenty, peace and plenty,
Peace and plenty shall displace
    Fierce strikes, and dire starvation;
Then peace and plenty shall displace,   55
Our wrongs, and every smiling face,
Shall tell the blessings all possess
    Through our Co-operation.

48. 'John Keats', by A. A., Kirkconnell. Published 17 April 1869.

'A. A.' is the well-known working-class poet Alexander Anderson, who at this point had not yet adopted his common pseudonym of 'Surfaceman'. Anderson was one of the most admired and successful of the *People's Journal* and *People's Friend* contributors, with a stronger relationship to the latter (which published most of his best-known poems in the 1870s) than to the former. He was a frequent winner in the *Journal* Christmas poetry competitions and his books were reviewed and praised lavishly. 'John Keats' was reprinted by the *People's Friend* on Wednesday 20 April, 1870, signed 'Surfaceman', inaugurating Anderson's relationship with the *Friend*. It was later republished in *Ballads and Sonnets* (London: Macmillan, 1879), p. 168, but without the title identifying Keats as the subject. While Anderson is remembered for his poems about railway work and the dignity of labour – which are those that tend to be anthologised, and show a clear development in skill from this early poem – he was a devotee of the Romantic poets and wrote a number of poems on Keats, Shelley and others. Like many poems by working men and women, 'John Keats' highlights an engagement with poetry in terms of comfort, inspiration and escapism. Keats (derided in his lifetime as a 'Cockney' poet) was highly regarded by working-class writers of this period.

See also: 107. 'Jenny wi' the Airn Teeth', p. 192.

He came from a land whose shadows   1
    Were brighter than our day,
And he sang of the streams and meadows,
    And then he went away.

Now I curse the heart that ever   5
    Will mourn for the clay behind,
When the soul is such glorious liver
    In the boundless realms of mind.

So at night when I grow dreary,
    And a sorrow is in my breast,   10
And the wings of life grow weary,
    And flutter, as if for rest:

Then I open my little bookcase,
    When the quiet is breathing low,
And I take from the shelf in silence   15
    A volume of long ago;

And I read and read by the firelight,
    Till quick and clear as chimes,
The man himself is with me,
    And is talking to me in rhymes.   20

Talking of waving meadows,
    And cunningly hidden brooks,
With the quietest gush of eddies,
    That the flowers may see their looks.

Babbling of summer and sunshine,   25
    And hills that reach the cloud –
And this – all this is in whispers,
    For he never speaks aloud.

So I read and read by the firelight,
    And listen to his talk,   30
As you would to a friend that joins you
    In your summer evening's walk.

Then betimes, when I shut the volume,
    To walk in the quiet street,
When the stars that are shadows of angels   35
    Have made its silence sweet,

He follows me still, like the shadows
    That none but spirits see,
And at every pause of the footstep
    The dead man speaks to me: 40

Whispers and speaks till the night-time
    Is fraught with all his tone,
And I cannot but let the pulses
    Of my being beat with his own.

So it fills with joy and gladness   45
    And the freshness of his prime;

And this all – this is only
From a volume full of rhyme.

From a volume of love and dreaming,
When youth was firm and strong;   50
But the dust is to me as nothing,
When the spirit is in the song.

So whenever I lift the volume,
Like summer beams that flow,
The dead man is still beside me,   55
And babbles of long ago.

49. 'The Tory Lords', by Will Harrow. Published 17 July 1869.

As noted above, Harrow (John Campbell) was radical in politics, and published several vehemently anti-Tory poems in the *Journal*. This poem responds generally to the aftermath of the Second Reform Bill. It is probably also a specific response to the dramatic revelations by Welsh Liberal MPs in the House of Commons on 6 July 1869 that Conservative candidates and landlords in Wales had threatened tenants with eviction if they failed to support the Tories – against their principles – in the previous election.

See also: 35. 'A Lay of Reform', p. 60; 37. 'Reform', p. 64; 88.
'Ring Up the Curtain', p. 155; 93. 'An Election Song', p. 165.

Crême de la crême are ye!   1
        Sweet Tory Lords,
The very pink o' lacteal oil,
        Creamy Tory Lords.
But some do speak a different way,   5
Ye're not even honest milk, they say,
But just a blash o' blinket whey –
        Sour Tory Lords.

An acrid taint is in your blood,
        Grim Tory Lords.   10

Your coronets are in the mud,
        Fouled Tory Lords.
Enveloped in your lordly pride,
The people's will ye have defied –
Scorned to hear them when they cried.   15
        Proud Tory Lords!

Ever for the wrong ye fight,
        Wicked Tory Lords;
Ever wrong and never right,
        Stupid Tory Lords;   20
For shadows of the past ye fight,
Scowling at departed night,
Howling at the coming light,
        Dreary Tory Lords.

The people spoke, and you must hear,   25
        Proud Tory Lords;
Or to reason or to fear
        Yield, Tory Lords.
The millions erst have you adored;
But now they do not fear a lord –   30
Yield, or topple overboard,
        Proud Tory Lords.

blinket – sour

50. 'The Herd Laddie', by Wolfhill. Published 11 September 1869.

'The Herd Laddie' is another poem in the popular suffering-child genre, which usually focuses on invoking pity for working-class children who are orphaned, abandoned or otherwise neglected. This poem lacks the standard Christian message, concentrating, more than most, on direct description of the physical suffering of the child. Herding cows was a common profession for young children in agricultural districts in this period, and a number of poets in this collection had worked as 'herd laddies' in their childhood. 'Wolfhill' is unidentified.

See also: 19. 'Nan Tamson's Wean', p. 33, 27. 'The Chappin' Laddie', p. 48.

See yon wee bit laddie   1
    That herds the farmer's kye,
Hooever coorse the weather be
    He aye maun stop ootbye;
He hisna ane tae care for him –   5
    No ane on a' the earth –
The wee bit orphan laddie
    That cam' frae the toon o' Perth.

He hisna a shoe upon his fit,
    His cleedin's unco' bare;   10
He's stannin' up against a tree –
    The puir loon's greetin' sair;
The rain has wet 'im to the skin,
    Yet hame he daurna gang;
Though it sud rain frae morn tae nicht,   15
    He's oot the hale day lang.

His kye are unco' ill to herd,
    Because the pasture's bare;
They'll no stay at peace a minnit,
    They wander here an' there;   20
He trachles an' rins after them
    Thro' corn an' barley weet,
Till on the whins an' chuckie stanes
    He's scartit a' his feet.

Fain wid he be tae rin awa',   25
   If he kenn'd whar tae rin;
But he disna' hae a mither,
   Nor a friend tae tak 'im in;
So he thinks he'll better be content,
   Altho' his comfort's sma';   30
As weel to trachle whar' he is
   As starve whan he's awa.

kye – cattle   *trachle – to limp, drag oneself along*
chuckie – pebble, small stone   *scartit – scraped*

51. 'A Tale of a Whale', by Harpoon. Published 20 November 1869.

On 3 November 1869, a large fin whale (known in the nineteenth century as a 'finner') was trapped in the Firth of Forth, shot, and stranded on the beach at Longniddry. The Longniddry Whale instantly became a tourist attraction, featured in a widely circulated engraving in the *Illustrated London News*, and in 1870 was the subject of two anatomical articles in the *Transactions of the Royal Society of Edinburgh* by William Turner, Professor of Anatomy at the University of Edinburgh. Whaling was a substantial industry in Dundee throughout the nineteenth century, and the occasional appearance of whales in Scottish waters caused great excitement – especially in the more famous 1884 case of the Tay Whale.

My tale's of a whale – the Longniddry whale –   1
Who stranded himself at the end of the gale
In the Frith of Forth. He had followed the trail
Of his comrade, who had been out for a sail,
They came cruising around the Head of Kinsale   5
Through the Pentland Firth, where the sea-bird's wail
Had assailed the ears of the doomed whale,
And warned him then to turn his tail,
And unless on a safer cruise he'd sail
He'd be scotched and killed as dead as a nail.   10
But he didn't care; and he flopped his tail,
And jumped and gamboled, the stupid whale,
Exactly as if he'd been drunk with ale.

His comrades (alas! advice is stale)
Advised him not to give heed to the tale;   15
For where was there ever a stronger whale,
Or one with so mighty and powerful a tail
To steer his way in the strongest gale?
He laughed in his fin as he heard their tale,
Held down the coast and came round by Crail,   20
And entered the Frith in the teeth of the gale,
And rushed as fast as the Limited Mail
On the London, Chatham, and Dover Rail.
But he soon found out he had entered a jail
That had puzzled the brains of many a whale   25
To escape from, or even get out on bail.
In despair he used his tail as a flail,
And lashed the water from green to pale;
And he rushed on the rocks, and, without avail,
He struggled to float himself off and sail;   30
But the grizzly rocks did his sides impale,
And the bold young fellows of Eskadale
Approached the monster with spike and nail,
And rifle and musket, and killed the whale.
And the Custom-house officer heard the tale,   35
And he said Her Majesty claimed the whale.
And the crowds came trooping by road and rail
To see and talk and attend the sale.
They said that he was a Roquhal whale,
And the whale, they said, was in gender a male.   40
The skin of his back resembled a snail,
And underneath it approached to pale;
He was thirty yards from snout to tail –
In short, he was a tremendous whale.
Mr Tait, from Fife, attended the sale;   45
He gave the best price, and he bought the whale.
Six scores of pounds was of money the tale
Her Majesty got for the monster whale.
As the whale began to scent the gale
With odour exceedingly vile to inhale,   50
Two steamers were hired, and a rope not frail
Was securely fastened around his tail.
The men on shore gave the steamers a hail,
And they tugged and strained and started the whale,
And floated him off, and away they sail   55

To Kirkcaldy, to boil and make oil of the whale.
They landed him there without any fail,
And this is the tail of the tale of the whale.

52. 'The Charge of the Light Brigade (Apollo's)', by J. D., Farnell, 23 November 1869. Published 27 November 1869.

This poem responds to the announcement that the *Journal* had received 600 entries for the annual Christmas prize competition in 1869. Due to the number of entrants, aspiring poets had been restricted to forty-eight lines or less. The poem parodies Tennyson's 'The Charge of the Light Brigade', one of the best-known poems of this period. The author is unidentified.

See also: 21. 'An Apology', p. 37; 29. 'A Voice from Parnassus', p. 51; 61. 'Defeatit', p. 104; 85. 'The Poet's Wail', p. 148.

Forty-eight, forty-eight,   1
Forty-eight lines each –
Climbing Parnassus' steep,
    Wrote the six hundred.
"Forward the Light Brigade!   5
Take the prize!" Apollo said;
For fame and for two pounds ten
    Wrote the six hundred.

"Forward the Light Brigade!"
Felt they no touch of dread?   10
What though poets born, not made,
    Oftimes have blundered?
Critics must ratify
What song doth sanctify;
Soaring in ecstasy,   15
Seeking Parnassus' top,
    Wrote the six hundred.

Pieces put up with care,
Pieces enough to scare

Critics a dozen there; 20
Charging an editor,
　　While the world wonder'd.
Through the Post Office came
Every day loads of them;
Postman and editor 25
Cursing their bulk and weight,
　　Thought, groaning under it,
When they come back they'll not –
　　Not be six hundred.

Critics to right of them, 30
Critics to left of them,
Critics behind them,
　　All stood dumfounder'd
Sneer'd at as doggerel,
Pegasus, and poet fell, 35
They that had wrote so well,
Safe from the critic's paws
Back from the bushel came
All that was left of them –
　　Left of six hundred. 40

When can their glory fade?
O the wild charge they made!
　　All the world wonder'd.
Honour the charge they made!
Honour the Light Brigade – 45
　　Noble six hundred!

53. 'The Tay Bridge', by J. B. M., Eglinton Street, Glasgow, April 1870. Published 23 April 1870.

In spring 1870, funding had just been found to build the first bridge across the Tay. J. B. M. celebrates this in the context of Dundee's rapid expansion and growth as a centre of trade and industry. The author, who is unidentified, shows his loyalty to Dundee and sense of himself as a Dundonian even though he is currently located in Glasgow.

See also: 80. 'An Address to Thee Tay Bridge', p. 138; 91.
'Lines, Suggested by the Melancholy Wreck of the Tay Bridge',
p. 162; 92. 'In Memoriam', p. 164.

Improvements vast our town has seen   1
    Since twenty years ago,
When enterprising schemes were few,
    And councils moved but slow.
But now-a-days our public men,   5
    We all are proud to see,
Are stirring with a heart and will
    To ornament Dundee.

The restless spirit of the age
    Now moves with rapid strides: 10
And engineering skill now laughs
    At floods and roaring tides;
For Tay's broad stream will soon be bridged,
    And critics all agree
'Twill give our rising town a lift,   15
    And famous make Dundee.

'Twill stimulate our local trade,
    Our busy hives increase;
Fresh vigour give our restless wheels,
    Nor let their noises cease;   20
The hidden "gems" of Fife we'll have
    At prices almost free,
When snorting engines o'er the Tay
    Come laden to Dundee.

And to extend our commerce down 25
    'Twill lend a powerful hand,
Until our present Royalty's
    Eclipsed at Broughty's strand.
Sir, changes great our "rising sprouts"
    Are destined yet to see, 30
And all through this gigantic scheme –
    The Tay Bridge of Dundee.

Come let us agitate at once –
    There's danger in delay –
To have a bracing pathway grand 35
    Above the glistening Tay;
'Twould grace the Bridge, a boon confer,
    Send scudding o'er with glee,
Right to the whinny braes o' Fife,
    The loons of huge Dundee. 40

May nothing mar its onward course –
    No danger unforeseen –
Till wedded be yon blooming knowes
    To Magdalen's famous Green.
May neither life nor limb be lost 45
    In piling through the sea,
Till, like an Iron Giant, it stands –
    The Wonder of Dundee.

Rejoicings great will greet the scene
    Upon the opening day, 50
When thitherward all grades will flock
    To line the banks of Tay.
This is no dreamy theme of mine –
    Such things are bound to be;
And say I with you all, my friends, 55
    "May I be there to see."

54. 'To My Auld Knapsack', by John Pindar. Gibraltar, April 1870. Published on 4 June 1870.

John Pindar (Peter Leslie) started his career as a coalminer in Fife before joining the 71st Highland Light Infantry, serving with them in India and Ireland: he was stationed in Gibraltar from 1868 to 1872. On his later return to Scotland, he developed a particularly strong relationship with the *Fife News*, which published his autobiography and supported a volume of his poems in 1893. Pindar is one of several soldier-poets who submitted their verse to the *Journal*. 'To My Auld Knapsack' shows the circulation of the *Journal* among Scots working overseas (Pindar claims here that he carried a year's newspapers with him) and incorporates familiar themes of nostalgia for home and family. It was republished in *Rambling Rhymes*, ed. Rev. A. M. Houston (Cupar: J. & G. Innes, Fife News, 1893), pp. 155–57.

See also: 6. 'The Dundee Maiden', p. 12; 22. 'Home Recollections', p. 40.

Guid frien' you've been to me, auld pack; 1
Nae mair you'll dangle on my back;
But let us hae a parting crack,
  For my heart's fou
Wi' grief an' sorrow noo to tak' 5
  Fareweel o' you.

'Tis noo eleven years an' mair –
Lang years to me o' joy an' care –
Since you an' I together were
  Acquainted first; 10
An' though you've made my lang back sair,
  I never curst.

You've kept my auld kit weel thegither,
In sunny an' in stormy weather,
An' a' the letters frae my brither 15
  That I hae gotten,
Forbye the Bible frae my mither –
  A sweet love token.

I've had you stowed so full o' shoes,
Stockings, towels, an' tartan trews, 20

Besides a year o' *People's News*,
        Which made you heavy;
You've made the sweat run owre my broos,
        Like draps o' gravy.

When wandering India's sunny clime,   25
'Mang grandeur stern an' sublime,
At night my head would oft recline
        Upon your tap,
Where I've enjoyed a sweet bit fine
        Refreshin' nap.   30

Yon day you fell in Ganges River
I thought to tine you a' thegither;
But auld Forsyth – so smart an' clever –
        Rescued you clean,
As you were sailing like a feather   35
        Adown the stream.

'Twas only ance that I can mind
That you, auld pack, was left behind,
When in a gloomy store you pined
        For saxty days,   40
While I was fighting pagans blind,
        On Indian braes.

Four times we've crossed the southern main,
An' traversed mony a fragrant plain,
An' now we've come abroad again,   45
        Alas! to part;
To leave you on the soil o' Spain
        Will break my heart.

If your successor chance to be,
Just like yoursel', a frien' to me,   50
Perhaps we'll whiles, in social glee,
        Enjoy a crack;
But I'll remember till I dee
        My auld knapsack.

fou – mad   *trews – trousers*
tine – lose, mislay

55. 'The Land That Rear'd Us A' ', by Backwoodsman. Published 24 September 1870.

Throughout this period, debates over whether and where to emigrate were a central feature of the *Journal*. Frequent letters and other seemingly authentic accounts were published in its columns from readers who had emigrated to different parts of the world, either extolling the advantages of particular locations (usually Canada, the United States, Australia, New Zealand or South Africa), or advising readers to stay at home due to difficult conditions overseas. Poems and songs about and by emigrants were very common. While almost all are deeply nostalgic for an imagined Scottish homeland, many also argue that the colonies offered greater freedom and democracy – particularly the freedom to own and work one's own land – than contemporary Scotland. The author of this poem is unidentified.

See also: 66. *'Epistle to Tammas Bodkin'*, *p. 112, 71. 'Happy Lamoo', p. 120, 96. 'Dakota', p. 170.*

(*Composed and Sung in a Backwoods Shanty.*)
O Scotia, mony is the sang   1
    We sing in praise o' thee;
And mony ane thinks unco lang
    Thy hills again to see.

For there's nae heather on our hills;   5
    We're sax months i' the snaw:
There's nought to see save muckle trees,
    Nor heard save "Gee! Wo! Haa!"

We've sair to toil to clear the soil,
    Right weary strokes we draw;   10
"Chop," "log" an' "fire" – we mauna tire,
    But drink and drive ava'.

Then eat our scrimp potato meal,
    Wi' bread as black's a craw;
Whiles bits o' cheese, whiles bits o' pork,   15
    And whiles we've nane ava'.

But we sit on our ain bit land,
    Frae laird and factor free;

Nae pettifogger fans the flame,
    When neebors disagree.   20

Nae sneakin' keeper spies around
    To trap our cat or dog;
We're everywhere as free as air,
    And happy o'er our grog.

And better days are drawing on;   25
    Our lands will soon be clear,
Our house and barn gi'e bield and bread
    To those we hold so dear.

Though happy here, we never will
    Forget our native ha';   30
Sae toom the horn, and cheer, my boys,
    "The land that reared us a'."

toom – empty

56. 'My Washing Machine', by M. W. W., Coupar Angus. Published 14 January 1871.

'My Washing Machine', although the author is unidentified, implicitly presents itself as a poem by a woman to her friends. Verse advertisements were not uncommon and are usually located on the front page of Victorian newspapers in the classified adverts and clearly identified as such. The *Journal* and other newspapers of the period, however, also print poems elsewhere which celebrate particular products and extol their virtues, seemingly from the position of a satisfied consumer. We might surmise that at least some of these poems were 'sponsored' productions, which the poet was paid to write or which were produced by an agent or employee of the company, but it is impossible to prove. Thomas Bradford & Co. was a company based in Salford and London, and became one of the first major manufacturers of washing machines from the 1860s onwards.

See also: 60. 'Gouldings Manur', p. 101; 63. 'Athole's Pies', p. 107.

With pleasure I call on my friends to behold 1
The wonderful works this machine will unfold;
Indeed, it is almost its weight worth in gold –
The Washing and Wringing and Mangling Machine.

We neither rise early nor stay at it late, 5
And yet it completes our large washing first-rate;
For we now do in four hours what occupied eight,
Through the Washing and Wringing and Mangling
    Machine.

Of washing day evils called legion we're quit;
Our limbs are not aching, our brows are not knit; 10
But with hearts truly thankful we sing while we sit
At the Washing and Wringing and Mangling Machine.

Though it cleanses so quickly, and wrings almost dry,
Though it mangles like satin, the best you can buy,
Yet foes to invention will stand and decry 15
My Washing and Wringing and Mangling Machine.

How prejudice hinders! – you'll find it indeed
Everywhere, but especially north of the Tweed;
Yet mid all opposition I know I succeed
With my Washing and Wringing and Mangling Machine. 20

We publish its merits wherever we go,
And whate'er be your judgment, this one thing I know
That we're deeply indebted to Bradford & Co.
For their Washing and Wringing and Mangling Machine.

57. 'Lines on the Death of the Glenlivet Poet', M., Dundee. Published 18 February 1871.

This poem, by an unidentified author, commemorates John Milne, a shoemaker born in 1792 who began to produce popular poems and songs in the 1820s. Milne 'travelled about the country, like Homer of old, singing and reciting his own poems, and selling them in broadsheets for the purpose of eking out a living' ('The Late John Milne of Glenlivet', 25 November 1871, p. 2) and was a well-known chanter and performer of his verses at fairs and other events. He specialised in political and election verse (he was radically inclined, and a passionate supporter of Liberal candidates) and in verse aimed at farm servants at feeing fairs, often warning about specific masters and their habits. Although much of his 'local' poetry did not survive or was con-sidered too scurrilous to print, the Aberdeen Free Press office published a selection after his death in 1871. In autumn of 1870 the correspondents' column contained a request for information about Milne and a response from a reader who knew him; on 25 November 1871, the *Journal* published a review of *Selections* and Milne's obituary. Like this poem, the obituary sees Milne as a late survival of a vital, but threatened, Scottish oral tradition.

See also: 114. 'Epistle to "Faither Fernie"', p. 209; 116. 'Epistle to Robert Wanlock', p. 213.

John Milne, the Bard o' Livet Glen,	1
The wale o' social, honest men;	
Grim Death, alas! awa' has ta'en	
That rhymester rare,	
An' ower leal Scotland mony a frien'	5
Doth mourn him sair.	
There's scarce a peasant in the North,	
Frae Inverness to winding Forth,	
But high esteemed his mental worth,	
For wit an' glee:	10
Though of obscure and humble birth,	
Yet great was he.	
The foe of tyranny and guile,	
The friend of manly sons of toil,	

He, like the mighty Bard of Kyle,   15
    High sang their praise,
And superstition did revile
    With scourging lays.

John aye was hamely, frank, and plain,
And scorned all actions mean and vain;   20
Though pomp an' pride he did disdain,
    He lo'ed mankind;
Ungrateful thoughts did never stain
    His gen'rous mind.

This worthy Bard, in "hoddin gray,"   25
Lang warstl'd up an' doun life's brae,
An' died in peace, without a fae
    To mar his name;
With Scotia's sons, frae Tweed to Spey,
    Shall live his fame.   30

Baith far an' near his lays he sung,
Rhym'd in the rare auld Scottish tongue;
While hypocrites wi' wit he stung,
    An' cow'd them weel,
An' richt frae wrang to auld an' young   35
    He did reveal.

I think I see him in his prime
Still pourin' forth his rantin' rhyme,
As he, with telling verse sublime,
    The truth extoll'd,   40
While cuifs an' knaves he did contemn
    With satire bold.

But ower his lays nae mair he'll croon,
Nor musing stray by Dee or Don,
Since he life's brief career has run;   45
    Yet, O! may he
With everlasting bliss aboon
    Rewarded be.

wale – the pick, the best   *warstle – struggle*
cuif – fool

58. 'The Tailor's Protest', G. L., Dundee. Published on 25 March 1871.

'The Tailor's Protest' concerns a specific local case: Hugh Sutherland, a Dundee tailor, had started a protest against the use of public funds to support a Corporation dinner in celebration of the wedding of Princess Louise (Queen Victoria's fourth daughter) to the Marquess of Lorne, on 21 March 1871. The editorial of 25 March, 'A Tailor Immortalized', is humorously supportive of Sutherland's stance. G. L.'s poem is more overtly political, and reminds the diners that the new influx of voters after the Second Reform Bill means that the people can show their displeasure at the ballot box. 'Nine tailors make a man' (referenced lines 3 and 11) was a common saying, and the term 'snip' is slang for a tailor; both are mildly derogatory. G. L. is unidentified.

See also: 35. 'A Lay of Reform', p. 60; 37. 'Reform', p. 64.

A tailor o' oor ancient toun	1
Has raised himsel' abune	
The proverb that demeans his trade –	
Guid service he has dune.	
At least he made a bold attempt	5
A grievance to redress;	
An' tho' he didna quite succeed,	
The glory's nane the less.	
We'll for his effort gi'e him thanks,	
An' study, if we can,	10
Never again a snip to ca'	
The ninth pairt o' a man,	
The tailor wadna interfered	
Had folk but haen the sense	
To gie their loyalty full swing	15
A' at their ain expense.	
But when they meet roond festive board,	
Wi' a'thing guid and grand,	
Syne pay the bill aff public rates,	
It's mair than he can stand.	20

We wadna grudge to do things richt,
 But, faith, we're growin' fear'd;
Because oor rulers hae for lang
 Been terribly mislear'd.

A' ye wha feast at oor expense,   25
 I winder ye can thole
To think an echo micht come back
 Oot o' yon quarry hole.

An' think upon election times,
 What voters then may dae;   30
Altho' they canna swamp ye a',
 Ae victim they will hae.

Noo, isn't angersome to think,
 Tho' folk strive a' their micht,
Employin' every proper means,   35
 They canna mak' things richt?

The thocht just mak's me doonricht wild;
 Sae, faith, I'd best get thro'
For fear my indignation mak's
 Me say what I micht rue.   40

Think muckle o' courageous snip
 There's proof that he's no fear'd;
He'd face the lion in his den,
 An' grip him by the beard.

Electors a', then shout hurrah!   45
 To him wha wields the shears –
To oor brave tailor errant knicht,
 Gi'e three richt hearty cheers.

syne – directly after, next   *thole – bear, stand*

59. 'Murder Most Foul', by T. N. D., Dundee. Published 24 June 1871.

The unidentified author of this poem, probably also the author of 'The Night Signalman' (below) asks working-class parents to teach their sons not to go birds-nesting, a common pastime, and so to make Baxter Park a place of safety for birds as well as people. The comparison of caged or persecuted birds to the suffering poor – and often to the suffering working-class poet – was very common in verse of the period, and the reference to 'houseless songsters' in the final line speaks to these analogies.

See also: 23. 'Rouse, Brothers, Rouse', p. 41; 24. 'The Opening of the Baxter Park', p. 43; 108. 'The Night Signalman', p. 194.

(On seeing a Linnet's nest and five young Linnets lying on
    the greensward of the Baxter Park, the nest torn and
    trampled on, and the young birds dead, with evident
    marks on them that cruelty had been practiced –
    Sunday, 18th June 1871)

By Baxter's bounteous hand this meadow fair,   1
    With all these walks and lawns and shrubs arrayed,
Was given unto the People, with the wish sincere
    That *all* would use it, and enjoy the shade
Of the green trees, and wander through those bowers   5
    Where "wood notes wild" would frowning brows
        unbend,
Soothe mingled griefs, and sweeten lonely hours,
    Until each songster seems a rustic friend,
Who, for protection given, their heaven-born music
    spend.

The humble Linnet sings that copse among,   10
    There Jenny Wren perks up her little head,
Aloft is heard the Lark's immortal song,
    The Blackbird's pipe sounds mellow down the glade;
Close by that rock, within his lowly bed,
    Poor Robin with the ruddy-breast sits all alone;   15
Tomtit and Master Yeldring overhead
    Call to Will Wagtail at the fountain stone,
"Safety is here, our dread of boys is gone."

Vain hope, poor birds! once more a gloomy fear
    Must take possession of each fluttering breast: 20
There is not safety for your nestlings dear;
    Here still your young are torn from out the nest,
And you are forced to fly at Cruelty's behest
    From your loved tree, because your frail abode
Is grimly ravished, torn up, and laid waste;   25
    Your murdered nestlings lie *above* yon rising sod,
Where pinks and daisies fringe the well-kept road.

Ye sons of labour! men of stifling streets,
    Ill smelling lanes and wynds, and dust and noise,
A warbler of the woods in sorrow greets,   30
    And asks you to reclaim these blackguard boys.
Tell them *our* nestlings are not torture toys;
    But that life beats in us with nervous glow.
We have our trials and cares, our fears and joys;
    Our life is not all singing on a bough.   35
Protect your houseless songsters evermo'e.

yeldring – yellowhammer

60. 'Gouldings Manur. a pome', by Poute. Published 18 November 1871.

In 'Gouldings Manur', Poute parodies the genre of advertising poetry, and plays on his own established persona as someone obsessed with growing giant vegetables (see 'Kale-Wurms'). In his praise of manure, he even comes up with an alliterative Scots advertising slogan for the company he celebrates, 'Goulding's graith gars grow' (Goulding's preparation makes [things] grow). Goulding's was an established Irish business. On 15 April 1871 the *Journal* printed an advert on the front page for 'W & H. M. Goulding's Manure, Cork and Dublin', which listed agents in Scotland and invited 'Applications for Agencies in Districts not yet represented': Poute's final footnote speaks directly to this. 'Keniwy' and 'Fruchy' are Kennoway and Freuchie, villages in Fife, and 'Backstir' presumably Baxter. As in Poute's other poems, much here is deliberately obscure in terms of dialect and references. 'Lums' in his headnote refers to a previously published poem addressing factory chimneys.

See also: 14. 'Untitled [Letter to Editor]', p. 25; 15. 'Odd to the Krokis', p. 27; 26. 'Apostroffe to the Rainbow', p. 46; 30. 'Kale-Wurms', p. 52; 56. 'My Washing Machine', p. 93; 63. 'Athole's Pies', p. 107.

> with nots And Annie tashens: Dedickted
>   to mr whyt stremigly fews.
> "having dun ampil Justiss to The lums
> They've got there Ditty – now my Mus Succum's
> to chang her texkst – brik praps must Now giv place
> what I'm to Cing's a Blessing to the rase."
>   from My skrap book.   Poute

Hail! Hail! Al Hail! thou goulding's Grate spiseefik!   1
that Maks deff erth eeld etibles prolific.
Thou Wundir of the World! Grate Fertilizer!
Aksepp this pome from Me thine advertizer.
in sweeter strans Than evir shaicksper Sung   5
I'll Cing thy prays As long's i have A tung.
thy feeding Powrs gav me in twathree Weeks
a Most enormis Crop of Monstris leeks.
like gosky sigs wi' Michty lang white rutes

& very neer as Thicks a plumans kutes. 10
the tails for sighs – wer like the laves o' Books
& ansird fine in hairsd to theck the stooks.
but leeks tho monstirs – al the peepil kno
Ar only *one* thing – gouldings graith gars grow.
My Karrits – losh preserv us – ar like Flails 15
Al fresh & helthy – And al free o' Snals.
And evry ing'n i have is like a Neep
hung up in nets, thats made for fensin' Sheep
and all the Kabitch Stoks i have in tack
Ar Just aboot As bigs a Little Stack 20
My Kurlies & My roobarb ar like Trees
They melt into my muth like snaw or greez.
But it wud tacts my Graffik powrs to show
the different things that gouldings graith gars grow
Pizz – fooshy's – Dalyez – raps – it's all the same 25
it gars al growe – on erth, that has A name.
Losh man! hoo Did it cum into yer powe
to study graith – for garrin taaties Grow.
The Hitt yev made – pruves that beyont a dout
Yer very nigh abowt as kliver's poute 30
That's No Sain littil na, no, – weel'a wat –
feu very Feu – gets honir such as that.
Ive study'd till my harenpan wus rackit
Tryin to find oot – to sea if i cud mak it.
Aha! Gudesooth! it bafils Me to tell 35
hoo it is made, nane kens except yersel.
Still, I beleev its micksed up wi' "Klute"
Hors-Banes – Swine lugg – Cod-liver Saat and Soot
al Steerd aboot – Syne Dryd upon a Kil
& grund like Neezin-Snuph into a Mill. 40
Then Sold in Shillin Kanisters of tin
When you lift Aff the lid you can See in.
For cleenlines – nocht on the erth can beat it
it is So Sweet – the very bees can eat it.
At Keniwy, it reer – Sich Dons! And "dawties" 45
that al the erth has hard Of *Backstirs* taaties.
It Swals them up like pudiks – & to Kleck
So Ryfe & beg – that thirteen fills a peck.
And backstir Says – but Backstir whyles can blaw
he filled a peck anse wi a Cingle Sha! 50
The Sha itsel – which meashurd 10 feet long

Cud made *Kreel-ribs*, It was so stiff and Strong,
And then – I wuss ye only Saw His neeps!!
ye cudna Keep yer tung – faw Sayin – "gude Keeps".!
Sic Awful Jiants o' neeps as he can rere   55
theyr al Like small balloons – as Shur's I'm hear –
They tak A gepin world by Mut Surpriz.
at evry Sho He take Th Foremest prize.
But not to backstir al the prays is Due
No.   Gouling i ascribe Most prays to you.   60
The Stranj Kompownd – i'll say no more About it
but this – No garden Man Shou'd Bee withowt it
One Singil pownd Note only Kills the Grub
But reres As mony leeks as fills A tub!
So Reedir if yev Any taste for Leeks   65
Try *gouldings* MANUR. & yell bet The greeks.
Now Gouling lad – I hop ye'll mind this *ae-thing*
if ye Don't Send a bocks to me for – nae-thing
i niver Mor, will Lift my Pen to prays –
Thy golden Ceerip – NIVER AL MY DAYS!   70
                                                    POUTE
Not. first. 1st. Sold in Tin Kanisters By dauvit normen &
co Keniwy at 1 ech bocks. Not. 2ndly. For a Publick good
Mr levyson Shud Be Apointed adjent for the fruchy.
     Est inch fruchy. Nov 3d 1871 –

gosky – *overgrown, rank, esp. of grass*   *kutes (cuit/coot)* – *ankles*
hairsd (hairst) – *harvest*   *theck* – *thatch*
graith – *preparation*   *gars* – *makes*
ingin – *onion*   *neep* – *turnip*
fensin' – *blocking out*   *powe* – *head*
'Klute' – *possibly reference to the Devil ('Clute/Cloot')*   *lugg* – *ear*
neezin-snuph – *snuff*
don – *leader*   *dawtie* – *darling*
pudik – *toad*   *sha (shaw)* – *leaves or foliage of a root vegetable*
kreel (creel) – *woven basket*

61. 'Defeatit', by Eriphos, Methven. Published 2 December 1871.

'Eriphos' published several other poems in the *Journal* during these decades – including 'Oor Mill' – but is unidentified (the pseudonym is borrowed from a classical comic poet; Methven is in Fife). The 'defeat' here is in the Christmas poetry competition, which once again had attracted a bumper crop of aspiring poets. Eriphos uses his defeat in the competition in a moral about the importance of practicing reading and writing poetry for 'mutual improvement', thus approving the motive of the editors in setting up such competitions. By this period, poems *about* the poetry competitions were themselves a significant subgenre in the run-up to the hotly anticipated results.

See also: 21. 'An Apology', p. 37; 29. 'A Voice from Parnassus', p. 51; 52. 'The Charge of the Light Brigade', p. 86. 68. 'Oor Mill', p. 115.

Defeatit again, sirs! Then what's to be done?   1
Get into the dumps and look doon at my shoon,
And mummel and yirn for the feck o' a day
Aboot favour to some and the want o' fair-play,
And firmly resolve, wi' my hands on my knee,   5
That I'll never fecht mair for a prize at Dundee!

It's a haver to think, when a chiel' wants the lear,
That he's fit to compete with three hunner and mair,
Wha, for oucht he may ken, hae been a' college bred,
Or if no, in book learnin' are unco weel read,   10
Wi' plenty o' time on their hands – no like me:
Troth, it's easy for them to compete at Dundee.

I'm glad, though, a gliffin o' sense yet remains,
And that something has come for my trouble and pains
For since e'er I began to put thochts upon paper,   15
I read and I write mair without ony caper;
Then I strive like a man, for Dame Fortune may jee,
And send me a prize yet frae "Bonnie Dundee."

I'm no verra sure but a prize I hae got
That will last me far langer than shillin's or note: 20

I hae learned to think – oh! the pleasure it gi'es me!
And my e'enin's are spent in a wye noo to please me.
E'en for this I'm content, so I canna weel see
Hoo there's muckle to grudge at wi' them in Dundee.

Then, courage! ye hunders wha enter the strife,   25
Ever think wi' a will, and then write as for life.
This yearly competin's a glorious movement,
Designed, without doot, for our mutual improvement.
To get a' siller prizes, that never can be,
But the motive's a grand ane they hae at Dundee.   30

mummel – mumble   yirn – whine, complain
feck – majority, most of   haver – nonsense, rubbish
lear – learning   gliffin – gleam (glimmer)

62. 'To the Domestic Servants', by Matilda, Dundee, 1872. Published 4 May 1872.

In spring of 1872, the debate over working conditions for female servants revived in a series of letters published in the *Journal*. On 27 April the *Journal* reported on a large meeting of servants in Mathers' Hotel, Dundee, at which participants argued that they should have a Sunday off each fortnight and a half-holiday every week, and objected to the principle that they were supposed to buy and wear particular caps (grievances about dress are referenced in lines 7 and 16 of 'To the Domestic Servants'). The Chairwoman argued that their treatment amounted to slavery, and announced, 'We have been subjected to a great deal of harsh and unfair treatment, and we have come here tonight to form a protective Union.' The meeting closed with the formation of the 'Dundee and District Servants' Protection Association.' This nascent union was met with praise from some quarters and satire in others. While 'Matilda' is both supportive and gently satirical, the *Journal* also reprinted two hostile poems satirising the new union and the servants' demands, one from *Punch* on 11 May 1872 (which may indicate less an editorial stance than interest in the fact that a local Dundee affair had made it into *Punch*) and an unsigned poem purporting to show the perspective of male servants, 'Jeames to the Rescue', on 18 May. The editorial of 4 May was cautiously in support of the women's union, but counselled moderation in its demands.

See also: 32. *'The Scottish Servant Maid', p. 56; 33. 'A Scottish Servant Maid', p. 57; 36. 'Song to the Servant Maids', p. 62.*

Ye servants in an' roun' Dundee,   1
    Ye noble band o' wenches,
Ye've let the haughty "*Madams*" see
    Nae more ye'll thole their pinches.

Nae mair ye'll stand their snash an' brag,   5
    Or mind their lang palaver;
Nae mair ye'll wear that silly "*Flag*,"
    Or ony sic like haver.

Nae mair ye'll spend the hallow'd day
    In cookin' beef an' mutton,   10
In roastin', toastin' (I micht say)
    Rubbin', scrubbin', cuttin'.

Nae mair ye'll sit till aifter midnicht
    Boilin' toddy-water:
Henceforth, ye'll wear whate'er ye think richt,   15
    And nane speir *"Wha's yer hatter?"*

Nae mair ye'll work frae week tae week
    At wark that's oucht but cannie;
But hauf a day ilk week ye seek
    Tae "catch" an' "coort" a *mannie*,   20

I've heard a deal 'bout *"woman's richt"*,
    But never cud see thro' it;
But, feth, ye dames hae clear'd my sicht,
    An' I'm fair buckled to it.

I wish ye weel wi' a' my heart,   25
    Ye sonsie weelfaur'd kimmers;
But "sneaks" I'd lash ahent a cart,
    "The supple-chafted limmers."

I houp ye'll a' amalgamate
    Tae gain the point ye've startit:
Tho' whiles ye've cause tae dreed yer fate,   30
    Yet never get doon-hearted.

thole – suffer   *snash – insult, abuse*
haver – nonsense   *speir – ask*
sonsie – attractive (often referencing figure, i.e. buxom)
kimmer – girl, lass   *supple-chafted – loose-tongued ('chaft' – jaw)*
limmer – rascal, rogue

63. 'Athole's Pies', by The Factory Muse, Dundee, 1872. Published 1 June 1872.

This is another ambiguous advertising poem purporting to be written by a satisfied customer, this time in praise of a local rather than national company. It incorporates deliberately overblown praise and poetic cliché for comic effect, as does Poute's mock-advertising poem 'Gouldings Manur'. Various poets in the *Journal* sign themselves as factory workers. 'The Factory Muse' is probably local Dundee poet Adam Wilson (b. 1850), who identified himself as such in an early twentieth-century handwritten collection, *Flowers of Fancy* (preserved in the A. C. Lamb collection in Dundee Central Library), with the dedication, 'To the Mill and Factory Operatives of Dundee these Poetical Trifles are Inscribed by their Sincere Friend and Fellow Worker, the Factory Muse, Adam Wilson' (see Scott, p. 43).

See also: 56. 'My Washing Machine', p. 93; 60. 'Gouldings Manur', p. 101.

Awake, my mirky muse! oh rise   1
And sound the praise o' Athole's pies.
For cheapness, quality, and size,
      Nane can them beat,
The sappy lumps that take the prize,   5
      For they're a treat.

Each minds me o' a baker's bonnet,
Sae round and big wi' flour upon it:
In fact, the chield deserves a sonnet,
      Whae'er supplies   10
These savoury clods; he is a don at
      Athole's pies.

O' a' the pies that e'er were eaten
At private board or social meetin',
There's no a pie like them in Britain,   15
    A'body cries;
Lease me upon the minch and dreepin'
    O' Athole's pies.

Yon hungry loon, whase craving kite
Is a' your care and chief delight,   20
If you wad try but ane some night,
    You wad be wise;
Then you wad see if I say right
    O' Athole's pies.

Sic lumps o' fat and dauds o' mutton   25
Atween their twa het sides lie shutten,
Aneath a cover ower them putten,
    Whaur temptin' lies
A sumptuous feast for ony glutton –
    Athole's pies.   30

The lad wha has an hour to pass,
If he is gaun to treat his lass,
To Athole's gangs, that place first-class –
    There ilk ane hies –
And gies'r a pie: nane can surpass   35
    The Athole pies.

Like humble bee that lightly skips
Frae flower to flower, and sweetly sips
The juice that issues frae their tips,
    And never shies,   40
Sae wad you smack an' lick your lips
    Ower Athole's pies.

don – leader   *minch – mince*
kite – belly   *ilk ane – everyone*

64. 'The Evening Hours, A Homely Rhyme', by J. Doubleyou, Dalcrue. Published 1 June 1872.

Published in the same issue as 'Athole's Pies', this is another poem that extols the pleasures of simple, Christian family life and the domestic circle for working men. The attraction of such poems is shown by the immediate response poem 'Address to J. Doubleyou.' 'Doubleyou' is unidentified.

See also: 20. 'The Bairnies at Hame', p. 35; 22. 'Home Recollections', p. 40; 65. 'Address to J. Doubleyou', p. 110.

When the toilsome day is yieldin'   1
    To the dark'nin' clouds o' nicht,
An' the stars begin to twinkle,
    Wi' a saft an' dreamy licht;
An' the shadows thick are flittin',   5
    In the gloamin' dim an' grey,
Then the labrer, tired an' weary,
    Plods his welcome homeward way.

But the weariness an' languor
    Frae his face are chased ere lang,   10
By the warm, ruddy firelicht,
    An' the kettle's cheery sang;
Syne as sune's the supper's endit,
    The bit bairnie's tae him gi'en,
An' it pu's his beard while mammie   15
    Mak's the dishes snod an' clean.

Then the younger anes are beddit,
    For wee, sleepy e'en are theirs,
An' the mither, bendin' ower them,
    Hears them lisp their simple prayers;   20
An' the aulder anes their lessons
    For the schule their faither learns,
But the grammar often puzzles
    Baith the faither an' the bairns.

Syne the man' an' wife sit crackin'   25
    Ower the plans they'll hae tae try
Tae mak' baith ends meet thegither,
    An' tae keep the wolf ootbye;

But as lang's they're weel an' able,
    An' while sickness 'bides awa',   30
Hard eneuch may be their trials,
    But they'll warsle through them a'.

When the yellow blaze has vanished,
    An' the fire has burned sae low
That there's naething left but embers,   35
    Wi' their changin', fitfu' glow,
To the Ear that's ever open,
    Saftly breathed's the nicht's request:
Then the lab'rer and his wifie
    Seek their peacefu' place o' rest.   40

snod – neat   warsle – struggle, wrestle with

65. 'Address to J. Doubleyou.' Unsigned. Published 22 June 1872.

This response poem to J. Doubleyou's 'The Evening Hours. A Homely Rhyme' is interesting in that the speaker suggests that the rather clichéd scenes of J. Doubleyou's poem, familiar from a great many such Scots poems in the period, read to him as domestic realism. It also again highlights the ideological function of poetry, and sentimental verse in particular, in the *Journal*: to offer moral support and strength 'for the fight'. The reading scene pictured here carefully positions the *Journal* as a family paper.

See also: 20. 'The Bairnies at Hame', p. 35; 22. 'Home Recollections', p. 40; 64. 'The Evening Hours. A Homely Rhyme', p. 109.

My weekly share of toil had just been ended,   1
    One summer day in June;
The cozy fire had just been stirred and mended,
    And I had sat me doon

Upon a chair, and, scancing ower the *Journal*,   5
    "A Homely Rhyme" I spied
A little lad, the eldest of my offspring,
    Was seated by my side.

As on I read, my interest still kept growing,
    So exquisitely fine   10
And tender were the beautiful allusions,
    They did my heart entwine;

But when I landed on the puzzling grammar,
    The picture was so true,
The little chap looked up and said right archly,   15
    "Father, that's just been you."

To this, of course, I gave a flat denial,
    But onward still I read
And still, as if reflected in a dial,
    My home was there portrayed.   20

I thank you, sir, for this your homely rhyming;
    It strengthens for the fight,
And makes one feel as if the bells were chiming,
    "Darkness shall soon be light."

May He who made and listens to the ravens,   25
    When crying for their food,
Make darkness light, and crooked things make even,
    And all things work for good.

And from your homely rhyme into your bosom
    May blessings back accrue;   30
May joy and gladness ever bud and blossom
    Around "J. Doubleyou."

66. 'Epistle to Tammas Bodkin', by Will Harrow, Salt River, Capetown, South Africa. Published 13 July 1872.

At this point, 'Will Harrow' (John Campbell) had emigrated to South Africa: the *Journal* wished him well in his new career there on 30 September 1871. Harrow sent several poems 'home' to the *Journal* from South Africa, including one framed as an epistle to Poute. Like some of the other emigrant poets in this volume, he is clear on the economic necessity for emigration, but unlike them, he is unremittingly negative about his new location and strongly advised Scots not to venture to South Africa. He returned to Scotland in the late 1870s. 'Epistle to Tammas Bodkin' references Edgar Allan Poe's oft-parodied 'The Raven' in its closing stanzas.

See also: 13. 'Epistle to Tammas Bodkin', p. 24; 25. 'A Voice from Stanley Mills', p. 45; 49. 'The Tory Lords', p. 81; 54. 'To My Auld Knapsack', p. 90; 55. 'The Land That Rear'd Us A'', p. 92; 71. 'Happy Lamoo', p. 120; 96. 'Dakota', p. 170.

      DEAR TAMMAS, –   1
I'm sittin' 'mang the burnin' sand,
    Elbow on knee and chin on loof,
Musin' on life's ravelled web,
    Entangled warp an' woof,   5
An' like tae greet wi' bootless grievin'
At the claith sae marred in weavin'.

Some folk hae talents nine or ten,
    Some only ane or twa;
The feck o' folk hae less or mair,   10
    But I had nane ava'.
An' though ye shak the napkin oot,
Ye'll no find ochtlins i' the cloot.

When folk wi' talents gathered gear –
    They wha had hands an' harns –   15
I boost be goavin' i' the air,
    An' glowerin' at the starns.
I hadna talents – what was worse,
I had nae siller i' my purse.

An' sae the wolf began to howl,   20
    An' chased me far away;
Far frae the Braes o' sweet Strathmore,
    An' flowery banks o' Tay;
Doon the Tay, an' ower the Tyne,
An' far besouth earth's central line,   25

An' here I am, 'mang burnin' sand,
    Whare rude sou'easters blow,
That lift the sand up bodily,
    An' drive it to an' fro,
An' whirl it through the blazin' lift   30
Mair fierce than e'en Kingussie drift.

There's no a rinnin' river here,
    In a' this parched land;
They're maistly a' a string o' pools,
    Slow sinkin' through the sand,   35
Or ower the scaurs, as at Lodore,
A gill a minute – less or more,

Musin' on my ain dear Tay,
    That fond remembered river,
That sweeps around my natal ground,   40
    Majestical as ever.
Musin' on that lovely stream,
I fell asleep and dreamed a dream.

I dreamed I lay on Table Bay,
The "sounding sea" before,   45
An' there I saw Poe's classic crow
    Hop, hopping on the shore –
Hopping, hopping, ever hopping,
Hopping on the sandy shore.

Wi' quivering lips, I cried – "Oh, raven,   50
Will I ever see Kinclaven,
Or Strathmore, or ony place
    On Scotia's classic shore?"
But the prophetic carrion crow –
The oracle of Edgar Poe –   55
    Sat croaking – "Nevermore!"

feck – the majority	*loof – palm*
ochtlins – anything	*cloot – cloth*
goav – to gaze stupidly or vacantly	*scaur – crag, precipice*

67. 'A Favourite Picture', by W. M. Published on 3 August 1872.

This is another poem written from an emigrant perspective, though the author does not give his or her location. While reflecting nostalgically on the pleasures of home, it also notes the changes caused by modernity, especially the advent of industry and railways to small-town Scotland. 'Oor Mill' offers a different take on the benefits of such changes. 'Tubal-Cain' is a Biblical character (Genesis 4.22), described as a metal-worker, used to signify the origins of industrial labour.

See also: 22. 'Home Recollections', p. 40; 68. 'Oor Mill', p. 115.

See also: 22. 'Home Recollections', p. 40; 68. 'Oor Mill', p. 115.

There hangs upon my parlour wall   1
    A picture my dear sister drew,
Which can the scenes of youth recall,
    And bring "the lost and loved" to view.

It shows the house where we were born,   5
    The gardens we as children made,
The birken-shaw, the waving corn,
    The stream by which we often played.

And well can mem'ry add to these
    All that gave early life its charm,   10
As parents, playmates, birds, and bees,
    The horse and kine upon our farm.

Alas, how changed! – my parents dead,
    My playmates in far distant lands;
Our house is down, and in its stead   15
    The station of a railway stands.

The stream, then free, is now a slave,
    Confined, and made mill wheels to drive;
No flow'rs nor willows o'er it wave,
    No birds now in its eddies dive.   20

The birken-shaw is now a street
    Where dwell the imps of Tubal-Cain;
The change all round was so complete,
    I could no longer there remain.

So I now in another land   25
    Have hung upon my parlour wall
That picture drawn by sister's hand,
    Which can the scenes of youth recall.

No painting artist ever drew
    Could be to me a tithe so dear   30
As that rude sketch; that homely view
    My darkest, saddest hours can cheer.

birken-shaw — birch wood

68. 'Oor Mill', by Eriphos, Methven. Published 15 February 1873.

This poem almost certainly refers to the establishment of a jute mill in the village of Methven, near Perth. It operated from a former Secession Church up until the 1920s. The jute trade was a major contributor to Dundee's success. From mid-century onwards 'over half the population' of the town were 'directly or indirectly dependent upon it' (Tomlinson, p. 2). As this poem suggests, the rise of jute had a knock-on effect on districts well beyond Dundee. Industry, here, brings new life and energy to the town and welcome winter employment. Eriphos is also the author of 'Defeatit'.

See also: 25. 'A Voice from Stanley Mills', p. 45; 61. 'Defeatit', p. 104; 76. 'Jute', p. 130; 82. 'King Jute', p. 142; 86. 'The Sack-Sewers of Dundee', p. 149.

There's a change in oor toon. Wad ye ken what it is?   1
Then just come awa' roun' – hear the clatter and whiz,
The blatter and click, wi' the bummin' and whirr,
As the shuttles flee quick, and the belts gie a birr;
And a half-hunder heads, a' sae eident ye'll see,   5
Busy tendin' the threads o' the wabs for Dundee.

And as wab after wab frae the loom tummels oot,
Some wi' strips in the drab – they're for vittal nae doot;
While thae ither thin anes, we can maistly be sure
Are for handin' crushed banes or some ither manure –   10
The phosphates or things which they bring owre the sea,
To spread wider the wings o' busy Dundee.

It surely maun thrive, that same toon on the Tay,
When the bees frae her hive glean their honey away
In the corners or nooks o' a county or shire,   15
Whaur the clear sil'er brooks gush through bracken and
   brier,
To join the big burnie that rins tae the sea,
Whaur ships aff a journey disload at Dundee.

The thrift in the traffic has spread owre oor toon,
Frae ilka auld wifie to hardie wee loon;   20
They are here for their bundle, or in wi' their "secks,"
Wi' a wheelbarrow's trundle, or slewed owre their necks;
Ay, frae auld Betty Bury to little Rab Lee,
They are a' in a hurry wi' sacks for Dundee.

Frae the east end o' toon to the west they are thrang: 25
See, yonder bit gumple that scampers alang,
He's juist oot frae the mill wi' a bundle o' fifty;
They can work wi' a will a' his folk, they're sae thrifty.
Noo, just hover a blink, if ye watch him ye'll see
He'll be back in a wink wi' his sacks for Dundee.   30

The shewin' o' sacks is a blessin' th' noo,
Wi' the coals sic a rax, and the tatties sae few,
And a' ither provisions at sic a dear rate
That we see but in visions a sheep's head for meat;
But yonder comes wark bowlin' in frae the sea –   35
It's a braw tradin' bark, wi' flax for Dundee.

Had the mill no been gaun when the winter set in,
E'en though prices had fa'n, eh! oor kail had been thin
A gey dowie season 'twad been at the best,
But noo wi' provision o' labour we're blest;   40
And oor shewsters are nimmel, fu' blithesome their glee,
As wi' needle and thimmel they work for Dundee.

Then speed to the beami', the shuttle, and loom;
While the sacks we are shewing the aumrie's no toom;
They will eke oot the rent and help claes to the back,   45
Wi' a surplus fornent it, if labour should slack;
Forbye, as we fend, there's the orra bawbee,
For the *Journal* and *Friend* ilka week frae Dundee.

And prosper the mill and the owners as weel,
Wi' work at their will and prosperity's weal;   50
Demand for their labour, their winnings when due;
Guid will to ilk neighbor, their enemies few;
Nae hindrance or hitches, by land or by sea,
On the warld o' riches that's stored in Dundee.

eident – industrious   wab – length of fabric on a loom
loon – lad   thrang – crowded, busy
gumple – obscure, may relate to 'gump' as rump, i.e. all that is seen of the boy
under a load of sacks, or to 'gump' as a plump child.
'sic a rax' – at extortionate price (cf. 'rack-rent')
gey dowie – very dreary ('gey' – excellent, great, but used ironically)
aumrie – cupboard, pantry   orra – spare

69. 'Coals', by W. T. E. Published on 22 March 1873.

Between 1871 and 1873, the price of coal in Britain rose sharply as demand outstripped supply. In late 1872 and the spring of 1873, as coal at one point tripled in price, the newspapers were particularly concerned about the impact of this 'Coal Famine'. As this poem suggests, the mine-owners or 'coalmasters' were regarded with great bitterness due to their high profits at a time when working people struggled to buy enough coal for their basic needs. This is one of several poems published in the *Journal* between January and March 1873 referencing the Coal Famine.

See also: 43. 'Hard Times', p. 72; 45. 'Woe', p. 74.

The shades of night were falling fast   1
As through a country village passed
A man who bore upon his back,
With trembling steps, an empty sack,
        In quest of coals.   5

His brow was black, his eye below
Was sunken deep with want and woe;
And from his hollow chest there rung
The accents of his Scottish tongue –
      "Oh, gie me coals!"   10

In humble homes he saw no light
Of cannel coal or anthracite;
Along the street no glimmer shone,
And from his lips escaped a moan –
      "Whaur's a' the coals?"   15

"Try not the Squire," the old man said;
"High o'er the poor he holds his head,
And to us would not deign to give,
Although without we couldn't live,
      A mett of coals."   20

"Oh, stay," the maiden said, "and warm
Thy chilly hands within my arm."
A tear stood in his sunken eye,
And still he made his longing cry –
      "Oh, gie's some coals!"   25

"Beware the store, and do not steal,
Else vengeance of the law you'll feel;
Six months imprisonment in jail –
That is the sentence without fail
      For stealing coals."   30

At break of day, as evermore
Counting the cash he had in store,
The coalmaster heard in his lair
This shriek upon the frosty air –
      "O for some coals!"   35

A man upon the frozen ground,
Stark-dead, was by the watchman found,
Still grasping in his hand so black,
With desp'rate gripe, an empty sack,
      That once held coals.   40

There in the twilight cold and gray,
Lifeless and motionless he lay,
Whilst from the crowd that gathered near
A cry like thunder strikes the ear –
    "We *must* have coals!"   45

mett – a measurement of coal (in Dundee, a sack of 1½ cwt)

70. 'Lily of the Vale', by Mrs Margaret Wallace, Coupar-Angus. Published 30 May 1874.

Margaret Wallace (born 1829) published a number of religious poems in the *Journal* in the early 1870s. Like Elizabeth Campbell of Lochee, she was one of the older women contributors to the *Journal*, though she came from a higher social class as the wife of a minister. Many poems, particularly by women writers, addressed wild flowers or smaller, hidden flowers, invariably drawing out the same moral about the virtues of obscurity and the beauties of natural as opposed to artificial or hothouse flowers. Wallace's collection, *Emblems of Nature* (Coupar-Angus: William Culross, 1875), published by subscription, includes 'Lily of the Vale' among many other flower-poems (p. 46).

See also: 15. 'Odd to a Krokis', p. 27; 73. 'Three Score and Ten', p. 126; 100. 'April Days', p. 177.

Beside an old gray wall, moss-grown,   1
    A bed of lilies grew;
A florist's care it scarce had known,
    And yet 'twas sweet to view.

Its cool broad leaves half-hid the stems   5
    Arrayed in snow-white bells;
It seemed a spot all decked with gems
    Where some bright fairy dwells.

Far from the world's broad glare and din
    It lived, and grew, and spread –   10
Pleased with the nook it sheltered in –
    And round its fragrance shed.

Thus virtue, howsoe'er obscure,
   In sweet content will grow;
Each task fulfil from motives pure,   15
   Though none but God should know.

71. 'Happy Lamoo* (Addressed to Intending Emigrants)', by Wandering Willie. Published 23 January 1875.

'Happy Lamoo' is a satirical pro-emigration poem, mocking the tendency of such verse to represent colonial destinations as agricultural and democratic paradises. 'Lamoo' (Lamu) is, as the endnote says, an island and town in Kenya, in East Africa (Zanzibar). In the nineteenth century, a major part of its economy was the slave trade until the British closed it down in 1873. David Livingstone briefly mentions Lamoo in a journal entry for 13 November 1870, as reputedly 'wealthy, and well supplied with everything, as grapes, peaches, wheat, cattle, camels, &c'; (p. 345); his *Last Journals*, published in 1874, are possibly a source for the poem's fantasy. The area was historically Muslim (hence, perhaps, the author's comments on punishments for drinking alcohol). 'Wandering Willie' is unidentified: an author using this pseudonym occasionally published riddles and acrostics in the *Friend* in the mid-1870s.

See also: 55. *'The Land That Rear'd Us A''*, p. 92; 66. *'Epistle to Tammas Bodkin'*, p. 112; 96. *'Dakota'*, p. 170.

Dear reader and friend, if you are in grief,   1
Or poverty cold, and despair of relief;
If friends stand aloof, and duns come too near,
Then what I've to say you'll be happy to hear.
So list – and I'm certain you never will rue –   5
To the tale of the wonderful town of Lamoo.
    There's a broad-bosomed river in the land of the
       swallow,
    Where rhinoceri roll and hippopotami wallow,
    With crocodiles basking asleep on its banks,
    And monkeys and apes all a-playing their pranks.   10
    And parrots and cockatoos chattering horrid,
    Which alone is good proof that the climate is torrid.

In this pleasant land it rains not nor snows
For summer's eternal: yet one would suppose
They'd have bad weather some time, sooner or later.   15
Not a bit of it, ma'am, for Lamoo's on the 'Quator.
Yet three days in each month come genial showers,
Fertilizing the earth and refreshing the flowers;
But umbrellas are needless, for you know ere they come,
As the birds stop their songs, and the wild bee its hum.   20
Then away flits the cloud, the sky becomes blue,
And sunshine again bathes lovely Lamoo.
    And miles on miles inland from the banks of the
       stream
    You may wander for hours like one in a dream,
    With forests of fruit trees before and behind,   25
    And the orange flowers sweetly perfuming the wind.
    Light-hearted and joyous. O! believe me, 'tis true,
    There is no land on earth like the land of Lamoo.
Every man is a king, and wherever he goes
No bloated aristocrat treads on his toes;   30
No poor rates to pay, no taxes, no rents,
For they don't live in houses, but only in tents;
They've no bothering business, no rotten ambition,
And no need of lawyer or priest nor physician.
    Then, there is no use for money, and no need of toil. 35
    Why, just wink at the earth and it yields up its spoil;
    And for garments, Lamooites are in no wise particular,
    False hair is unknown, so's the severe perpendicular.
    All you want is a shirt, and for that don't you see,
    You'll have no tailor's bill, 'cause it grows on a tree.   40
So, if you go to Lamoo you'll be happy and frisky
As the lambs on the lea; but you mustn't touch whisky.
If 'tis even as much as smelt on your breath,
If a former offender, you'll be punished with death.
If not, then, just by way of a warning,   45
You'll get fifty good blows with a stick in the morning.
    So, now my good friends, if you long to be happy,
    Take out the pledge, bid farewell to the "nappy;"
    Leave false friends and foes, leave your creditors too
    Pack – a very few traps – and be off to Lamoo.   50

*Lamoo, a large town and district on the east coast of
    Africa, second in importance only to Zanzibar.

72. 'My First Attempt', by John Stargazer. Published 15 May 1875.

One of the many poems published in the *Journal* which reflected, with humour, on the would-be poet's effort to write a poem that would satisfy editorial criteria, 'Stargazer's' effort is particularly notable because of the way in which it satirises the clichéd image of the young, ambitious, physically frail poet, misunderstood by his vulgar family and community. Stargazer may have in mind fictional heroes, such as Walter in Glasgow working-class poet Alexander Smith's very successful 'A Life-Drama' (1853), or such real-life figures as David Gray. The poem sets up a comic contrast between poetic aspirations and the writer's actual domestic situation, signalled in part by the disparity between the author's standard English and his family's reported speech in Scots. No other poems appear under this pseudonym from these years.

See also: 4. 'A Young Rhymester's Address to the Editor', p. 9; 42. 'The Bard of Caldervale', p. 70; 61. 'Defeatit', p. 104; 85. 'The Poet's Wail', p. 148.

I lingered in the shady nook, beneath the spreading trees, 1
I wandered by the babbling brook and listened to the
    breeze;
I dreamed away the broad daylight, I "burned the
    midnight taper,"
In the high hope that I might write a poem for your paper.

With throbbing brow and aching heart I sat in act to
    write, 5
Before me reams of paper spread – a surface snowy white;
The farthest corners of my brain I searched for thoughts
    of gold
And treasured every glittering grain within the snowy fold.

In calmer moods I viewed my store of golden thoughts
    next day,
Alas! I found them basest ore, as worthless as the clay. 10
I dug a gem from thought's deep mine – a precious gem I
    thought it –
I seized my pen – my diamond fine was only paper
    blotted.

I soared aloft on fancy's wings far past the common ken;
And bird's-eye views of various things I painted with my
    pen.
I poised aloft and rubbed my eyes and looked my painting
    o'er   15
When lo! I saw to my surprise, a blot, and nothing more.

At length my health began to fail, my form grew thin and
    wasted,
My bowl of brose and dish of kail I often left untasted;
My cheeks were pale, my eyeballs glared, my looks were
    wan and sad;
And vulgar people as they stared said – "What a
    moonstruck lad."   20

My mother's anxious-looking eye kept following me
    about;
I knew her watchfulness would pry and worm my secret
    out.
So telling her my hopes I bade her let none other know it,
She shook her head, "Ah, John," she said, "I doot ye're
    nae a poet."

But mother is a woman, who – the truth I am revealing – 25
Though loving, gentle, kind and true, has no poetic feeling
A family council she did call, where, with deliberate air,
Met brothers, sister, each and all – my father in the chair.

I stood myself behind the door, and, peeping through a
    hole,
I saw my father reading o'er a blurred and blotted scroll. 30
Good gracious! How my spirits fell at such a dismal sight.
That scroll of verses I knew well; for many a day and
    night

I spent o'er it, with anxious thought, in study and
    revision;
And now, ill-luck! my friends had got the very worst
    edition.
Besides, my father – though the best of men – if you
    would know him,   35
He's not the man you would select to read your MS poem.

That little art, which, unto us, is known as punctuation,
With all inflection of the voice, he holds in detestation.
Nay more, it must be freely own'd, although my sire it
  shames
Some words, not in the Bible found, he awkwardly
  misnames.   40

I'm sure I can't tell how I felt, nor how the rest did
  wonder,
As line on line he read or spelt in tones as loud as
  thunder.
The blotted words, the lines scor'd through, the interlined
  correction,
The notes upon the margin, too, he read all in connection.

The tender thing that I caress'd, the first-born of my brain,
That – like a girl her doll – I dress'd, redress'd, and
  dress'd again,
He now held up in all the tags with which I tried to deck
  it;
No wonder 'neath its cast-off rags no one knew what to
  make it.

My sister said, "He is in love;" my brothers muttered
  "Lazy;"
My father, looking up above, remarked, "The lad is
  crazy."   50
My mother quietly did suggest my stomach might be
  wrong,
Then one and all declared 'twas best I should take physic
  strong.
"A double dose of Epsom salts, with senna to the bargain;
Twill purge frae aff his brains the swauts o' that
  confounded jargon."

I turned away in deep disgust; that vulgar observation   55
Convinced me they could have no just or true
  appreciation
Of my poetic talents, which I now resolved to test,
And show as plain as print how much of genius I
  possessed.

My poem I wrote out with care, looked sharply to the
　　spelling,
And put some dots in here and there to make the points
　　more telling.　　　　　　　　　　　　　　　　　　　　60
I signed my name and full address, that all the world might
　　know it –
That John Stargazer of Duhl-ness had now become a poet.

How fancy pictures to my view my neighbours' look of
　　wonder
When, as they read the poem through, they see the name
　　that's under.
And there is ane – a fair-haired girl, low folk call carr'ty
　　Nancy,　　　　　　　　　　　　　　　　　　　　　　　65
Whose rosy cheek and golden curl for ever haunts my
　　fancy.
How will that maiden's bosom swell with rapture at the
　　thought
That she – a simple village belle – a poet's taste has
　　caught?

How will the man of culture pause each stanza lingering
　　o'er;
How will the critic's ruthless claws lay open every sore.　　70
How will – but no, I need not tell the various fancies vain
That in succession rose and fell – air bubbles of the brain.

I bought the paper, inside out I laid its columns bare;
I looked – could I my optics doubt? – my poem is not
　　there!　　　　　　　　　　　　　　　　　　　　　　75
The reason why is told me soon, although I didn't ask it:
"Stargazer's 'Ode unto the Moon' has gone to the waste
　　basket."

73. 'Three Score and Ten', by Elizabeth Campbell – The Lochee Poetess. Published 15 May 1875.

Elizabeth Campbell (1804–1878), like Margaret Wallace of Coupar-Angus, was an older woman poet supported by the *Journal* for her pious attitude and ability to write well-produced, conventionally smooth and moral verse. She was entirely self-educated and had worked in service and then in the weaving trade from the age of seven. When her husband was disabled and became unable to work, she single-handedly attempted to support her large family by having some of her poems printed locally and 'tried to eke out a subsistence by selling them' (*Songs of My Pilgrimage* (Edinburgh: Andrew Elliot, 1875), p. vii). During 1875, when she was 'discovered' as a poet by Rev. George Gilfillan, the *Journal* made several appeals for financial aid for Campbell, who was living in severe poverty. Her poetry, in showing her high moral character, sensitivity and intelligence, was used both to justify this charitable support, and to move readers' hearts on her behalf. This apparently biographical poem was published immediately above a list of contributors to the fund for her assistance, and appears in her collection (p. 63).

See also: 40. 'Despondency', p. 68; 70. 'Lily of the Vale', p. 119; 100. 'April Days', p. 177.

I sit in the shade of a lilac tree,   1
    Dreaming of days that are gone,
The lilies and roses are nodding to me,
    And warblers sing merrily on.

The sunbeams blink on my silvery hair –   5
    Now its auburn hue has fled –
And midges dance in the balmy air,
    While clouds are creeping o'erhead.

And music's sweet strains fall soft on my ear –
    Now swelling, now dying away –   10
From the magical voices to me so dear,
    That bless my declining day.

Though roses may blush, and fair lilies smile,
    And music in torrents be gushed,
The rose has its thorn, the lilies will fade,   15
    The strains of the singers be hushed.

I long to be free from sin's weary load,
    That long my soul has oppressed;
May I through His Lamb be welcomed by God
    Up to his eternal rest!   20

74. 'The Lassies o' Bonnie Dundee', by Auld Betty. Published 14 August 1875.

This poem is concerned with the 1875 Dundee millworkers' strike, caused by a proposed wage cut of twenty per cent: on the same date, the editorial notes that thirty-five works were stopped and 12,000 people were on strike. One of the most notable aspects of the 1875 strike was how heavily female mill-workers were involved. On the same page as 'Auld Betty's' poem, the *Journal* reported a speech at the mass meeting on Magdalen Green by J. Bruce in which he commented, 'I am certain that if the females take the matter on hand – those who are in work and who are able, and think it is their own battle they are fighting – those who are out on strike just now will never go in until the intimation of the reduction is pulled down.' (14 Aug 1875, p. 2). On August 21, the *Journal* reported an opposition meeting claiming that women had started the strike, 'The women went out of their own accord, while we men were kicked out (Laughter and applause)' (p. 2). As other poems in this collection show, Dundee had a reputation as a city with a large and visible population of working women, actively involved in politics. Auld Betty's poem – the only poem identified under this pseudonym – proposes a narrative where the male mill-owners are deliberately conspiring to bring down the over-proud factory lasses, and suggests that this is a women's strike. The poem is aimed at readers outside Dundee and is part of the effort to raise money for the Relief Fund to support the strikers. Baxter, Cox and Grimond were prominent millowners, known for their generosity to the city. The lyrics and rhythm here deliberately echo the well-known song, 'Bonnie Dundee', a Jacobite song with lyrics by Sir Walter Scott to an old tune.

See also: 28. 'The Working Lasses', p. 49; 62. 'To the Domestic Servants', p. 105; 75. 'Ane Strikeing Ballant', p. 129.

To the Jute Lords o' Dundee Sir Avarice said –   1
"A lucky thought, lads, has come into my head:

The wages we're payin' are ower big, do ye se,
We maun hae a reduction in bonnie Dundee.

"The factory lasses they a' gae sae braw,   5
Oor ladies hae often to gie them the wa';
Wi' their silks and their satins they bear aff the gree,
We ne'er saw the like o't in bonnie Dundee."

"A month syne or mair we pat on the screw,
An' ten per cent aff them we easily drew;   10
Tho' the pill wasna sweet, it was wholesome, ye see,
Sae we'll e'en try anither in bonnie Dundee."

He paused for an answer, an' a' the sma' fry
Flocked round him like dirt-flees aboot a pig-stye,
An' loudly they cheered him, as each did agree   15
To bring doon the braw bonnets o' bonnie Dundee.

But to Baxter, Cox, Grimond an' a the brave band,
Be honour recorded throughout a' the land,
Wha scorned frae the workers to wrench a bawbee,
For they are the nobles o' bonnie Dundee.   20

But when oor brave lassies they heard the ill news,
They cower'd not, they blanched not before the hard screws.
"Keep shouther to shouther!" they shouted wi' glee,
"An' we'll keep up the bonnets o' bonnie Dundee."

Frae Brechin an' Forfar, Arbroath and Montrose,   25
Blairgowrie and Alyth subscriptions arose;
An' toons that to name are ower mony for me
Send help to the lassies o' bonnie Dundee.

The battle they're fechtin' may sune be yer ain,
The cloud in the east may come wast wi' its rain;   30
Ne'er grudge what ye're able, but cheerfully gie
To support richt an' justice in bonnie Dundee.

Some wiseacres say we're weel paid for oor wark –
Anonymous writers that stab in the dark –
They daurna come forward, sic cowards they be,   35
Wi' their name an' their standing in bonnie Dundee.

bear aff the gree – to hold or win first place

75. 'Ane Strik(eing) Ballant', *Air* – "Bonnie Dundee", by Mistress Lapstane, 12 August 1875. Published 28 August 1875.

This is one of several poems published on the major Dundee millworkers' strike of July and August 1875, caused by a proposed wage cut of twenty per cent. The *Journal* reported extensively on the strike throughout the period, often devoting a full two pages of coverage to it, and representing varied opinions in published correspondence and articles. Like 'Auld Betty', 'Mistress Lapstane' is a semi-comic pseudonym (playing on the pseudonym of another comic *Journal* poet, Geordie Lapstane (Robert Ford)), but the poem is highly supportive of the women on strike. As in the previous poem, the verses closely follow the language as well as the form of 'Bonnie Dundee'.

See also: 28. 'The Working Lasses', p. 49; 62. 'To the Domestic Servants', p. 105; 74. 'The Lassies o' Bonnie Dundee', p. 127.

Tae the Lords o' Juteopolis the weavers hae spoke –   1
"If ye rug doon oor wages, as sure as the cleck
We'll fling up the shuttle; we'll sune lat ye pree
The pluck o' the lasses o' Bonnie Dundee."

Chorus – Then hurrah for the lasses, sae dauntless an' fair,   5
        Let them stand by their colours, an' tyranny dare;
        While there's hearts that can feel, an' hands gleg
            tae gie,
        Nae fear o' starvation tae Bonnie Dundee.

The lasses hae struck, they march up the street;
They cry, "We'll ne'er yield while there's shune on oor
    feet;"   10
An' ilka douce neebour says, "E'en lat it be –
There's room for improvements in Bonnie Dundee."

Chorus – Then hurrah for the lasses, &c.

There are weavers in Forfar an' weavers in Perth,
There are weavers in Belfast an' ilk ither airth;   15
An' the cry frae ilk point is, "We're willin' tae gie;"
An' subscriptions are hurlin' tae Bonnie Dundee.

Chorus – Then hurrah for the lasses, &c.

Noo, defy ilka bribe, though the shuttles sud rust –
Be ruled by your leaders, they're worthy o' trust;   20
I'm nae sworn prophet, but bide ye awee,
An' ye'll get a' ye're wantin' in Bonnie Dundee.

Chorus – Then hurrah for the lasses, sae dauntless an' fair,
          An' three cheers for the strike that'll sune be nae
          mair;
          Sin' there's hearts that can feel, an' hands gleg tae
          gie,   25
          Nae fear o' the weavers o' Bonnie Dundee.

rug – to pull   *pree – to try, to taste*
douce – kindly   *airth – direction (variant 'airt')*

76. 'Jute', by D. Taylor, Dundee. Published 10 March 1877.

Taylor, also the author of anti-Tory poem 'Ring Up the
Curtain', worked as a handloom weaver from the age of thirteen,
eventually moving to a powerloom factory and becoming an
overseer. He was secretary of the Dundee movement for the
Nine Hours Factory Bill, debated and eventually passed (in
relation to women workers) in 1874 (Edwards, I, p. 26). 'Jute'
reflects on the many uses of Dundee's most famous product and
its ubiquitous, disguised presence in the consumer goods of the
period. The final verses lament the slump in trade in the 'long
depression' of the 1870s.

See also: 68. 'Oor Mill', p. 115; 82. 'King Jute', p. 142;
86. 'The Sack-Sewers of Dundee', p. 149; 88. 'Ring Up the
Curtain', p. 155.

That stuff we ca' jute has monie a name,   1
    An' gangs thro' maist a'body's hands;
It's made intae bags, an' sent tae bring hame
    The produce o' far awa' lands.
Wharever you gang, at hame or abroad,   5
    You're aye sure tae find that it's there;
Whiles in a raw state in braw cushioned seat,
    And even in women's back hair.

It's mixed amon' silk, an' ca'd by that name,
    In cotton, tae, often it's tried; 10
It looks gey weel on the back o' some dame,
    When in braw, bricht colours it's dyed.
It's intae *oor* hets, it's intae *your* shawls,
    It's mixed in maist a'thing wi' wear;
An a' the gaudy an' gay fal-de-rals 15
    Three-fourths o' them's jute you may swear.

The blankets you haup yoursell wi' at nicht
    An' think o' pure wool they are made,
Are mixed up wi' jute, though kept frae yer sicht,
    Wi' tricks that are wrocht in the trade. 20
The glossy black coats you see on great swells,
    Look nobby an' braw there's nae doot;
But if they're close scann'd, I'll wager my hand,
    You'll find that they're no free fae jute.

When settin' up hoose, it's likely you'll buy 25
    A sofa, or braw easy chair;
But I think you'll be a bit o' a "guy"
    Gin you think the stuffin's a' hair.
When worn a while the claith'll get bare,
    What's in will begin tae come oot; 30
Just look at it weel, you'll ken by the feel
    What you took for hair is just jute.

When bousters you want tae pit in your bed,
    Wi' pillows o' wool just tae match,
Tak' ye my word for't, you hae there instead, 35
    Some stuff that was ance in a "batch."
You'll sune find it oot, it gathers in lumps,
    An' wi your head winna weel suit,
Till anxious to see what on earth it can be,
    You open't an' find your freend jute. 40

In fact, there's scarcely a thing you can name
    But it's mixed up wi' mair or less;
Frae big tattie sack wi' rough lookin' seam,
    Tae newest come oot satin dress.
You wad think, when used in sae mony ways, 45
    There cudna be o't half enough;

But it's been sae slack this year or twa back,
    The trade in't is no worth a snuff.

The orders are sma', an' prices sae low,
    Tae think on't juist mak's your heid sair;   50
But ither things tae hae got a sad blow
    As weel's the jute trade, I'm aware.
No in it alane, but a' the warld o'er,
    Dull trade wi' a'body's the cry;
I houp the warst blast o't a' is noo past,   55
    An' guid times we'll see by-an'-by.

haup – cover

77. 'Rapidly, Rapidly. A Good Templar Song', by C., Forfar. Published 10 March 1877.

The Good Templar temperance movement or IOGT (International Order of Good Templars) arrived in Britain from America in 1867 and rapidly spread, particularly in Scotland, where it became enormously popular with working men and women. The Good Templars stood out for their emphasis on equality across class, gender and (in the US) racial divisions. Many working-class writers were ardent members, including poets Alexander Anderson and James Nicholson. These verses, clearly designed to be sung at meetings, though no tune is given, use very common imagery, familiar from Evangelical hymns, of the river and the brighter shores of Heaven.

See also: 19. 'Nan Tamson's Wean', p. 33; 101. 'Advice to Blue Ribboners', p. 178.

Rapidly, rapidly flows the River   1
Of Time, on whose banks ye stand;
Embark with us, and help our endeavour
To quell the curse of our land!
For pirate-like, its black flag floats   5
Athwart the azure sky;
Its darksome shadow mars and blots
In man God's majesty!

But we are striving onward
To a brighter, better shore,   10
Where drink-born demons downward
Shall drag men's souls no more!

Rapidly, rapidly flows the River
Of Time to th' Eternal Sea;
O waver not: Hell's chain dissever,   15
And from its bondage flee!
Our Templar banner proudly waves
And still the Fiend defies;
We glory, while *he* madly raves,
To hear a brother's cries –   20
    "O help me, help me onward
    To that brighter, safer shore,
    Where drink-born demons downward
    Shall drag men's souls no more!"

Rapidly, rapidly flows the River   25
Of Time o'er rock and shoal; –
Our barque is strong and buoyant ever,
And soon must reach its goal;
When all mankind in unison
From evil shall abstain,   30
And with "Our Father's" benison
Shall chant the glad refrain –
    Now we are striving onward
    To a brighter, better shore
    Where drink-born demons downward   35
    Shall drag men's souls no more.

78. 'Only', by Lisa M. Smith, Dollar. Published 14 April 1877.

This is a typical example of the poems on lost love that were so popular in newspapers of the period. The *Journal* published hundreds of love-poems, all very similar in content and imagery, and often implicitly designed to be set to music and performed. Such first-person poems about betrayal and heartbreak were especially popular with woman poets composing newspaper and periodical verse, because they were considered an integral part of the genre of women's poetry in the period and were thus highly publishable. Lisa M. Smith is unidentified and did not appear to publish other poems in the *Journal* in this period.

See also: 98. 'A Year Ago', p. 173.

Only a mildewed casket	1
That I hid in the chest years ago,	
Containing the proofs of a story –	
Of a life-story fraught with woe;	
Open the casket gently,	5
And safely reposing there,	
Tied by a faded blue ribbon –	
Only a wave of hair.	
Only a moss-rose withered,	
That was gathered long years ago	10
From a tender rose branch swaying	
In the land where the roses blow;	
Only a few love letters –	
Only a broken vow,	
Only *one* heart faithless	15
One – only one, I trow.	
Only a true heart bleeding,	
Only a wasted life –	
Only a lonely woman	
Who'd have made a faithful wife;	20
Only care-blanched tresses,	
Only a broken heart –	
And this is the old, old story	
That the casket has to impart.	

79. 'Naething New', by Mrs Duthie, Dun Cottages, by Montrose. Published 28 July 1877.

Jane Allardice Duthie (1845–1928) worked as a nursemaid, a seamstress and milliner, and as a shopgirl in Glasgow before settling near Montrose in Angus, around forty miles from Dundee. In January 1877, she published her first poem under the initials 'J. D.', and from March was signing her poems 'Mrs Duthie'. From the 1870s to 1890s, she became one of the *Journal's* regular contributors. Her correspondence with Tammas Bodkin from 1893–94, and a selection of her poems (not including this one) were published in *Rhymes and Reminiscences* (Brechin: D. H. Edwards, Advertiser Office, 1912). This poem, implicitly addressing the editor, discusses the difficulty of finding an original topic for newspaper verse, running through the most popular themes, songs and authors of the day. 'Kailworms and nettercaps' in line 12, for instance, are a specific reference to Poute, and 'Yang-Yang-tse-Kiang' alludes to a comic song by that name by the minister and poet Thomas Davidson (reprinted in full in the *Friend*, 9 May 1877). Established international authors like Longfellow ('Excelsior') are commingled with local Scottish working-class poets, like Alexander 'Sandy' Rodger, Glasgow radical weaver and journalist and author of 'Robin Tamson's Smiddy'. 'The Forfar Pensioner' was composed by David Shaw of Forfar (c.1786–1856), and also has the repeated 'sir', refrain in its line-endings. It is reprinted in Alan Reid's *Bards of Angus and the Mearns* (pp. 407–08), along with some of Duthie's verse.

See also: 85. 'The Poet's Wail', p. 148; 97. 'Reminiscences of the People's Journal', p. 171.

(*Tune* – "The Forfar Pensioner.")

I kenna what I'll sing aboot, although I hae the time, sir;   1
For maistly a'thing, in or oot, has been strung up in
    rhyme, sir.
I've rypit and I've turned aboot this empty muddled brain,
    sir;
But feint a thing can I mak' oot but some auld-farrand
    strain, sir.

I've heard folk sing o' hills and dales, o' sun and moon
    and stars, sir;   5

I've heard them sing o' glens and vales, and Irish jauntin'
    cars, sir;
O' bonnie wavin' corn or bere, o' muirs or baggy mosses,
    sir;
Some vaunt aboot their warl's gear, some rave aboot their
    losses, sir.

Some bardies sing aboot their bairns, and ca' them lovely
    dears, sir;
While ithers sing o' flooers and ferns, or cranky, auld
    arm-chairs, sir;   10
Some sing o' lions, whales, and bears, or ither sic-like
    chaps, sir,
As horses, kye, or even hares, kailworms or nettercaps,
    sir.

There's mony a sang aboot a hoose, frae gentle ha' to cot,
    sir.
A poet ance addressed a louse, and a gude job he made
    o't, sir.
The shamrock, rose and thrissle bauld hae gotten a' their
    share, sir.   15
I've read aboot a whissle auld, 'twas by the bard o' Ayr,
    sir.

The sangs they sing aboot the sea wad fill a book theirsel',
    sir;
And rivers – lat me think a wee – their names I cudna tell,
    sir;
But here's a few – the Tay and Doon, but some hae sic a
    twang, sir,
I fear my tongue wad ne'er get roun' the Yang-Yang-tse-
    Kiang, sir.   20

Some sing aboot the deadly force o' whirlwinds on the
    plain, sir;
While ithers praise the iron horse – that's what we ca' a
    train, sir.
We've heard folk sing o' bonnets blue; o' bonnie lads and
    lasses, sir;
O' hearts that aye were leal and true, and green grow the
    rashes, sir.

We've heard o' Italy's sunny sky, and ower the sea to
 Charlie, sir;   25
We've heard o' comin' thro' the rye, and the bonnie
 Hoose o' Airlie, sir.
Sweet Afton water has been sung, and my boy Tammy,
 sir;
Likewise the lass that was ower young to gang and leave
 her mammy, sir.

We've heard o' Willie Wastle's Wife, wha lived at
 Linkumdoddy, sir,
And a miller, wha ance lived in Fife – he was a drucken
 body, sir;   30
O' cauld kail in Aberdeen, and the gallant weaver laddie,
 sir;
The charms o' Burns's bonnie Jean, and the deuks dung
 ower my daddie, sir.

Some folk strike up Excelsior, some Robin Tamson's
 smiddy, sir.
I yet could gie you score on score, but my heid is turnin'
 giddy, sir;
And why need I spin oot this sang? it's naething but a
 blether, sir;   35
Sae I'll lay doon my pen, and gang ootbye to see the
 weather, sir.

nettercap – spider   *rypit – ransacked*

80. 'An Address to Thee Tay Bridge', by William McGonagall, Dundee, 1877. Published 15 September 1877.

William McGonagall was no stranger to the *Journal*. In 1872, for instance, 'An Old Stager' had published a biography of McGonagall in the *Journal* (see Watson, pp. 41–42); in 1875, McGonagall was engaged in a dispute over the millworkers' strike on the letters page, in which his theatrical interests were cited, and in January 1876 readers were expected to know he was the 'local tragedian' of 'Lines on a Well-known Local "Tragedian"'(!)', also by 'An Old Stager'. This 'Address', however, appears to have been the only poem by McGonagall in this period originally published in the *Journal* as well as in partial form by its rival the *Weekly News*, which McGonagall had chosen as his preferred venue for his first poem in July 1877. What is significant about 'An Address' is that the variant spellings and particularly punctuation reproduced in the *Journal* (and not in later republished versions of this poem), present it as far closer to Poute and his imitators than is evident outside this context. Indeed, it appeared immediately underneath a poem by Poute. Readers knew this genre of mock-bad verse very well by 1877 and would naturally have questioned whether McGonagall was another conscious contributor to it. The satirical editorial note hedges its bets on whether McGonagall's poem is intentional or not. As in Poute, the reader assumes that the printed copy exactly reproduces the unorthodox layout and punctuation of the handwritten poem submitted (this is doubtful only on 'array' and 'Inverness', which were typeset to fit the column width).

See also: 53. 'The Tay Bridge', p. 88; 83. 'An Epistle to "Poet M'Gonagall!"', p. 144.

[We feel that by the publication of this exquisite poem we are conferring an inestimable boon upon the literature of the nineteenth century.]

1 – Beautiful, railway bridge of the Silvery Tay,   1
   with your numerous arches, and pillars in so grand
     array,
   and your Centere girders, which seems to the eye,
   to be almost towering to the sky, . . .   5
   the greatest wonder of the day, . . .
   and, a great beatification, to the river Tay.
   most beautiful to be seen near by
   Dundee, and the Magdalen Green –

2 – Beautiful, railway bridge of the Silvery Tay,   10
    that has caused the Emperor of Brazil, to leave
    . . . his home far away,
    Incognito, in his Dress,
    and view Thee 'ere he pass'd along en route to
      Inverness.   15

3 – Beautiful, railway bridge, of the Silvery Tay,
    Thee longest of the present day, . . .
    That has ever, cross'd o'er a tidal river stream,
    Most gigantic ! to be seen . . . .
    near by Dundee, and the Magdalen Green –   20

4 – Beautiful, railway bridge of the Silvery Tay,
    which will cause great rejoiceing on the opening day,
    and hundreds of people will come from far away,
    also Thee, Queen, – Most Gorgeous to be seen,
    near by Dundee, and the Magdalen Green –   25

5 – Prosperity to Provost Cox, who has given
    Thirty Thousand Pounds, and upwards away,
    In helping to erect, the bridge of the Tay,
    Most handsome to be seen . . . .
    near by Dundee, and the Magdalen Green –   30

6 – Beautiful ! railway bridge of the Silvery Tay!
    I hope, that God ! – will protect all passengers,
    by night, and by day. . . . .
    and no accident befal them while crossing,
    The bridge of the Silvery Tay – for that   35
    Would be most awful ! to be seen –
    Near by Dundee. – and the Magdalen Green –

81. 'Burns's Lament', by W. S. T., Botriphnie. Published 2 March 1878.

A comic poem denigrating the host of Burns' admirers and imitators in the poetry columns, via a conversation with Burns about their effect on his afterlife. Ironically, of course, this poem also borrows from Burns in its language and in using the habbie stanza for humour and satire. In placing Burns beside King David in heaven, the author comments sardonically on the veneration with which Burns was regarded in Victorian Scotland. W. S. T. is unidentified.

See also: 29. 'A Voice from Parnassus', p. 51.

The nicht was young, and shadows shy   1
Were flittin' o'er the dusky sky;
The amorous breeze's gentle sigh
    Faint-breathed I heard;
Nae streamlet chanted soft reply,   5
    Nor warbling bird.

Musing I lingered, free of care,
Watching the softening landscape fair;
And then, I ween, each rebel hair
    Stood swift on end;   10
A figure ghastly white stood there,
    "Heaven me defend!"

I muttered; but its ice-like han'
The ghaist held oot; my bluid cauld ran,
My tremblin' knees refused tae stan',   15
    But bowed by turns;
"Frien'," quoth the spectre, "ye're my man,
    I'm Robbie Burns."

"Gled tae see ye," I chattered oot,
I believe I was as white's a cloot;   20
At all events, I hae nae doot
    The draps stood thick
Upon my broo; I tried tae shout,
    But Rob spak' quick: –

"Dear Brither Willie, list tae me,   25
I'm in an unco fix, d'ye see;
An' sae I hope a friend in thee
        I hae found oot,
Wha will my stern avenger be."
        Quo' I, "Nae doot."   30

"See, here, he said, "I wander lane,
And coort the Muses a' in vain;
A wheen accursed rhymin' men –
        The deil their necks thraw –
Hae driven me frae the fair domain,   35
        Like some puir jackdaw.

"Snugly I sat at Davie's side,
Tae tune his harp my fondest pride,
Till some infernal carle tried
        Tae soon' my praise;   40
Then thick as weeds on every side
        Their clamours raise.

"A little sprite for postman stuid
At Heaven's yit; on wings o' speed
Their rhymes he brocht, then 'gan tae read   45
        Wi' mony a 'hail!'
An' mony a lingo-jingo screed,
        'Thoot head or tail.

"Sadly I mourned my hapless lot,
I'd selt my fame for half a grot   50
Tae ony chiel' wha wad hae shot
        Ilk bletherin' ass.
Ae day he swift approached the spot,
        Mair rhymes alas!

"'Hail, son of song,' the imp began –   55
I cracked him owre the harn-pan;
The harp in bits flew frae my han' –
        Snap gaed the strings,
An' David 'gan tae sairly ban,
        Like ither kings.   60

"His guid harp that he aften played
By Babel's streams broken! he said;
Nae langer should I share his bed,
     But straight depart,
And wander as a ghostly shade   65
     Wi' broken heart

"Until this string o' rhyme should cease,
Then I micht back return in peace;
Oh, if ye hae a heart o' grace
     Within your breast,   70
In pity stop that rhymin' folk
     Think on puir Burns."

cloot – cloth   lane – alone
thraw – wring   yit – gate
harn-pan – skull, brain-pan   ban – curse

82. 'King Jute', by Auld C., March 20, 1878. Published 7 April 1878.

Like 'Oor Mill', this is a celebration of Dundee's rise to become
'Juteopolis' and a paean to the benefits of industry. It makes
specific reference to the new bridge over the Tay, and to the
purchase of the Law hill by the city. 'Auld C' is identified by
Edwards (13, p. 198) as John Smith, born in 1836 in Alyth: he
worked in warehouses, as a salesman, and from 1872 ran a
draper's in Alyth. He published monthly pamphlets of his
poems for a penny each during 1888, collecting them as *Poems
and Lyrics* (Perth: Miller & Gall, Printed for the Author, 1888).
'King Jute' appears on p. 36.

*See also: 68. 'Oor Mill', p. 115; 76. 'Jute', p. 130; 86. 'The
Sack-Sewers of Dundee', p. 149.*

     What tongue shall be mute   1
          To honour King Jute?
Free trade to the land o' the free;
          They honour the toast
          Wha labour the most,   5
There's no use for drones in Dundee.

Now flax, hemp, and tow
To jute all must bow,
Its might gives 't a right so to be;
Who needs to be told   10
Of its strength and hold
O'er the name and the fame of Dundee?

Hark! Each whistle shrill,
From loom-shed and mill;
King Jute is the cause of their glee.   15
We'll never say fail,
While jute shall prevail,
Then "Up with your bonnets, Dundee."

Shall sack, web, or twine,
Jute's powers confine?   20
Ten thousand more potent they'll be –
Take facts, not fiction,
Open conviction –
King Jute's the backbone of Dundee!

King Jute holds his sway –   25
See yon bridge o'er Tay,
He built it, and made our Law free;
Should any one doubt
How this came about,
Ask the Provost, douce man, in Dundee.   30

Who then shall dispute
The power of King Jute?
Like the wind or the waves he is free;
Give to tongues unknown
The fibres ungrown,   35
The fibre, King Jute! rules Dundee.

83. 'An Epistle to "Poet M'Gonagall!"', by An Old Stager. Published 25 May 1878.

'An Old Stager' was a regular antagonist of McGonagall's, the author of several derogatory poems about his acting and his poetry in the Dundee press, as well as biographical material. By 1878, the 'Old Stager' could safely assume that readers were familiar with McGonagall and his work. He refers here to the well-known anecdote about McGonagall's walk to Balmoral to see the Queen, and to the topics of several of his poems. 'Book' is sarcastic, given that McGonagall's 1878 *Poems and Songs* 'by William McGonagall, Poet to Her Majesty' was a cheap pamphlet containing only four poems. The final line alludes to the notion of poets as 'moonstruck', also referenced in other poems here.

See also: 31. 'An Epissel to Poute', p. 54; 80. 'An Address to Thee Tay Bridge', p. 138; 114. 'Epistle to "Faither Fernie"', p. 209; 116, 'Epistle to Robert Wanlock', p. 213.

Ech! Willie, man, I've seen your BOOK!   1
    An' read it *through* an' *through*,
Sae hing your harp up on a hook
    For you're immortal noo.
Tae future ages you'll gae doon   5
    A bard sae high respeckit,
That statues inta ilka toon
    Tae you will be ereckit!

The banks o' Ayr an' bonnie Doon
    Were classic made by Burns;   10
But in the shade you hae them thrown
    Wi' *your* poetic turns.
Tay's bonnie banks their place hae ta'en
    At your sweet muse's call,
An' noo you stand forth a' alane –   15
    THE GREAT M'GONAGALL!!!

The Tay Brig an' the Maidlen Green,
    Wi' Balgay's bonnie braes,
You've laid afore oor gracious Queen
    In your seraphic lays.   20

A pension you will get I'm tauld,
 If you just wait a wee,
For Tennyson is gettin' auld
 An' sune he's sure tae dee.

Sae what wi' "Poet tae the Queen,"   25
 Your poems intae a BOOK,
Fame starin' you atween the een
 As hard as she can look,
You weel may snap your thooms at a'
 Base critics, wha wi' sneer   30
Say that nae poet you're ava,
 But juist a little "queer."

But, Willie, man, there's ae thing yet
 I think that you shud try;
When aince that you that pension get –   35
 Which you will, by-an'-by –
Start you a paper wi' the gains,
 An' independent be
O' Editurs, wha's muddle brains
 Your genius canna see.   40

What though you dinna ken *the trade*,
 There's naething comes *you* wrang;
For, Willie, man, you hae a heid
 That's extraord'nar' lang.
Sae houpin' my advice you'll tak',   45
 As you afore hae dune,
I'll stop noo my auld-farrant crack,
 An' *gang an' see – the mune.*

84. 'The Millennium of Capital', W. W., July 1878. Published on 20 July 1878.

Trade unions, although they existed throughout the century, were legalised by a Royal Commission in 1871. The epigraph to this poem explains its impetus: it presents the perspective of the ironmasters, who see an opportunity to use the depression of the 1870s to form their own 'union', crushing their workers. Iron production was a vital part of Victorian Scottish industry, especially in the 'iron towns' around Glasgow. 'Blue books' usually referred to published reports from parliamentary committees and commissions, information from which could be deployed by unions. W. W. is unidentified.

See also: 62. *'To the Domestic Servants', p. 105;* 74. *'The Lassies O' Bonnie Dundee', p. 127;* 113. *'The Workmen's Cry to the Masters', p. 207.*

"The sixth annual report of the Iron Trades Employers' Association indicates a widening breach between capitalists and employees. The Executive Committee strongly urge employers to take advantage of the present condition of trade to enforce piece-work, lengthen the hours of labour, reduce the pay, and crush, where possible, trades unionism." – *A London correspondent.*

Brave kings o' the great iron kingdom proclaim   1
    Your lang-day desires in ilk city and toun;
Though labour protest in humanity's name,
    Gie piece-work a lift and strike big wages doun.

The trade union tyrants, rough-bred and low-born,   5
    Carouse on our profits – a great social bane;
But we'll hurl them back wi' the cannon o' scorn,
    To find their ain level in serfdom again.

They'll starve at our gates, and be hooted and hissed
    For breaking auld rules that are dear to us a',   10
And the rottenest half o' the press will assist,
    Till their funds are a' squandered and wasted awa'.

A' points o' dispute we'll refuse to discuss,
    In vain will their leaders put forward their claims;
And if they reject what is offered by us,   15
    We'll pervert their "blue-books" and blacken their
        names.

The guid time is comin' on wings that are fleet,
    The dogmas o' labour in fragments we'll shiver,
And non-union men will be doun at our feet,
    And the death-knell o' strikes will be rung out for
        ever.   20

We'll hide the class hatred that burns in our souls,
    And rough-shod through poverty's ranks we shall
        ride;
And though in the earth millions burrow like moles,
    The wealthy maun prosper whatever betide.

Then huzza for the will and the power, and huzza   25
    For the guid that our dignified union effec's!
As foiled and defeated the workers shall fa'
    Wi' capital's heel on their stubborn necks.

Yet, if retribution tak' haud o' their mind,
    And changes o' fortune should mak' them rebel,   30
Wi' union and non-union tyrants combined,
    We'd better import the warst devils o' hell.

THE MORAL

And as the haill nation seems honey-combed ower
    By trade union bees, unco soon they may see   35
How truly their honey mak's greatness and power,
    Sae gude help us a' to reflec' for a wee!

85. 'The Poet's Wail About the Balaam Box', by Mrs Duthie, Dun Cottages, by Montrose. Published 23 November 1878.

The 'Balaam Box' (a term attributed to critic Christopher North and *Blackwood's* in the 1820s) was the supposed repository for poems too weak for inclusion in the paper, and is the subject of frequent humorous poems and commentary from rejected poets and the editors. The poem mimics typical editorial commentary from the 'To Correspondents' column about the faults of plagiarism, imitation and poor grammar and spelling. It closely parodies the Victorian period's best-known piece of inspirational verse, Henry Wadsworth Longfellow's 'A Psalm of Life', which opens 'Tell me not, in mournful numbers,/ Life is but an empty dream.' Duthie, author of 'Naething New' in this collection, contributed several poems to the *Journal* in this period.

See also: 61. 'Defeatit', p. 104; 72. 'My First Attempt', p. 122; 79. 'Naething New', p. 135.

Poets wail in mournful numbers –   1
    "If that box were but a dream,
Peaceful then would be our slumbers,
    Gentle as the rippling stream.

"But, alas! that box is earnest;   5
    And when once within its goal,
No piece to the poet returneth,
    Howe'er precious to his soul."

Few the pleasures, great the sorrow,
    Each poor rhymer has to bear;   10
Not a line he dares to borrow –
    Prying eyes are everywhere.

Lonely o'er a poem he ponders;
    And his heart, tho' stout and brave,
Sinks, as now and then he wonders   15
    If that box will be its grave.

Poets, in this field of battle,
    Earnestly invoke the Muse;
Lest vile critics storm and rattle,
    Look well to your p's and q's.   20

Trust not friends, tho' they may flatter,
    Keep the Balaam box in view;
O'er your poem its lid may clatter,
    No sham there – that box is true.

"Much your 'Ode to Spring' reminds us   25
    Of a poem we've heard before;
'Tis in vain you try to blind us;
    Do not send us any more."

"Your grammar's bad, your spelling fearful
    It may please *you*, not other folks;"   30
You may read, with eyes all tearful,
    The words of Balaam Box!

Poets! then, be up and doing,
    Strive to earn a better fate,
While the path of fame pursuing,   35
    Labour still, in patience wait.

86. 'The Sack-Sewers of Dundee', by E. Lindsay, 51 North Wellington Street, Dundee. Published 1 March 1879.

This poem offers another take on the Jute trade and the women who worked within it. The author is unidentified.

See also: 27. 'The Chappin' Laddie', p. 48; 68. 'Oor Mill', p. 115; 76. 'Jute', p. 130; 82. 'King Jute', p. 142.

The poor sack-sewers of Dundee,   1
Their sorrows few may know
When looking for their bundle
Out through the frost and snow.
They wander here, they wander there,   5
Till hour by hour goes by,
With scarce a shoe upon their feet,
The tear oft in their eye;
The little ones oft left behind
In some lone garret high,   10

Or in a lowly lonesome room,
With scarce a watcher by.
And think a minute, only think
How hard they have to win
The coppers for their bundle.   15
When work they do begin,
A juty hair doth fly from them
When sacks they do unfold,
Which dirties every corner in
Their little homes they hold.   20
Ninepence for fifty they do get,
To fold and stitch them well;
If not close sewed, no money,
The truth to you I'll tell –
Not speaking of the time that's lost,   25
Again I do repeat,
Returning with the bundle
Through many a dirty street,
Many a one would gladly throw
Sacks down upon the way,   30
If it were not for starvation,
So near their homes to-day.
Ye rich, that move through plenty,
Just think of poor Dundee,
And a penny throw the sack-wifies   35
When that ye do them see.

87. 'Died on the Street', by James Y. Geddes, Dundee. Published 22 March 1879.

'Died on the Street' was reprinted in *The Spectre Clock of Alyth and Other Selections* (Alyth: Thomas McMurray, 1886), pp. 54–58, with a note stating 'The foregoing was written after witnessing the death of a millworker on the street in Dundee', but without the epigraph which gives the name and date – indicating the immediacy of Geddes' poetic response – of the woman commemorated. Born in 1850, at this point Geddes was a tailor and clothier in Dundee. He is one of the more experimental newspaper poets of this period, and has been regarded by twentieth-century critics as one of relatively few such poets to produce genuinely innovative verse (see Bold). Geddes had a stronger relationship with the *Dundee Advertiser* than with the *Journal*, its sister paper, and this is the only one of his poems to appear in the latter during this period. Although in some respects it has a conventional religious message, and follows the *Journal*'s poetic doctrine of equality between rich and poor and the need for sympathy and charity, it is more questioning and less resigned than is the norm. Geddes' compressed lines, often with only two stresses, are also unusual in newspaper verse.

See also: 19. *'Nan Tamson's Wean', p. 33; 69. 'Coals', p. 117.*

> *In Memoriam* Mary Fox.
> Died March 17th, 1879.

Thy love is over all,	1
Thou mark'st the sparrows fall;	
Thou, with a tender care,	
Feedest the fowls of air.	
Yea, Lord, who can divine	5
Thy care complete?	
Yet, Lord, a daughter Thine	
Dies on the street.	
Lord of our life and days,	
Who knoweth all Thy ways?	10
Birds of the air,	
Art thou, then, more than we?	
Showeth the Father thee	
More of His care?	

Out in the morning grey   15
Death greets her by the way,
Pillowed on stones;
None but a curious crowd,
Talking or whispering loud,
Hear her last groans.   20

No friends or kindred nigh
Heard her last dying sigh;
Fain would we rest –
Fain would we have our head,
When death's decree is said,   25
Laid on loved breast.

Why make us reason *why*
When nought can satisfy?
Happy the birds in bower,
Knowing not reason's power,   30
To whom the present *is* –
Future – but nothingness.
God, art Thou Love?
Lov'st Thou them more than us?
Why treat Thy children thus,   35
Father above?

So we, 'twixt earth and sky,
Ask on, but no reply
Silences break.
Is there a love which lies   40
Far from our prying eyes?
Shall we when life is done –
When last its race is run –
Shall we awake?

And yet perchance it is   45
Simplest of mysteries
Under the sun.
So would He save from scaith,
So fill with fuller faith
Till unbelief is laid –   50
Till with a lowly head,
Free from our former doubt,

"Lord," we can murmur out,
"Thy will be done."

Leaving Thy earthly land,   55
Is there no kindly hand
Death wreaths to twine?
Lost from life's labyrinth,
Though not of amaranth,
Though but of uncouth make,   60
This my poor tribute take,
Sister of mine.

Shall I restrain my tongue?
Should sad requiems be sung
Only for woes   65
Wrought in the royal sphere?
Shall I reserve the tear,
Sackcloth and ashes wear
Only for Prince or Peer?
'Gainst her low-lying head   70
Sympathy close?

Ancient of Life and Days,
Who knoweth all our ways,
Pity her fate.
Still, though we see not yet   75
He who can ne'er forget,
Safe in his circling arms
Kept thee from death's alarms,
When on the snowy ground
Saw thee with host around   80
Dying in state.

Little He cares above,
Who ruleth all in love,
Princess or drudge,
Whene'er a duty's done   85
Then shall His praise be won;
Though it be kingly toil,
Though it be work and moil,
God, His approving smile,
Never will grudge.   90

Stay yet and do not stir;
I charge you think of her –
Life – is it sweet?
Think of her constant strife,
Warring with want for life;   95
Think of the end of all –
Death at a moment's call –
Death on the street.

Ye with your pride in birth,
Are ye of better worth?   100
Who gave it so –
Gave her the harder lot –
Toil and the troubled thought;
Gave you the wealth and ease –
Handmaids to wait and please –   105
Comfort below?

Then in a milder mood
Think of the sisterhood
Born but to spin.
Think not by merit is   110
Dealt out the preferences –
Granted the proud estate –
Given them the lowly fate
Wages to win.

Come from your homes and halls,   115
Speak not from pedestals
Down to their destinies;
Grudge not their little doles,
Stand not by starving souls,
Preaching economies.   120

Yours be the kindlier part –
Give them within your heart
Truest of sympathy.
Think them *thy* sisters – mine,
Though chance the will Divine   125
Gave thee a pleasant place,
Grants them but little grace.
So, may God prosper thee,
If this thy watchword be –
God help humanity.   130

88. 'Ring Up the Curtain', by D. Taylor, Dundee, April 1879. Published on 19 April 1879.

In 1874, Benjamin Disraeli defeated Gladstone in the General Election, and his Conservative government set about pursuing an aggressive foreign policy. This led to war in Afghanistan from 1878 to 1880, designed to prevent the Russians from gaining a foothold in central Asia within reach of British India; and to the Anglo–Zulu War from January to July 1879, which aimed to bring independent Zululand under British control. (While both wars arguably owed more to the actions of colonial governors than Parliament, the Liberal public squarely blamed the Tories.) The staunchly Liberal *Journal* and its poets were firmly against these campaigns, which (in their view) achieved little, involved enormous expense and loss of life, and placed Britain in a morally dubious position in its questionable justification for warmongering. More anti-government and anti-war poems appear in the late 1870s and early 1880s than at any other point in this period. 'Your' in this poem refers to the Tory rulers, whose government would fall a year after 'Ring Up the Curtain' appears. Taylor contributed other poems, including 'Jute', to the *Journal* in this period.

See also: 76. 'Jute', p. 130; 89. 'Isandula', p. 157; 90. 'Ketchwayo the Zulu', p. 160; 93. 'An Election Song', p. 165; 95. 'The Dogs of War', p. 169.

Ring up the curtain! Let us see	1
The plot and purpose of your play;	
Deal now no more in mystery,	
But come forth to the light of day.	
In Asian tricks you've dealt too long;	5
Your power at length is on the wane;	
On even the dull unthinking throng	
You cast your glamour now in vain.	
Ring up the curtain! Tell us what	
You mean by all these sounds of war.	10
What are the tricks you would be at	
In Africa and Ind, afar?	
We hear the groans of dying men,	
The orphan and the widow's wail,	
And try to find, but try in vain,	15
By what right 'tis such ills prevail.	

Ring up the curtain! Clear the stage,
    Till through the darkness we can pierce,
And see what roused the horrid rage
    Of Afghans wild and Zulus fierce.   20
You say the cause is right and just,
    But what we daily hear and see
Makes us your words and acts mistrust,
    And look on them as trickery.

Ring up the curtain! Bring more light,   25
    If you speak truth, what need to fear?
Who feels his cause is just and right
    Cares not how soon it is made clear.
'Tis only those that do the wrong
    Who try their acts, from light, to hide,   30
Or, knowing that their power is strong,
    Gloss over them with mocking pride.

Ring up the curtain! It is time
    We had a peep behind the scenes;
It may be that your plot's sublime,   35
    Although we know not what it means.
But while our soldiers fight and die,
    'Tis surely right that we should know
If all their deeds of bravery
    Are meant injustice to o'erthrow.   40

89. 'Isandula', by Per Mare Per Terram, Montrose. Published on 6 November 1879.

The Battle of Isandlwana (Isandula is an alternative spelling) took place on 22 January 1879 and was the opening salvo in the Anglo–Zulu War. It was a decisive defeat for the British, who had signally underestimated the Zulu forces, and a staggering blow to British imperial pride. By November, the war was over, but discontent over Britain's actions in Africa continued to simmer. This poem is notable because of its dramatic switch from standard patriotic rhetoric in the opening stanzas, to an anti-war position (signaled in the pointed questions of line 22), and then to a pro-Zulu position in which God, disgusted by British hypocrisy, will support the Zulu people in their rise to a prosperous, peaceful and Christian future. Although still displaying some of the typically racist attitudes of its period, a statement like 'The Zulu now becomes your king' shows the author's opposition to Britain's behaviour. No other poems were published under this pseudonym.

See also: 88. *'Ring Up the Curtain'*, p. 155; 90. *'Ketchwayo the Zulu'*, p. 160; 95. *'The Dogs of War'*, p. 169.

Stand back to back, stand firm, stand true,	1
Stern deeds to-day you have to do	
This day at Isandula;	
Ere sets yon glorious orb of light,	
Our sun may set in death's dark night –	5
Dark night at Isandula.	

Stand back to back, stand firm, stand true, 1
Stern deeds to-day you have to do
    This day at Isandula;
Ere sets yon glorious orb of light,
Our sun may set in death's dark night – 5
    Dark night at Isandula.

Behold yon mighty horde advance
With masked shield and deadly lance –
    Advance on Isandula;
So quick they come flight would be vain, 10
Nor shall we Britain's banner stain
    With flight at Isandula.

And now in front, in flank, in rear,
Nearer they come and still more near –
    Ah fatal Isandula; 15
They close, Oh God, the awful fight,
Fiends well might sicken at the sight –
    Dread sight at Isandula.

Enveloped in that column dark,
As in a tomb, Oh, Britain, mark   20
  Thy sons at Isandula.
Who brought them there? What brought them there?
To death amid their wild despair –
  Despair at Isandula.

Now British blood like water flows,   25
Commingled with their savage foes –
  Thrice bloody Isandula.
Oh God, assert thy might and power,
Rob Satan of his cursed hour –
  Curst hour at Isandula.   30

And now the fatal hour is past,
Behold yon bleeding column fast
  Retire from Isandula;
That column in whose dread embrace
Four hundred of our British race   35
  Were crushed at Isandula.

.—.—.—.—

A thousand years since then has flown;
Behold yon obelisk of stone
  That stands on Isandula;
While round its base there may be seen,   40
With beaming eyes, with manly mien,
  Some men of Isandula.

Their skin is black, their hair like wool,
Thick lips they have, receding skull –
  Those men of Isandula;   45
But heavenward now they cast their eyes,
To Heaven's Great King their anthems rise –
  Rise up from Isandula.

Their land now blossoms like the rose,
Their Sabbath bells peal out repose,   50
  God's rest at Isandula.
Long since are turned to hooks their spears,
To shares their swords, and now for years,
  Peace reigns at Isandula.

Ah, Christian Britain, hide your face,   55
Your Master's name you did disgrace –
   Disgrace at Isandula,
When to these dark benighted slaves,
You sent your sons to find their graves
   At fated Isandula.   60

You had the light, you had the power,
To give those men that heavenly dower –
   Those men at Isandula.
What did you give? Cold steel and shot,
Your sons 'neath tropic skies to rot –   65
   To rot at Isandula.

The Zulu now becomes your king,
God took him 'neath his sheltering wing
   Since bloody Isandula.
He saw your cruelty and pride,   70
He saw you set His laws aside –
   Aside at Isandula.

90. 'Ketchwayo the Zulu', Natal, January 1879.
Unsigned. Published on 22 November 1879.

Like 'Isandula', this is a firmly pro-Zulu poem. The note
supplied at the end of the poem enhances the international
liberal credentials of the *Journal* by suggesting that it offers a
home for radical sentiments unpublishable in the colonies. The
January date in this note implies that the poem was composed at
the opening of the Anglo–Zulu war, which was partly justified
as an effort to protect British Natal from the Zulus. By com-
paring Cetshwayo kaMpande, king of the Zulus, to Horatius, the
defender of Rome in Thomas Macaulay's very well-known *Lays
of Ancient Rome* (1842), the author casts him as noble hero and
the British invaders as villains. Cetshwayo was captured and exiled
in September 1879, after which he came to be regarded as a
tragic and kingly figure: parts of the British media campaigned
vigorously for his restoration as ruler. He was frequently
pictured and discussed in the press, particularly in relation to
his later visit to London in 1882.

See also: 89. 'Isandula', p. 157; 95. 'The Dogs of War', p. 169.

I ask myself how can such things be done, and in God's
    name,   1
As try to quench the spark of life from some heroic frame.
Has not the proud Ketchwayo, savage chief although he be,
As good and just a right to fight the battle of the free
As any ancient warrior who stood in stern array   5
To spurn the proud invader from the land they trode that
    day,
Or as the noblest Roman sung of in Macaulay's lay?
Breathes there a worm that will not turn, and thus itself
    defend?
And why should not Ketchwayo's soul be burning to that
    end?
Lives there a man in any land who calmly would sit still   10
And watch the proud invaders crown the crest of every hill,
And never dare to stop or stay the burning of his home,
Nor seek to intervene between the plunder sure to come,
Nor seek the sword to turn aside from wife and children
    dear?
Alas! for such as this there's none on earth will shed a
    tear,   15

But he that will his foes retard or hurl them to the tomb
Will in his country's story like the spring-time ever bloom.
Ketchwayo, rise in all your strength and barbarous display,
Deal death to those who seek to steal your land and life
    away.
Fight for your home and household gods, as all great men
    have done   20
Fight for your right with all your might, and save your
    crown and throne.
God gives the race not to the swift, nor victory to the strong,
And He of all alone can judge if you are in the wrong,
And happ'ly you may conquer yet if right is on your side,
But if you're wrong remember, vengeance comes with giant
    stride.   25
With noiseless step and ruthless grasp, that none have yet
    withstood,
That overpowers its victims as are wrecks in some wild
    flood.
But fight you on, fight strong and long, then though at last
    you fall,
Your stern defence will cover you with glory's gorgeous
    pall;
Fight on, for what is life but death if won ingloriously?   30
Lead on your men to conquer, or if not to conquer, die,
Death or subjection is the ultimatum offered you,
So either way you're bound to fall whatever you may do;
But when your foes triumph o'er you no glory will they gain,
And every laurel leaf will bloom with foul dishonour's
    stain.   35

NOTE. – This is a poem sent by a friend of mine from
Natal. As it was inconsistent with the views entertained by
the colonists, it would have been heresy to publish it there,
so I transmit it now to you, sir. If you think it worthy of a
place in your *Journal*, it would no doubt give the author
some satisfaction to know that the opinions are still held by
some that every man has a right to defend his own to the
utmost of his power. There are many professing Christians
in Natal that would have hung Ketchwayo like a dog, if they
had had the power to do so.
                    D. P. C., Edinburgh.

91. 'Lines, Suggested by the Melancholy Wreck of the Tay Bridge', by G. W. Donald, Abbey Buildings, Arbroath, 31 December 1879. Published 3 January 1880.

G. W. Donald (1820–1891), from 1866 Keeper of the Abbey grounds at Arbroath, and formerly a herd boy, weaver and self-taught schoolmaster, was a well-known contributor to newspapers and periodicals, and had considerable success in the *Journal's* poetry competitions. He published collections in 1855 and 1867, and a complete volume of *Poems, Ballads and Songs* in 1880 (Arbroath: T. Buncle). This poem would have been written just too late for inclusion. The central section of the Tay Bridge collapsed as a train crossed it in the evening of Sunday 28 December 1879, during a violent storm. The train plunged into the Tay and seventy-five passengers drowned. This was one of the worst, and most famous, railway disasters of the century, and the Dundee press reported on the disaster and its aftermath very extensively throughout 1880. Donald's poem appeared in the first issue of the *Journal* after the disaster, alongside a 'Review of Local Events for the Past Year', which described the fall of the bridge as 'the most awful and notable mark in the history not only of the catastrophes of 1879, but of the century.' Numerous other poems appeared in the Dundee and Scottish press in response to the Tay Bridge disaster.

See also: 53. 'The Tay Bridge', p. 88; 80. 'An Address to Thee Tay Bridge', p. 138; 92. 'In Memoriam', p. 164.

'Twas Sabbath e'en, the pale moonlight	1
Was streaming from on high,	
Save when the clouds, like sheeted ghosts,	
Were drifting 'cross the sky.	
The storm fiend, in his wildest mood,	5
Impell'd the scowling blast;	
And trees and towers were scatter'd wide,	
By every gust that passed.	
E'en those who sought the house of prayer	
Oft trembled with alarm,	10
And closer clung to Him who rules	
The whirlwind and the storm.	
The mother by her lonely heart	
Pray'd for her sailor boy,	
The new-made bride, 'mid tears and sighs,	15
Forgot her hour of joy.	

Strange sounds of fear fell on her ear,
    And 'mid the dire alarms
"Oh Heaven," she cried, "what could betide
    To keep him from my arms."   20
Yon group who from the lattice peer
    Why turn their lips so white
While on the foaming billows' crest
    Appear those streaks of light.
That redd'ning flame – 'tis seen – 'tis gone –   25
    And yet the sparks arise
Like shooting stars that pierce the gloom
    Beneath the northern skies.
Ah! now 'tis gone, nor spark nor flame
    Salutes the gazer's eye.   30
'Tis gone – 'tis gone but not alone
    The hungry waves reply,
A murmur passed from lip to lip,
    And spread from home to home,
That o'er the Bridge that spans the Tay,   35
    That hour a train should come.
Through wreck and ruin, fast they sped,
    And sought the truth with care;
Still all was doubt and darkness round,
    Suspense and deep despair.   40
Yet through the tempest's madd'ning wrath,
    One venturous soul would go,
And battling o'er the angry flood
    That yawning surg'd below,
He dar'd what mortal man might dare   45
    Till he could dare no more;
The mountain waves on either hand,
    Now bounding, stretch'd before.
The truth was found – oh sadd'ning truth,
    As mortal lips might tell,   50
That brings to many a home and hearth
    Despair and anguish fell.
The glory of the Tay was gone,
    Her crown was rent in twain,
The learn'd, the lov'd, the good, the brave   55
    Were buried with the train.
Buried beneath the swelt'ring brine,
    None heard the crash – the cry –

The stifled groan – the fearful plunge,
     None save their God on high.   60
A gloom has spread o'er all the land
     By this sad overthrow.
Stand still, proud man, and weigh the worth
     Of all thy works below!

92. 'In Memoriam', by J. S. M. Published 10 January 1880.

Another of the many poems published on the Tay Bridge disaster, this short poem borrows the well-known rhyme-scheme of Tennyson's *In Memoriam* (abba, the 'In Memoriam' stanza) for its elegy. It suggests that the victims were pioneers, in that they were part of the fight for progress and enlightenment represented by new technologies and works.

See also: 53. 'The Tay Bridge', p. 88; 91. 'Lines, Suggested by the Melancholy Wreck of the Tay Bridge', p. 162.

There shines a light high o'er the mass   1
Of darkened life, shot past the flood
Of Time's swift river, though the blood
Stands frozen at the awful pass.

They fell as in heroic charge   5
Of battle for the true and right;
Before the unmeasur'd, viewless might
Of heaven's artillery, vast and large.

They trusted Man's proud handiwork
Of venture, in supremest hour;   10
They pioneer'd the newer power
Which air's dire forces shall not burke.

All royal roads are paved by death:
We only reach the mount of light,
We only find the vision bright,   15
Through valour, and by parted breath.

Honour the brave, the sacred band
Who fill the breach, and make for us
The pathway safe, and new, and bless,
And leave them in their Maker's hand.   20

93. 'An Election Song', by John Rae, Glasgow. Published 20 March 1880.

John Rae – born on the Burns Centenary, 25 January 1859 – worked in the drapery business in Glasgow, and then in London (see Edwards, 3, p. 216). 'Willie' is William Gladstone, who was the MP for Midlothian. His campaign in March and April of 1880, known as the 'Midlothian campaign' and featuring stirring speeches lambasting Disraeli's foreign policy, was widely reported in the media and helped the Liberals to a landslide victory in the election of 5 April, when Gladstone became Prime Minister. On 17 March, Gladstone had spoken to a large meeting in Edinburgh. The *Journal* published more poems in relation to this election than any other in the period, and in an editorial on 27 March, warned readers that 'Never in the history of Scotland was there so important an election as this' (p. 2). 'Asian mysteries' commonly refers to Disraeli's foreign policy in this period, and was also a phrase used, with a strong anti-semitic sense, to imply that Disraeli himself was tricksy, untrustworthy and did not have Britain's best interests at heart.

See also: 88. *'Ring Up the Curtain', p. 155; 94. 'An M. P. Non Est', p. 167.*

The bubble's burst, the win' is blawn,   1
The Tories canna langer stan'.
Come north again noo, Willie, man,
    An' gie's some grand oration.

You'll aye be welcome tae the north,   5
For weel we ken yer noble worth;
A Scot despite your English birth,
    You're sterling like your nation.

A master in politic art,
A' daubin' loons you gar them smart,   10

Wha daur tae play a roguish part
    In name o' this great nation.

We "British interests" a' revere,
Tae Britons aye they will be dear,
But "Asian mysteries" we fear,
    An' jugglin' declamation.   15

You aye can keep the nation's cash
Richt weel, an' settle ony hash,
If need be, wi' the nation's lash
    An' patriot animation.   20

An' noo, ye voters a', attend,
Frae John o' Groat's unto Lan's En';
Do each, wi' a' your micht an' main,
    What ye can in your station.

Return the men that's guid an' true,   25
Despite the "faggot" laden crew;
Mak' this a reg'lar Waterloo
    For Liberal legislation.

An' 'neath the sun o' gowden trade
Oor sickly commerce, well-nigh dead,   30
Shall rise in micht, an' grandly spread
    Again ower a' creation.

daubin' – pecking, stabbing   *gar – to make*

94. 'An M.P. Non Est', by Jacob Moon, Dundee.
Published in 'Election Verses', 27 March 1880.

The MP in question, and the speaker of this election poem, is James Yeaman, who was elected as a Liberal for Dundee in 1873 but then aroused anger among his constituents by voting with the Tory government on their foreign policies in Afghanistan, Turkey and in the Zulu wars. In Liberal Dundee, this had earned him the title 'Tory Jeamie' (also the title of a second poem on his candidacy in the same issue of the paper). The 27 March editorial on 'The Representation of Dundee' noted that Yeaman had sided more with the government than any other Liberal MP, and very strongly opposed his re-election, citing 'the depth of the degradation to which Dundee will fall should a supporter of the Government be returned.' (p. 5). Yeaman, now standing as a Conservative, lost his seat in the Liberal landslide. Five poems on the election were published on 27 March, three dealing with Yeaman.

See also: 93. 'An Election Song', p. 165.

Alas! alack the day, man;   1
My title is away, man;
No longer now I may, man,
        Call myself M. P.
Alas! alas for Tory ways,   5
That I in London crown'd with bays,
Should meet down here such scanty praise.
        Alas! alas for me!

I don't know what to say, man;
I'm fit to weep to-day, man,   10
For now I'm plain James Yeaman;
        My glories many spurn.
Oh! for those days my heart held dear,
To hobnob with our great Premier –
I'll never see him more I fear –   15
        They're past, ne'er to return.

Unearth'd are all my Tory ways,
E'en where Liberalism pays;
And each true Liberal smartly says
        That he'll have none of me.   20

I'm badger'd day and night, man,
To rag me's their delight, man,
With all their fearful might, man;
       They will not let me be.

Oh! how I wish I knew the way   25
To blind them on the polling day;
And after that they'd have their say
       For many years to come.
But, ah! to think that day is near
That'll leave me as a private here;   30
For, when the votes are counted clear,
       Defeat is sure the sum.

I wish I'd kept my faith, man,
For that had pleased us baith, man,
And then I'd met no scaith, man,   35
       In Liberal Dundee.
But what's the use of sighs and cries?
I'll e'en arise and dry my eyes;
I can't pretend 'tis a surprise,
       Alas, alas for me!   40

95. 'The Dogs of War', by Jessie R. McIntyre, Edinburgh. Published 10 April 1880.

Appearing immediately after the General Election, this is another poem critical of Conservative foreign policy, which hints in the final lines at the poet's hope for the new Liberal government. McIntyre is also the author of 'A Year Ago'. She is unidentified.

See also: 88. *'Ring Up the Curtain', p. 155;* 89. *'Isandula', p. 157;* 90. *'Ketchwayo the Zulu', p. 160;* 93. *'An Election Song', p. 165;* 98. *'A Year Ago', p. 173.*

The dogs of war are hungry still,   1
    Though from their reeking jaws
The heart's blood of a nation drops
    Upon their restless paws.

Their hot eyes glare from out the gloom   5
    Of widowhood and woe,
And through the awful stillness comes
    A mutt'ring deep and low,

Which stronger grows, till rock and sea
    And every traversed shore   10
Shall hear, and dread the meaning of
    That fierce, menacing roar.

Oh! that some brave and daring hand
    Would chain them down for aye,
And from a night of horrors lead   15
    Our land to peaceful day.

96. 'Dakota', by P. Mitchell, Kensington, D. T., USA, 28 July 1880. Published 21 August 1880.

Another emigrant poem, this advertises the beauty and fertility of Dakota, and the status of America as the 'land of the free', to readers in Scotland. Settlement in Dakota Territory grew very rapidly in the 1870s and 1880s, supported by the expansion of the railway network in North America. North and South Dakota were admitted into the United States in 1889.

See also: 55. 'The Land That Rear'd Us A'', p. 92.

Dakota, how lovely thy valleys and hills,   1
Gladdened by rivers and watered by rills;
Broad are the plains where the husbandman tills
    His own fertile land in Dakota.

Fruitful Dakota, her fields spreading wide,   5
Waving with plenty, like flow of the tide;
We rival the world, and carry, with pride,
    The banner for grain in Dakota.

Wild let the winter winds bellow and blow;
Rage in their fury the frost and the snow;   10
My log burning bright shall fill with a glow,
    My house and my home in Dakota.

Hail to my brothers far over the sea –
A welcome we give to the land of the free;
Cast off the yoke; come, enjoy liberty –   15
    No tyranny reigns in Dakota.

97. 'Reminiscences of the *People's Journal*', by Grandfather. Published 29 March 1881.

'Grandfather' was the pseudonym of Henry Syme, a weaver from Dunfermline. He had published one collection, *Local Musings* (Dunfermline: A. Romanes, Press Office, 1876). This poem is important in suggesting the established reputation of some of the *Journal* contributors: Syme particularly identifies the comic prose characters Tammas Bodkin and Jamie (James) Thacket (the latter a druggist created by Alexander Whamond), and poets Will Harrow and Poute, showing an ability to reference, and in Poute's case imitate, details from their productions. 'Reminiscences' also highlights the significance of the Christmas competitions, alluding to the essay and letter-writing competitions – some aimed at child and women competitors – as well as those for fiction and poetry, and defends the virtue and Christianity of *Journal* readers ('some wha dress in black' are ministers).

See also: 44. 'Lines on Receiving a People's Journal', *p. 73; 79. 'Naething New', p. 135.*

While sittin' by the ingle-cheek I've read the *Journal* mony
    a week,   1
The number now I cudna tell, in case I might tell lees,
But aething I can brawly min', I read the first ane at the
    time
When "Jamie Tacket" was on tramp, and ate the ale-wife's
    cheese.
There's Bodkin Tam the tailor, baith a landsman and a
    sailor,   5
Better far at writin' stories than he is at making breeks;
At the twinnies' mule and funnel, Tibbie kissin' in the
    Tunnel,
I have seen a housefu' lauchin' till the tears ran down their
    cheeks.
We were wont to hear frae Tammas baith at Hogmanay
    and Lammas,
But his jaunts are grown like angels' visits, few an' far
    atween;   10
How in Feugh he hookit herrin' to mak' Tibbie dainty
    fairin',
An' gaed a sable huntin' in the town o' Aberdeen.

Next comes our friend "Will Harrow", you wid scarcely
    find his marrow.
A racy story clad in rhyme that worthy weel can tell;
That great chieftain, Mr Poute, weel deserves a muckle
    shout,   15
The king o' a' his countryside 4 growing Leeks and Kail.
Then you can get the local news for ony district you may
    choose;
Through a' the kingdoms three and Wales the *Journal* is
    weel kent;
To a' the Colonies abroad, whaur Scotsmen hae abode,
The *People's Journal* weekly has for mony years been sent; 20
And mony a servan' callant wha cud scarcely read a
    ballant,
Like Davock at his carritches, they noo hae grown sae
    gleg,
They can screed you aff the news about the Afghans an'
    Zulus,
And tell ye wha's the Dorkin' hen that laid the muckle
    egg;
The Christmas poems and stories, with rewards for the
    victorious,   25
Whaur a' hae opportunity their mental powers to test;
The youngsters at the schule are ay busy before Yule
Awritin' to the Editor, and tryin' wha is best.
The thrifty wives and lasses among the working classes
Hae shown us how to keep a house upon a pound a-week, 30
And how to guide the youth in ways of righteousness and
    truth,
Because God's blessin' rests on those who early grace do
    seek.
Lately some wha dress in black the *Journal* readers did
    attack;
They had shown a better spirit had they let the matter
    rest.
Some of our modern teachers hae forgot the Prince of
    preachers,   35
Wha plainly wrote, "Of all the graces charity is best."
When the clouds are rent asunder and the Judge descends
    in thunder,
An' the hills are whummelt ower an' there is neither loch
    nor sea,

When the folk are a' forgathered, when the good an' bad
  are severed,
We'll see readers o' the *Journal* whaur we a' wid like to be.   40

98. 'A Year Ago', by Jessie R. McIntyre, Edinburgh. Published 21 May 1881.

'A Year Ago' presents itself as a standard poem of lost love and betrayal, until the twist in the final line. It shows McIntyre's awareness of the codes and themes of women's poetry and her ability to manipulate them. A response poem published on 4 June 1881, 'To Jessie R. M'Intyre, After a Period of Severe Illness', by G. J. M. L., dated 30 May 1881, expressed sympathy for McIntyre as an invalid.

See also: 46. 'Sweet', p. 76; 78. 'Only', p. 134; 95. 'The Dogs of War', p. 169.

'Tis only a short, short year ago,   1
In the swift glad time when roses grow,
When scented winds o'er the hill tops blow,
    And days are long.

A year ago, in the gloamin' sweet,   5
Unheeded flew time's radiant feet,
For love, with its harmonies complete,
    Was all our song.

A year ago, and beside the shore,
Where the sad waves murmured o'er and o'er   10
"You may meet again, ah, nevermore,"
    We said good-bye.

A year ago, and I know that now
You've broken each whispered kiss-given vow,
I sigh not, weep not, but meekly bow,   15
    For so have I.

99. 'Eviction', by John Rae, 46 Paternoster Row, London. Published 23 July 1881.

This is almost certainly the same John Rae, employee in a draper's firm, who features in the poetry columns in 1880 and was the author of 'An Election Song', now giving his new address in London. The Highland Clearances were the subject of a great many poems in the Victorian period, in Gaelic, Scots and English and by writers across Britain and in overseas colonies, but few poems on this topic appeared in the *Journal*. In the years leading up to the Crofters' Act of 1886, agitation about land reform, and indignation at the treatment of Highlanders, was gathering pace. This poem takes a familiar line about the importance of the Highlands in supplying brave fighters for the British armies.

See also: 93. 'An Election Song', p. 165; 103. 'The Battle of Tel-el-Kebir', p. 182.

A *Protest against the Depopulation of the Highlands, and the Substitution of Deer Forests for Human Dwellings.*

Why should honest men be hunted   1
    From the land that gave them birth,
Making room for game to flourish
    In their place upon the earth?

Why should aged sires and mothers,   5
    With their children at their knee,
Thus be driven forth as felons
    From a land that's boasted free?

Surely God who made the peasant
    Meant him not to houseless roam,   10
Nor empower'd a lordly mortal
    Thus to waste his lowly home.

Famed were Britain's peasant soldiers
    In the past and noble days,
When her ranks were filled with thousands   15
    Fresh from Scotia's heathy braes.

By the hearths where grew those heroes
    Now the red deer grazes free,
But the men are gone for ever,
    And their race no more we'll see.   20

Britain, in the hour of danger,
    Where will be thy peasant shield?
Where the arms that drove thy bayonets,
    Hearts that know not how to yield?

In that hour when help is needed   25
    Will the lordlings of the land,
With their game preserves and forests,
    Prove a strong defensive band?

Spain hath seen proud Gallic armies
    Tremble at the ringing cheer   30
Of our gallant Highland "kilties;"
    Will they tremble at our deer?

Lords there are who earn the title
    By their dignity and worth;
Men who gain their meed of honour   35
    For themselves and not their birth.

Men who bravely aid and labour
    Striving for the common good,
And who scorn in heart to mingle
    With the lazy gilded brood.   40

Patriots they of manly virtue,
    Nature's nobles to the core;
May our country, to its credit,
    Nurse and cherish many more.

Let us fill the glens and forests   45
    Once again with sturdy men;
Better sight than sportsmen's rifles
    Are the mowers 'mong the grain.

Bring us back those men, they're wanted
    In this nineteenth century time;   50

Men of mind and men of muscle,
    Fit to live in any clime.

Honour men not for their station,
    Nor their silver, nor their gold;
Honest worth in manly bosoms 55
    Is not bartered, bought, or sold.

Gift it is from mighty Donor,
    Maker of both high and low;
Rank and title are but bubbles
    Rising as life's waters flow. 60

Study how to help a brother,
    How to cheer a fellow-man;
Aim at good that's universal,
    Help to make all peoples one.

Yours may then be honours brighter 65
    Than are won by shield and sword;
Yours a name of fame for ever,
    Living, lasting, and adored.

100. 'April Days', by Annie S. Swan, Mountskip, Gorebridge. Published 29 April 1882.

Annie S. Swan (1849–1943) was better known as a writer of popular romantic fiction for the *People's Friend* and other periodicals and magazines: in 1881 the *Friend* had serialised her novel, *Wrongs Righted*. The income from her writing enabled her to help her husband through medical school, and to move to London to pursue her literary interests. Swan was active in Liberal politics and in the suffrage movement, and a strong supporter of the Church of Scotland. Her poetry and fiction generally tended to eschew overtly political themes and was associated, by the twentieth century, with the 'kailyard' school. 'April Days' is representative of two of the most common genres of newspaper poetry: seasonal poems, always printed at the appropriate time of year, and elegiac verse with a Christian conclusion.

See also: 78. 'Only', p. 134.

Hoo green an' fresh the buddin' trees,   1
    Hoo sweet the birdies' lays,
They lilt a blithesome welcome tae
    The bonny April days.

The gowan and the sweet blue-bell   5
    Are bloomin' on the lea,
The glen is decked wi' primrose pale
    An' shy anemone.

Hoo fresh and sweet the gentle wind,
    The sun, hoo bricht an' clear.   10
Ay, this should be a heartsome time –
    The spring-time o' the year.

Ah! me, I canna see the buds
    For mist o' blindin' rain;
The birdies only chant for me   15
    A bitter, sad refrain.

Dear hands hae slippet frae my clasp –
    Dear hands I'll touch nae mair;
I canna bide the gledsome spring,
    My heart's sae fou o' care.   20

Dear God, hoo sair and hard tae thole
    The pairtin's we hae here;
I pray we a' may meet abune
    I' the spring-time o' the year.

101. 'Advice to Blue-Ribboners at the Fair Holidays', by Jas. Burns, Lochee. Published 24 June 1882.

'Blue-ribboners' are those who took the temperance pledge, for-mulated by the popular Irish-American temperance reformer Francis Murphy, and who wore a blue ribbon to signify their abstinence from alcohol. Murphy's blue ribbon movement spread very rapidly in Scotland, particularly after he held large-scale meetings in Forfar and Dundee between September 1881 and January 1882, signing up thousands to the cause. The poem is addressed to those inexperienced converts who may be tempted to backslide from their commitment while enjoying the summer fairs.

See also: 19. *'Nan Tamson's Wean'*, p. 33; 77. *'Rapidly, Rapidly'*, p. 132.

You people with the Ribbon Blue,   1
Beware how at the Fair you do;
Temptations they are not so few
    As you may think.

Be sure your Ribbon Blue you show,   5
No matter to what place you go,
And then the people they will know
    You do not drink.

The public-houses always shun,
And never take a glass for fun,   10
Or else the devil he will run
    Within your veins.

And if a non-abstainer say,
"Come, it is very cold to-day,
We'll take a glass and then away –   15
    See how it rains" –

Then all that you have got to do
Is let him see your Ribbon Blue,
And if he then remains with you
       He will not drink.   20

But still the safest way of all
Is not to be with him at all;
The staunchest of us sometimes fall –
       So you may shrink.

The way your Ribbon it should be   25
Is so that everyone may see
Without an eyeglass to their e'e;
       You've nought to fear.

For then they know they need not try
To ask you if you don't feel dry,   30
And as you don't drink whisky, why
       You'll taste some beer.

102. 'Victory', by J. M. K., Dundee. Published 23 September 1882.

This poem commemorates the Battle of Tel-el-Kebir, of 13 September 1882, in which the British army, with the Highland Brigade in the lead, resoundingly defeated Egyptian forces under Ahmed Urabi. It was the decisive incident in the Anglo–Egyptian War of 1882, fought to protect British interests (particularly the Suez Canal) in the region after a nationalist uprising. The *Journal* was supportive of this war, led by a Liberal government, unlike Britain's other interventions in the East in the period. The editorial, 'Our Egyptian Victory', on 23 September emphasised that Britain was fighting in defence of her rights and in order to restore the legitimate government to power, arguing that those Radicals who saw Urabi ('Arabi') as another William Wallace or Garibaldi were misguided. It did disagree, however, with calls for Britain to annexe Egypt in the wake of this victory. Poems on this battle in the Scottish press are naturally invested in emphasising the importance of Highland soldiers, perhaps in order to make the same points that John Rae had made in his 'Eviction' (p. 174).

See also: 89. 'Isandula', p. 157; 90. Ketchwayo the Zulu, p. 160; 95. 'The Dogs of War', p. 169; 103. 'The Battle of Tel-el-Kebir', p. 182.

Hark! the summer air	1
Is filled with sudden sound,	
And the cool winds bear	
The echoes all around;	
And from the deep-mouthed bells	5
The wild mad music swells,	
Telling in joyful melody	
The regal news of victory.	
To peaceful harvest fields	
The thrilling peal is borne,	10
And caps are flung in air	
And shouts rise 'mid the corn;	
While in the city din,	
'Mid whirling shaft and pin,	
Grave business lifts a sober eye	15
And joins the proud triumphant cry.	

See from dizzy height
    The flaunting pennons wave,
And Scottish lion bright,
    In memory of the brave;   20
And almost lost to sight,
Drowned in excess of light,
St George's banner floating free
In honour of the victory.

And over Highland glen   25
    The bonfire crowns the hill –
Whence spring the gallant men
    Whose deeds the country fill;
While cannon greets the ear
With salvos loud and clear –   30
Proclaiming joy with deep hoarse voice,
And bidding land and sea rejoice.

The storied East is ours,
    With hoary mystery crowned,
Its battlemented towers   35
    From which muezzins sound;
While pibroch's mountain cry
Mingles with liquid sigh,
Of Oriental summer fair,
Enthroned in sultry Eastern air.   40

And all the land is glad,
    And we forget to weep
In concert with the sad,
    Whose loved ones are asleep,
Far beyond cannon's boom,   45
Or passing glow or gloom –
The steadfast gallant hearts that die
To make and swell the conq'ring cry.

And still the bells ring out,
    And we keep holiday,   50
In memory of the rout
    Of foreign foe to-day;
And all in joyful mood
Thank Heaven for the good

Which mingles with all grief and pain, 55
Sunshine with shadow, weal with bane.

103. 'The Battle of Tel-el-Kebir', by G. Bruce, St Andrews. Published 14 October 1882.

This poem, on the same battle as 'Victory', was republished in George Bruce's *Poems and Songs* (Dundee: John Leng, 1886), pp. 104–05, and is one of the poems Bruce alludes to as 'verses condemning the *present fashion* of falsifying History and Geography, by substituting *"England"* for "Great Britain and Ireland"' (p. i). He uses the failure of the British press to recognise the heroism of the Highand Brigade in this battle in a nationalist (though British as well as Scottish nationalist) poem, which argues that England deliberately stole Scottish glory and thus shamed the name of Great Britain, whereas Scotland upheld 'British', as opposed to 'English', pride and 'soul'. Bruce was a self-made businessman, originally trained as a joiner, in St Andrews; he was a keen amateur naturalist, historian and marksman, as well as a poet, and was a leading member of the Town Council (Edwards, I, pp. 217–18).

See also: 102. 'Victory', p. 180.

"The Highland Brigade bore the brunt of the battle." –
   Telegram
"The Highland Brigade hardly got justice in the official despatches." – *The Press*

Turkey noo has met her match; 1
Scotland's sent her auld "Black Watch"
Order in the East to patch
   Tartan on the Nile!

Scotched Rebellion made a stand – 5
Britain halted on the sand,
Waiting for the kilts to land –
   Tartan rank and file!

Weel she kent the bluidy cause
Made the Anglo-Saxon pause – 10

Long to ancient Britain fa'se –
    Scotland grim did smile!

Scotland marched unto the front –
Scotland "bore the battle's brunt" –
Fought and conquered – as her wont –   15
    Caledonia's style!

Tel-el-Kebir only tells
Britain's *soul* in Scotland dwells! –
Floating still ower Campsie fells –
    Anglo-Saxon spoil.   20

England stole Great Britain's name –
Tries to hide auld Scotland's fame –
What she does is burning shame!
    Anglo-Saxon guile!

Anarchy must hide her dead   25
Deep beneath auld Freedom's head –
Heiland bluid's no' vainly shed
    On the plains o' Nile!

She will be Great Britain yet –
The suns o' Scotland only set   30
Brighter mornings to beget.
    God protect our Isle!

104. 'In the Net Factory', by E. W., Lundin Mill. Published 14 April 1883.

E. W., from Lundin Mill in Fife, is unidentified. 'In the Net Factory' is spoken from the perspective of a working woman, whose job enables her to support her family, and is thus comparable to other poems about virtuous women or child factory workers.

See also: 27. 'The Chappin' Laddie', p. 48; 28. 'The Working Lasses', p. 49; 86. 'The Sack-Sewers of Dundee', p. 149; 108. 'The Night Signalman', p. 194.

Clink, clank, clatter: 1
    Harsh music for those weary and sad;
This ceaseless and hopeless monotony
    Will certainly drive me mad.

I'll away to service or emigrate; 5
    Why should I toil on here
While my eyes are burning, burning?
    But I dare not shed a tear.

I work from morn till night,
    I jump on this weary machine, 10
Till my poor limbs ache and heart seems to break
    For a joy which might have been.

Clink, clank, clatter:
    Oh, let me a moment think –
Is duty a thing ignoble, 15
    From which I impatiently shrink?

There are those at home would miss me –
    My poor little cripple brother,
His face beams with smiles when he sees me;
    For me alone and no other. 20

And for thee, dear Jamie, I'll labour,
    For thee honest wages will gain;
In thinking and acting for others
    Forget my own restless pain.

Clink, clank, clatter: 25
 The iron may enter the soul,
But healing may come with duty well done,
 If faith make Heaven its goal.

POETRY FROM THE
PEOPLE'S FRIEND

105. 'The Trappit Mouse', by Maggie, Keir. Published in the *People's Friend*, 4 August 1869.

'The Trappit Mouse' was published along with two other poems in the eighth number of the new *People's Friend*. The poetry column initially appeared on the back page, p. 16 of the journal, along with a 'To Correspondents' column, first titled 'Friends in Council', emphasising the community feel of the *Friend*. Rather than relegating poetry and criticism on poems received to a minor place in the new journal, this placing made it easily accessible. 'Maggie' is unidentified, and no other poems from this pseudonym have been traced: Keir is a parish in Dumfries and Galloway. 'The Trappit Mouse' takes its cue from Burns's 'To a Mouse', but uses the mouse in a specific commentary on the state of 'feral children' in the Victorian city. Writers in Victorian Scotland were deeply concerned about street children, especially in the slums of Glasgow and other cities, and this poem can be seen as part of the discourse around the Ragged Schools movement and other charitable efforts to 'rescue' a class of neglected children from becoming adult criminals.

See also: 19. 'Nan Tamson's Wean', p. 33; 50. 'The Herd Laddie', p. 83.

Puir, little, pokin', hung'red thing,   1
Ye've nibbled thro' the treach'rous string,
An' noo cauld justice' iron ring
        Grips ye fu' ticht,
E'en tho' ye kenned na what ye did   5
        Was wrang or richt.

In simmer days ye fended weel,
Afore the crap was aff the fiel';
Noo ye maun either starve or steal
        Yer bite o' meat;   10
An' stealin's nat'ral whan ane
        Has nocht to eat.

An' ye hae stown sin e'er ye mind –
Born as ye were o' thievin' kind,
Your morals early undermined   15
        By bad example:
A parent's precepts 'neath yer feet
        Ye ne'er did trample.

Gin ye had haen a cosy hame,
Presided ower by thrifty dame,   20
An' borne an honest, decent name,
      I muckle doot
If this nicht, on sic pilferin' trade,
      Ye'd vent'red oot.

An' dark the social mystery froons,   25
When ane thinks on the hameless loons
That forage thro' our muckle toons
      Nicht after nicht,
Scarce daurin' e'en to show their face
      In God's daylicht.   30

Lord help them! they had nocht to lead them
But what twa sinfu' craturs gied them,
An hunger's cruel goad tae speed them
      Doon Ruin's road,
An Misery's cauld breath blawin' oot   35
      The licht o' God.

Than shallna we, whom Fortune's blest
Wi' bread to spare an' cosy nest,
Put oot our hand, an' dae our best
      Tae aid the plan   40
That aims tae mak' our thievin' loon
      An honest man?

We're muckle what our fortunes mak' us;
But gin the reck'nin' day o'ertak' us,
Wi' maybe gifts abused tae rack us,   45
      Wi' shame we'll see
The hunted, hung'red *human mouse*
      Win aff 'maist free.

106. 'With You', by Dorothea. Published in the *People's Friend*, 15 March 1871.

'Dorothea' is Dorothea Ogilvy, one of Victorian Scotland's better-known women poets. She published a number of poems in the *Friend* in these years, and attracted at least one response poem, 'To Dorothea', by W. Robertson (8 September 1875). While still in the genre of love-poems by women poets, 'With You' speaks of a strong relationship between woman poet and the wilder landscapes of Scotland. As a highly accomplished poem about the beauty of the Highlands – one of hundreds – it hits two of the top genres for Scottish newspaper verse at once. It was reprinted in Ogilvy's *Poems* (Edinburgh: Edmonston and Douglas, 1873) [printed at the Advertiser office, Dundee], p. 43.

See also: 70. 'Lily of the Vale', p. 119; 100. 'April Days', p. 177.

A freshet on a mountain gushes   1
Through blue forget-me-nots and rushes;
There breckan green and yellow bent
With gold and silver march-flowers blent,
Dot emerald moss with dew besprent,   5
Where Highland sheep do eat their fill,
There runs a rill adown the steep.
To hear the crooning of the rills,
     The whistle of the wild curlew –
To see the purple of the hills,   10
     I'll go with you, I'll go with you.

I've listen'd long with bated breath,
All was so silent on the heath –
So still the mighty mountains lay,
In their calm grandeur, stern and grey,   15
They seemed to draw my soul away;
With very bliss my bosom swells
'Mid heather-bells sweet as thy kiss.
To hear the corncraik in the grass,
     The clarion of the glad cuckoo –   20
To see the misty mountain pass,
     I'll go with you, I'll go with you.

A lovely Grampian slope I know,
Where sweeter flowers than roses blow –

Where heath-fowl brood, where dun deer browse   25
On birken braes, on broomy knowes
Beneath the fir trees' red-stain'd boughs,
Where berries shine like coral beads,
Their silken threads where spiders twine.
To hear the plashing of the springs,   30
    The cooing of the cushie-doo,
To see the heron's blue-grey wings,
    I'll go with you, I'll go with you.

107. 'Jenny wi' the Airn Teeth', by Surfaceman. Published in the *People's Friend*, 26 November 1873.

As noted on 'John Keats', Alexander Anderson's (Surfaceman's) reputation in the twentieth and twenty-first century rests on his poems about railway life and labour. But in the Victorian period, he was arguably most admired for his poetry for and about children, in the genre known as 'nursery verse'. The *Friend* was devoted to promoting nursery verse and published hundreds of poems in this genre during this period. They are invariably in Scots, often based on traditional nursery rhyme and spoken from the perspective of a harassed mother, and usually deal with mischievous but dearly-loved small children. The origin of this genre, in its Victorian incarnation, lies well before the establishment of the *Friend*, with Glasgow wood-turner William Miller (author of 'Wee Willie Winkie', a bogeyman poem with a clear influence on Anderson's 'Jenny') and the 'Whistlebinkie' school of poets in the 1840s. But it was the *Friend* that made it a mainstream genre of Scots verse in the mid-late century, and helped to ensure that virtually every working-class poet produced poems of this type. They can be read as part of the growing 'cult of the child' in the late Victorian period, and also as an effort to position working-class male poets as loving parents with an understanding of and attachment to family life (even when, as with Anderson, they never became parents themselves). In nursery verse male poets frequently, as here, adopt a maternal persona. Anderson's other highly successful poems in the same vein include 'Cuddle Doon' and 'The Bowgie Man'. His 'Jenny' was set to music by Alexander Stewart, subeditor of the *Friend*: the music and lyrics were printed in the *Friend* on 31 March 1875.

See also: 48. 'John Keats', p. 79; 111. 'Jenny wi' the Lang Pock', p. 202; 115. 'A Shetland Lullaby', p. 211.

What a plague is this o' mine,   1
    Winna steek his e'e,
Though I hap him owre the head
    As cosie as can be.

Sleep! an' let me to my wark,   5
    A' they claes to airn:
Jenny wi' the airn teeth,
    Come an' tak' the bairn;

Tak' him to your ain den,
    Where the bowgie bides,   10
But first put baith your big teeth
    In his wee plump sides;

Gie your auld grey pow a shake,
    Rive him frae my grup –
Tak' him where nae kiss is gaun   15
    When he waukens up.

Whatna noise is that I hear
    Comin' doon the street?
Weel I ken the dump-dump
    O' her beetle feet.   20

Mercy me, she's at the door,
    Hear her lift the sneck;
Whist! an' cuddle mammy noo
    Closer roun' the neck.

Jenny wi' the airn teeth,   25
    The bairn has aff his claes,
Sleepin' safe an' soun', I think –
    Dinna touch his taes;

Sleepin' weans are no for you;
    Ye may turn aboot   30
An' tak' awa' wee Tam next door –
    I hear him screichin' oot.

Dump, dump, awa' she gangs
    Back the road she cam';

I hear her at the ither door,   35
    Speirin' after Tam.

He's a crabbit, greetin' thing,
    The warst in a' the toun;
Little like my ain wee man –
    Losh, he's sleepin' soun'.   40

Mithers hae an awfu' wark
    Wi' their bairns at nicht –
Chappin' on the chair wi' tangs
    To gie the rogues a fricht.

Aulder weans are fley'd wi' less,   45
    Weel aneuch, we ken –
Bigger bowgies, bigger Jennies,
    Frichten muckle men.

steek – close   *hap – cover*
rive – tear, wrench   *beetle – a pestle, a wooden implement for mashing*
sneck – latch   *speir – to pry, question*
fley – to frighten, scare

108. 'The Night Signalman', by T. N. D., Dundee. Published in the *People's Friend*, 5 May 1875.

Alongside its standard fare of romantic, elegiac, pastoral and nursery verse, the *Friend* did publish a substantial subset of poems about industrial labour. Railway poems, often written about and by railway workers, were popular in this period (they were one of Surfaceman's specialities) and often took their impetus from the tension between immense and dangerous machines and their human controllers, who bore huge responsibility for avoiding accidents and disasters. Poems about such disasters, real or imagined, were common. The repetitive language and rhythms of this poem imitate the tiring mechanical actions that the signalman has to perform. T. N. D. also published in the *Journal*.

See also: 59. 'Murder Most Foul', p. 99; 91. 'Lines, Suggested by the Melancholy Wreck of the Tay Bridge', p. 162; 92. 'In Memoriam', p. 164; 104. 'In the Net Factory', p. 184.

All through the long, dull night, 1
    With brow o'ershadowed with pain,
The signalman sat in his signal hut,
    Watching each coming train.
The wires magnetic rang 5
    In low, monotonous tones,
And murmured like a choir of bees
    Led by the king of drones.
Click, click, click
    Sang the nimble needles quite low – 10
Click, click, click
    They said, so sure and slow;
Quite low, so sure and slow;
    They said it again and again,
While the signalman sat in his signal hut 15
    Waiting each coming train –
Sat, sat, sat,
    Along through the dreary night –
Sat, sat, sat,
    To pass each train all right. 20
No time had he to pause,
    Scarce a moment to think,
Watching the needles spell out the words
    Without a pen and ink.
Click, click, click, 25
    Repeated the needles again –
Click, click, click –
    Look out, here comes the train.
To work with a fitful start,
    His signal obeys the train; 30
Then back again the needles to watch,
    And wait for another train.
Watching and waiting alone,
    All through the weary hours,
No time has he to think of home, 35
    Or birds, or trees and flowers.
Sleep, sleep, sleep,
    He has no time to see
The wife and children whom he loves
    Come clambering on his knee. 40
No, he must keep by his post,
    Through the midnight hours so deep:

When morning comes, like a pale-brow'd ghost,
    He hies him home to sleep.
Sleep, sleep, sleep,   45
    Till twilight comes again,
Then back to his lonely signal hut
    To watch and wait the train.
He must wait and watch with a care
    Which gives scarce time to breathe;   50
Let vigilance sleep but a moment, beware
    Of the terrible foes beneath.
Watch, watch, watch,
    To grumbling never give vent;
Watch, watch, watch,   55
    With the patience of a saint,
For Destruction is leagued with Death,
    And Death with grim Despair;
Already it seems as if their breath
    Was wafted on the air.   60
As crash, crash, crash,
    They shout with might and main;
Ho! crash, crash, crash,
    Death claims another train.
What a wreck of sorrow and woe!   65
    O Life, how short thy span!
Made shorter still by the dire mistake
    Of a railway signalman.
O, man, in pride and power,
    Who earth's vain baubles chace,   70
Remember every day and hour
    Death follows you in the race.
Then race, race, race,
    With muffled sound and low,
Death's pace, pace,   75
    Follows you fast or slow
Until the goal is made.
    Then a sting of sharpest pain –
A flash of light – a shape – a shade –
    And you – have joined Death's train.   80

109. 'I'll Hae My "Freen"', by J. W. R. Published in the *People's Friend*, 23 June 1875.

A semi-comic poem about how highly a reader values his copy of the journal, this spoke to the *Friend*'s marketing of itself as by and for the people, embedded in a loyal working-class community of readers and writers. Bank Street in Dundee was the now-famous location of the newspaper offices.

See also: 44. 'Lines on Receiving a People's Journal*', p. 73; 97. 'Reminiscences of the* People's Journal*', p. 171.*

Ye readers o' the *Freen*', look here,	1
You'll speak in favour o't, I'm sheer –	
At least, to me it's jist as dear's	
My darlin' Jean;	
I'd sooner lose her an' her gear	5
Than lose my freen'.	

'Twas ance neglecket for some days,
I travelled till I'd blistered taes.
At last the postman coolly says –
      "What mak'st for ane?"   10
Says I, "As sure's I'm in my claes
      I'll hae my freen'."

While thinkin' ower the thing a wee,
I started, sayin', "The plan will be
To write to 'Bank Street in Dundee',"   15
      'Twas said an' dune;
Twa days elapse, then brocht to me
      My welcome freen'.

So overjoyed to see't again,
I grasped it fondly, after then   20
I wandered far up through the glen
      'Mang trees so green;
I canna gang nine yards (or ten)
      Withoot my freen'.

What can excel the "Mysteries o' Crime?"   25
The anecdotes, stories, an' rhyme?

'Tis like a doctor come in time
    Wi' skilfu' een;
Sud I gang till some distant clime,
    I'll hae my freen'.   30

110. 'The Storming of Perth', by Nisbet Noble. Published in 'Standard Readings, Original and Selected', in the *People's Friend*, 19 January 1876.

'Nisbet Noble' is the pseudonym of James Ferguson of Stanley in Perthshire (born 1842), who worked in the mills, as a grocer's apprentice in Dundee, as a labourer in an engine shop and then clerk in its counting-house, as a surfaceman, and in a dye-works in Perth. He was a frequent contributor to the *Friend* in its early decades and a key part of its community of poets (see also his 'Epistle to Robert Wanlock', below). In 1880 he published *Lays of Perthshire*, according to Edwards (1, p. 147). Edwards cites his recollections on having an early piece published in the *Journal*, 'Being literally and truly a first effort, you may fancy my feelings when I saw it in print. Earth seemed too small for me. I needed wings' (p. 147). The *Friend* published a regular 'Standard Readings' section which included both poetry and prose readings, intended for private or public recitation. In keeping with this purpose, Noble's contribution is a dramatic narrative, designed to arouse patriotic spirit in listeners by invoking Robert the Bruce and the run-up to the battle of Bannockburn, 1314. The poem commemorates Robert's defeat of the English and taking of Perth in January 1313.

See also: 112. 'The Thistle Yet', p. 204; 116. 'Epistle to Robert Wanlock', p. 213.

Night sweeps o'er the land with gentle power,   1
    And the noisy world grows hushed and still,
And darkness settles on town and tower,
    Or silently creeps o'er the crest of each hill,
And they vanish from sight as softly o'erhead   5
The heaven unveils its star-studded forehead.

We hear the river's lap-lapping waves
    Licking the walls of the ancient town,

And the measur'd tread of the watching braves,
    And the sudden challenge at intervals thrown   10
From their rugged throats, and the faint replying,
And the hurrying feet into distance dying.

But war-batter'd Perth like a desert seems
    As the solemn midnight nearer moves,
And its sleepers roam through the realm of dreams,   15
    With its mimic passions, terrors and loves;
While over its streets, and towers, and turrets
Float silence and peace like guardian spirits.

But we hear a hum like the rising blast
    Moving in murmurs upon our ears,   20
And the ringing clatter of something cast
    On the frowning walls, and the clank of spears;
Then a shout and a curse, dread, fierce, and bloody,
And the dull dead thud of a falling body.

"God! what a glorious King and a Knight" –   25
    (See the Bruce as he leads thro' the sluggish moat.)
"God! what a glutton for danger and fight" –
    They cry as already he holds by the throat
The drowsy warder, and hurls him under,
As if stricken to earth by bolt of thunder.   30

Then wildly the Scottish slogan rings
    Through the sleeping air from a thousand throats,
And rage and terror, on frenzied wings,
    Fly howling abroad at the war wild notes –
"The Bruce is upon ye, up knight, and up, yeoman –   35
The Bruce is upon ye, your mightiest foeman."

His battle-axe falls like the hammer of Thor,
    Impelled by his arm's resistless might,
And bolts, and bars, and steel-studded door
    Go down 'neath the blow like the foe in fight,   40
And the awe-stricken braves, wherever he bore him,
Flew scatter'd like sheep from the wolves before him.

The morning dawns in the wintry skies
    O'er bleeding bodies and broken brands,

And the victors gaze with exultant eyes   45
    On the red work of their valiant hands,
And grasp meets grasp with stern emotion,
And look meets look with freemen's devotion.

The gate of the Highlands driven ajar
    By one night's work, what may they not still?   50
Their voices roll thunderous, fierce, and far,
    "We'll drive the caitiffs from valley and hill."
And no idle words were theirs for they harried
The English side ere the sounds were buried.

For the force of freemen is like the sea,   55
    And the will of freemen like rocks in strength;
And they who have sworn they shall be free
    Will bask in the beams of the sun at length.
No power on earth can baffle persistence
In stern resolve and in stern resistance.   60

Bleak, bare and bloody the onward way
    Of that fearless band; but bloody and bare
Their paths had been for many a day;
    Houseless and homeless everywhere,
With their lives in their hands, housed like cattle,   65
They had toiled and endured and thronged to battle.

Rivers had redden'd as o'er them they passed;
    Hamlets around them had perished in flame;
The screams of their loved had startled the blast,
    And stricken their hearts with horror and shame,   70
Wherever they turned till ruth was trod under
The heels of their vengeance 'mid battle and thunder.

Great is the land that a story can frame
    Like unto ours, wild though it be;
Great is the land that its heroes can name,   75
    Like unto ours the sires of the free,
The land that the leaves of the past can o'erturn,
And point to a Bruce and a Bannockburn.

Our great King Robert, we see him now,
    And feel the sweep of his far-reaching eyes,   80

And the conquering strength of his mighty brow
    As the field of battle before him lies;
And he stands cool, bold, and self-reliant,
With the will of a god and the strength of a giant.

Outnumbered by thousands he faces the foe   85
    (As he'd faced them oft) in the morning light
Outnumbered by thousands his dead lie low
    On that awful field, with the coming night,
While liberty rides at the heels of disaster,
As he strides o'er the plain its lord and master.   90

Give him the glory for freedom won,
    Give him the praise, though as great a name
In the army of heroes the struggle began;
    Crown them alike with the chaplet of fame,
Our Bruce and our Wallace; and may we inherit   95
    Their patriot power and their patriot spirit.

111. 'Jenny wi' the Lang Pock', by James Nicholson. Published in the *People's Friend*, 20 September 1876.

Nicholson's response poem appeared almost three years after Anderson's 'Jenny', which in that period had become well-known as both poem and song. Like Anderson's poem, it is a contribution to the nursery verse genre, as a bogeyman poem spoken by an exhausted mother. Nicholson's poems were often intended for performance, so the longer lines might offer a spoken contrast to the shorter sung or recited lines. He was a tailor at Govan Poorhouse in Glasgow and a self-educated writer, who began as a factory worker (aged seven) and herd-boy: his biography was given in a review of his poems, 'A Poet of the People', *Journal*, 9 May 1863 (p. 2). In this period Nicholson was one of Scotland's better-known working-class poets, especially as a poetic temperance campaigner and ardent Good Templar, though he also published works on botany and on religion. He is the addressee of Crawford's 'Epistle to "Faither Fernie"' and published a number of other poems in the *Journal* and *Friend*, as did his daughter Ellen Nicholson. 'Jenny wi' the Lang Pock' was republished in *Kilwuddie and Other Poems, with Life-Sketch and Portrait of the Author* 4th edn (Glasgow: James McGeachy, 1895), p. 163, a late collection which also contains a biographical sketch of Nicholson. Like Anderson's poem, it was set to music by Andrew Stewart, *Friend* editor.

See also: 107. 'Jenny wi' the Airn Teeth', p. 192; 114. 'Epistle to "Faither Fernie"', p. 209; 115. 'A Shetland Lullaby', p. 211.

A Companion Song to "Jenny wi' the Airn Teeth."

> Jenny wi' the lang pock,   1
>   Haste ye owre the main,
> Lampin' wi' yer lang legs,
>   Plashin' through the rain;
> Here's a waukrife laddie   5
>   Winna steek his e'e,
> Pit him in yer lang pock,
>   An' dook him in the sea.
> Oh, dear me! whan'll Jenny come?
> Wheesht! I think I hear her cryin' doon the lum;   10
> Fye, awa', Jenny! we dinna want ye here –
> A' the bairns are in their beds – a' but Jamie dear.

Gudesake, noo I hear her,
    There she's on the stair,
Sapples o' the sea-bree   15
    Stickin' in her hair,
Hushions on her bare legs,
    Bauchles on her feet,
Seekin' waukrife bairnies
    Up an' doon the street.   20
Oh, losh me! There she's at the sneck,
Stoitin' owre the stair-heid – may she break her neck!
Cuddle doon fu' cosy – that's my ain wee lamb;
Dinna spurtle wi' yer feet, or ye'll wauken Tam.

Jenny's nae awa' yet,   25
    Sae ye mauna greet;
There she's on the door-mat
    Scufflin' wi' her feet,
Wabblin' wi' her lang legs,
    Sneevlin' through her nose,   30
Hirslin' wi' her lang pock,
    Aff Jenny goes.
Oh, losh me! there she's back again,
Listenin' wi' her lang lugs for a greetin' wean;
Fye, gae bar the door, Jean, thraw aboot the key –   35
Na, she winna get ye, ye're owre dear to me!

Whaur's the body gaun noo?
    Up the ither stair,
At oor neebor's door she's
    Tirlin' I declare!   40
Cryin' through the key-hole
    Like a roupit sheep,
"Hae ye ony weans here
    Winna fa' asleep?"
Oh, losh me! hae they let her in?   45
Wha's that sprechin, makin' sic a din?
No oor Jamie, for he is sleepin' soun',
Like a bonnie rose-bud in the month o' June.

Jenny wi' the lang pock,
    Ye may tak' the road,   50
A' the bairns are safe noo
    In the land o' nod;

> Losh, can that be John's fit
>   Comin' up the stair?
> No ae bit o' supper yet   55
>   Ready I declare!
> Oh dear me! rest for me there's nane,
> Pity on the mither that's plagued wi' sic a wean;
> Yet at him the very cat daurna wink an e'e,
> For he's the darlin' o' my heart, an' a' the warl' to me!   60

pock – bag, sack   steek – close
sapples – soap-suds   bree – wet, moisture
hushion – footless stocking ('hose')   bauchle – old, worn-down shoe or slipper
sneck – latch   stoit – stagger
spurtle – stir around   hirsle – slither, slide
lug – ear   tirlin' – rattling (the latch)
roupit – hoarse, raucous   sprech – to shriek

112. 'The Thistle Yet!', by Alexander G. Murdoch. Published in the *People's Friend*, 20 December 1876.

'The Thistle Yet!', though following patriotic themes common in *Friend* poems, did not appear as a standard original poem, but was given in the fictionalised context of a Christmas gathering of contributors, 'Face to Face, or Stories Told at the Editor's Party' (20 December 1876). The conceit is that the editor bumps into a provincial agent for the *Journal* and *Friend* who has missed his train from Dundee, and invites him to the party at A. C. Lamb's famed Temperance Hotel, where fiction-writers and poets take turns presenting their special Christmas stories and songs to the gathering. The agent is, of course, overwhelmed at meeting so many luminaries – especially 'Surfaceman'. When Sandy Murdoch, another self-made poet, working as a mechanic in Glasgow and a very frequent contributor to the *Friend*, appears, the editor and agent have this exchange:

> "By the way, Mr Agent, I may tell you that Mr Murdoch has a volume of songs in the press. It will be issued very soon, and I hope you will succeed in disposing of a goodly number."
>   "I'll try sir, I'll try. I sellt a gey curn o' 'Surfaceman's' book."
>   "So did the other agents, and I shall be glad to know that Mr Murdoch's volume has a similar success. This reminds

me that he has written a song for the present occasion,
and now is the time for him to sing it."

The song is 'The Thistle Yet'. It is thus a Christmas song for
a communal gathering, and an advertisement for Murdoch's
collection. In common with most nationalistic poetry of
the period, which was content with freedom within the
Union, it is unlikely (though not impossible) that England is
implied by 'foreign state'.

*See also: 103. 'The Battle of Tel-el-Kebir', p. 182; 110. 'The
Storming of Perth', p. 198; 116. 'Epistle to Robert Wanlock',
p. 213; 118. 'Song of the Clyde Workers', p. 217.*

Let other craven lands forget   1
    Their watchwords, battle-tried;
Ours be the sturdy thistle yet –
    The heather by its side.
We rivet not oppression's chain;   5
    We flaunt nae flag o' show;
But while we mar the peace o' nane,
    We fear nae braggart foe.

      For never shall a foreign State
        Gie ancient Scotland law;   10
      She wears her plaid her ain auld gaet,
        And nane daur say her – na.

The shades o' Wallace and o' Bruce
    Still bear the lifted sword.
That held wi' Tyranny nae truce   15
    Till Freedom was restored.
Their names, a shining symbol, set
    In Scotland's jewell'd Croon;
Then up, lads, wi' the thistle yet,
    Whatever else gangs doon.   20

      For never shall a foreign State
        Gie ancient Scotland law;
      She wears her plaid her ain prood gaet,
        And nane daur say her – na.

For Christ and for the Covenant,   25
    Our brave forefathers stood,
And dared wi' steel the lying cant
    Born of the Papal brood.
The martyr-scroll auld Scotland brags,
    Nae vain remembrance craves,   30
For wild and well the thistle wags
    Above her guarded graves.

      And never shall a foreign State
        Gie ancient Scotland law;
      She wears her plaid her ain stern gaet,   35
        And nane daur say her – na.

Is there a Scottish heart wad see
    The thistle flow're forgot,
And no bleed tears? If such there be,
    Let shame erase the blot;   40
A prouder legacy than ours
    Na ither land can claim;
Then let us wreath the gift wi' flow'rs,
    And hand it on to fame.

      For never shall a foreign State   45
        Gie ancient Scotland law;
      She wears her plaid her ain auld gaet,
        And nane daur say her – na.

113. 'The Workmen's Cry to the Masters', by W. M. W. Published in the *People's Friend*, 13 June 1877.

Overtly political poems and poems about social injustice were much rarer in the *Friend* than the *Journal*. While this poem offers a bleak picture of relations between master and men and the conditions of labour, its solution is a nostalgic paternalism and charity ('like the good old sires of yore'), rather than political change. W. M. W. is unidentified.

See also: 84. *'The Millennium of Capital'*, p. 146; 87. *'Died on the Street'*, p. 151; 104. *'In the Net Factory'*, p. 184; 108. *'The Night Signalman'*, p. 194.

For wages, oh, my masters,	1
For the price of daily bread,	
Do we work from early morn	
Till the sun's last ray is fled.	
Youth and manhood in your service	5
Day by day we throw away;	
And, prematurely aged,	
We are toiling still for pay.	

At the end of labour's journey
    There's no dream or hope of rest,   10
Like golden-tinted sunset
    Luring traveller to the west;
But as black cloud o'er the mountain,
    Whence, perforce, our ships are driven,
Stands the pall of death before us,   15
    Only place where rest is given.

You, my masters, have your leisure,
    And in evening of your day
Can relax the long strung muscles,
    And from labour steal away;   20
But we, who build your fortunes,
    By whose sweat and toil and pain
All the visions are illumined
    That cross your busy brain,

Have no hope to see e'er broken   25
    The cords that bind us down
To work for daily wages,
    That a crust our board may crown.
We are far from you, my masters,
    Though by book we brothers be,   30
And no tie have we to serve you
    But the craven one of fee.

In your far off place of master,
    As sun in moonlight night,
You are cold and distant from us   35
    By the gaffer's borrowed light.
All the springs of human action –
    Those by which the heart can feel –
You have left untouched for ages,
    And forget the workmen's weal.   40

Come nearer, then, my masters,
    Like your good old sires of yore;
Make us feel we're of your family,
    Though perchance but near the door;
Though above the salt we never   45
    May hope in time to win,
Yet beneath its clear distinction
    Let us know we still are kin.

114. 'Epistle to "Faither Fernie" (Jas. Nicholson)', by W. P. Crawford. Published in the *People's Friend*, 19 January 1881.

The Crawfords of Catrine were a family of poets, and Nicholson certainly knew them; he worked with temperance poet James Paul Crawford ('Paul Rookford') in the Govan Poorhouse, Glasgow, collaborated on joint publications with him, and was friends with his son, also a poet and composer. W. P. Crawford probably belonged to this family, but cannot be definitely identified with any of the known poetic Crawfords. The poem references Nicholson's reputation as a leading performer at temperance meetings and his botanical pursuits. His book on botany, *Father Fernie, the Botanist*, had been published in 1868 and was well-received. Epistle poems to fellow-poets were popular in the *Friend*, as in other Victorian newspapers, because they helped to cement the image of a friendly community of writers.

See also: 13. 'Epistle to Tammas Bodkin', p. 24; 31. 'An Epissel to Poute', p. 54; 66. 'Epistle to Tammas Bodkin', p. 112; 111. 'Jenny wi' the Lang Pock', p. 202; 116. 'Epistle to Robert Wanlock', p. 213.

I say, guidwife, the table clear 1
O' cups an' flets an' a' sic gear;
Bring pen an' ink an' paper here
    Till I write Faither Fernie.
For since I was aboot fourteen
My help botanic he has been: 5
In Temp'rance wark my richt-han' frien'
    Was willing Faither Fernie.

At Temp'rance gala or soiree,
When young folk's hearts danc'd wild wi' glee,
The wale o' treats was then tae see 10
    And hear blythe Faither Fernie.
His stories an' poetic lore
Aye kept the house a' in a roar,
While mony a loud an' lang encore
    Was gien tae Faither Fernie. 15

An' weel I mind, in byegane days,
Wi' merry lilt I sang his lays;
Delighted still I am tae praise
    The strains o' Faither Fernie.
Like him I lo'e in leisure hours   20
To seek the shade o' sylvan bowers,
Or hunt the glade for ferns an' flowers
    Alang wi' Faither Fernie.

On Saturdays, when free frae toil,
Wi' him I've wander'd mony a mile,   25
By Kenmuir's bank an' fair Carmyle,
    Tae seek rare plants wi' Fernie.
By winding Cart or Cambus Glen,
Where rare anes grew weel did he ken,
Nae won'er that I like tae spen'   30
    An afternin wi' Fernie.

He kens ilk ferlie ye could name,
The history tae o' mony a stane,
An' noo, sin' tae the stars he's ta'en,
    We'll learn queer things frae Fernie.   35
But simmer's pleasures soon flee past,
The fields wi' sna are noo o'ercast,
Fell winter's reign is in at last –
    Wae's me for walks wi' Fernie.

But I maun quat, it's wearin' late,   40
Look up the *Frien'*, see what's the date;
Dear me, it's noo the twenty-eight!
    Twa months sin' we saw Fernie.
Dear Fernie, I wad like tae see
Ye stap alang some nicht tae tea,   45
The wife an' bairns, as weel as me,
    Will welcome Faither Fernie.

Sae fix a time, an' let us ken
Upon what nicht ye'er coming then,
An 'oor or twa wi' us tae spen'   50
    And gie's yer crack, frien' Fernie.

flet – saucer   *wale – the pick, the choice*
ferlie – wonder, marvel   *crack – talk, gossip*

115. 'A Shetland Lullaby', by L. J. Nicolson. Published in the *People's Friend*, 10 August 1881.

Nicolson, born 1844 in Lerwick, was a leading nineteenth-century Shetland poet. Trained as a journeyman, he moved to Edinburgh to find work, and then became a clerk and eventually business traveller (Edwards, I, pp. 355–36). He published a number of poems in the *Friend* and other papers, some collected as *Songs of Thule* (Paisley: Alexander Gardner, 1894). 'A Shetland Lullaby' is reprinted in this volume as 'A Lullaby', pp. 23–24. This is the only poem I have identified in these years in Shetland dialect, or in a named dialect from any part of northern Scotland. Its unfamiliarity to readers is shown by Nicolson's inclusion of a glossary. Outside the language, the subject matter is very familiar, as the *Friend* published quantities of cradle songs and nursery verse.

See also: 107. 'Jenny wi' the Airn Teeth', p. 192; 111. 'Jenny wi' the Lang Pock', p. 202.

Hushyba, my curry ting.	1
Cuddle close to mammie;	
Cuddle close an' hear me sing,	
Peerie mootie lammie.	
Glancin' goold an' siller shells	5
Fae da mermaid's dwellin',	
Bonnie flo'ers fae fairy dells,	
Past a' mortal tellin';	
Wha, oh wha sall get but de,	
Hert o' my hert, life o' me.	10
Saftly, saftly, heumin grey	
Owre da sea is creepin',	
An' it's nedder nicht nor day,	
Waking time, nor sleppin';	
But da waves upo' da shore	15
Whisper still my lammie,	
Doun da lum, an' troo da door;	
Cuddle close to mammie.	
Cosier du couldna be –	
Hert o' my hert, life o' me.	20

Bonnie blue een blinkin' fast,
    Peerie mootie lammie;
Sleep has ta'en de noo at last,
    Cuddlin' close to mammie.
Blissens be attendin' de,   25
    Happy be dy wakin',
For wir ain comes fae da sea,
    Whin da day is breakin'.
Daybreak, licht-o'-hame is he –
Hert o' my hert, life o' me.   30

NOTE. – Curry – Neat, bonnie, lovable, are included in this comprehensive word, and do not exhaust its meaning. Peerie mootie – very small; ting – thing; fae – from; nedder – neither; da – the; du – thou; dy – thy; upo – upon; troo – through; de – thee; blissens – blessings; wir – our; heumin – twilight.

116. 'Epistle to Robert Wanlock', by Nisbet Noble. Published in the *People's Friend*, 4 January 1882.

Like 'The Storming of Perth', this shows Noble (James Ferguson) in patriotic mode. It is also an emigrant poem, because at this point the newspaper poet 'Rob Wanlock' (Robert Reid of Wanlockhead) had emigrated to Montreal. Noble suggests that whatever the virtues of Canada, Scotland's history and literary heritage retain his loyalty; and urges Reid to become the Canadian Burns. Reid was part of the poetic community that also included Anderson, Murdoch, postman poet and *Friend* contributor Robert Tennant, and editor Andrew Stewart, among others. Some of their poems addressed to Reid, including this one, were incorporated in the appendix to Reid's *Poems, Songs and Sonnets* (Paisley: Alexander Gardner, 1894).

See also: 66. 'Epistle to Tammas Bodkin', p. 112; 83. 'An Epistle to McGonagall', p. 144; 110. 'The Storming of Perth', p. 198; 114. 'Epistle to "Faither Fernie"', p. 209.

DEAR WANLOCK,   1
        Though it's unco late,
I'll write th' nicht, as sure as fate,
     Or else I'll be forsworn,
For ilk day an' nicht goes by,   5
An' weeks an' months hiv heard me cry
     "I'll Wanlock write the morn."
Procrastination, lazy jaud,
     Ye've ever been my bane;
Ye're dull, ye're deaf, ye're a' thing bad,   10
     For aince let me alane,
Or else I'll up, an' crack my whup,
     Though ye shood sweat an' swear,
An' fling my tae an' trip ye up,
     An' kick ye doon the stair.   15

Yer letter cam', an' made me fain,
     But oot on ye, an' ower again,
     What gar'd ye no come north?
I wid hae liked tae shak' yer han',
An' seen ye in yer native land,   20
     On this side o' the Forth.

Aweel, aweel, it mak's nae odds,
    I winna grin nor greet;
I doot nae ye'd ower monie road
    For ae puir pair o' feet   25
Tae travel ower, for a' the time
    Ye brought tae Scotland wi' ye
(This line is juist put in for rhyme).
    Be happy – I forgie ye.

Eh, man, I'd like tae cross the brine   30
Tae that adopted land o' thine,
    An' a' its wonders scan;
Its lakes like oceans spreadin' far,
Its plains that end th' guid kens whaur,
    Woods measureless by man,   35
Its rivers, cataracts, an' a',
    An' mair than I can name;
I think on't wi' a kind o' awe,
    An' half despise my hame,
Wi' its bit puny lochs an' linns,   40
    Its mountains bleak an' bare,
Its muckle sung o' brooms an' whins,
    Its – ah, but haud ye there –

Its THISTLE! At the soon my saul
    Looks backwards strang an' clear;   45
I hear the freemen fearless call,
    The clash o' sword an' spear
Rings tae my heart, our sires are round,
Our land becomes a storied ground,
    Ilk hill an' rocky scaur   50
Gives voice, an' seems to grow in size
An' grandeur 'fore our very eyes,
    An' flings its shadow far
Across the world; your land becomes
A place we'd cover wi' our thumbs   55
    Compared to Scotland then.
The little history ye've made
Is bound within a Scottish plaid,
    An' writ by Scottish men;
An' Britain views yer fields, an' cries –   60

"I give ye peace, bid plenty rise
    From swelling sea to sea!
Who dares to raise an angry word,
Or o'er ye shake a threatening sword,
    Must square accounts with me."   65

Hech, hey! when I get on this strain
Methinks I'd soond it till amen,
    My heart sae heated turns,
For isna ours the land o' Bruce,
O' Wallace, an' o' John de Luce –   70
    The land, the land o' Burns.
Ne'er may ye need a Bruce's hand,
Nor Wallace's death-dealing brand
    Tae keep yer country free.
Its Burns may come. An' wha can tell   75
But ye may be its Burns yersel'.
    Sae cock yer cap on hie,
An' let the inspiration come
    Frae oot yer lips in fire.
Look roond ye on yer wond'rous hame,   80
    The theme micht weel inspire
A heart an' saul like yours tae sang –
    Its grandeur micht impart
Force tae yer wirds, till swellin' strang,
    They stir the world's heart.   85

But I maun end, I weel ye wush,
An' houp ye'll ne'er be at a push,
    When oucht ye need tae crave;
A guid New Year tae yours an' you,
An' a' th' friends ye ever knew,   90
    Mysel' amo' the lave.

gar – cause   *linn – waterfall*
lave – the rest

117. 'A Song of the Clyde', by Sailon. Published in the *People's Friend*, 10 May 1882.

This song – no tune is given, but the chorus indicates that it is intended to be sung – presents the perspective of a happy fitter's wife, and thus celebrates both industrialism (for providing gainful employment) and contented domesticity. The *Friend*, perhaps reflecting the friendships of its sub-editor Stewart, who came from Glasgow, featured a number of Glasgow-centred poets and poems. 'Sailon' is unidentified.

See also: 118. 'Song of the Clyde Workers', p. 217.

The bonnie Clyde, the famous Clyde, richt weel I lo'e tae
   hear   1
The clamour frae her busy yards – it's music tae my ear.
Six months this day hae pass'd away sin' I became a bride,
And Jack my lad he toils for me – a fitter on the Clyde.
     A toiler's wife am I; wi' sweet content I try   5
     Tae keep my hoose baith trig and clean – and sae the
        days run by;
     And blessings on us bide, for this is a' my pride –
     Tae be a richt guid wife tae Jack – a fitter on the
        Clyde.

The whistles blow, the hammers go, and willing hands
   begin
Tae work for hame, and wife, and weans amid the cheery
   din,   10
The whistles' soun' again comes roun' the tools are laid
   aside;
Wi' grimy faces hameward speed the toilers on the Clyde.
     A toiler's wife am I, &c.

There's no a soun' in a' the toon that mak's me half sae
   glad.
It tells me that he's coming hame, my blithesome fitter lad,
Comes up the street the tramp of feet, amang the crood
   sae black
I see the ane that's dear tae me – my handsome fitter Jack.
     A toiler's wife am I, &c.

Fu' weel I ken amang the men wha socht this hand o'
    mine,
Some ne'er wad need tae grease their hands or soil their
    cheeks sae fine;   20
But far awa' abune them a', despite their plush and pride,
In my esteem stood honest Jack – a fitter on the Clyde.
    A toiler's wife am I, &c.

Sae, man and wife, oor start in life we've made, and we're
    content
Wi' what we hae! come ither joys, we'll praise them as
    they're sent.   25
Jack lo'es me well, and I can tell sin' I became a bride
Nae lass but micht be prood tae mate a fitter on the Clyde.
    A toiler's wife am I, &c.

trig – neat

118. 'Song of the Clyde Workers', by Alexander G. Murdoch. Published in the *People's Friend*, 3 January 1883.

Like Alexander Anderson, Murdoch published a number of 'songs of labour' in the *Friend* and elsewhere, celebrating working men for their masculinity and determination, and singing the praises of industry and the dignity of labour. By 1883 he had given up his work as mechanic in an engineering firm in Glasgow and was making his living through literature; he had already published four volumes of poetry, was completing an anthology of *The Scottish Poets, Recent and Living* (1883), and was also selling short fiction set in Scotland to the newspapers. Edwards provides a very complimentary account of his life and works (1, pp. 177–81). Murdoch was a leading light in working men's poetic communities and in Glasgow's literary societies, and knew most of the other key contributors to the *Friend* personally. As 'A Song of the Clyde' also indicates, shipbuilding and engineering works along Glasgow's Clyde were major employers in Scotland in this period.

See also: 34. 'The Navvies', p. 58; 117. 'A Song of the Clyde', p. 216.

Ho, men of the Clyde, I will sing you a song,   1
For I, like yourselves, to the "black-squad" belong;
A bred engineer, I can handle the "file":
Can "chip," "fit," and "polish" – a true son of toil!
And what I would sing is no song of a sigh,   5
No mawkish, soft song with a tear in its eye,
But a right good refrain – and I sing it with pride –
Hurrah for the shipbuilding men of the Clyde!

    The men of the Clyde, Glasgow's honour and pride;
    Three cheers for the black-squads that work on the
       Clyde!   10

Ere the dawn greys the sky, hark! the "bell" calls to toil!
Then we don our white "ducks," stain'd with "red-lead"
   and oil;
And off to the "yard" or the "foundry" we go,
Finding each our own "job," be't above or below.
Day by day, week by week, as the year's records tell,   15
We build mighty ships, and we "engine" them well,
Fit the ocean to sweep, and her storms to outride –
Hurrah for the shipbuilding men of the Clyde!

    The men of the Clyde, Glasgow's honour and pride;
    Three cheers for the black-squads that work on the
       Clyde!   20

Lay the "keel" straight and strong; curve the "ribs" to
   their sweep;
Rear the "bulk-heads" across that her strength she may
   keep;
Make the spacious "compartments" stand "water-tight"
   all,
That the good ship in storm may toss safe as a ball;
Shaft the giant "propeller" that smites the sea-foam,   25
Wield the heavy "swing-hammer" and drive the "keys"
   home;
Hang "feed-pumps" and "bilge-pumps" in place side-by-
   side –
Hurrah for the shipbuilding men of the Clyde!

The men of the Clyde, Glasgow's honour and pride,
Three cheers for the black-squads that work on the
   Clyde!   30

Let rank and wealth boast of their honours and powers,
On earth there's no royalty nobler than ours;
Be it that of a Prince, be it that of a King,
Toil-arm'd, truer honour and service we bring;
For the sweat that is born of the struggle for bread,   35
And the scars and rough hands to such strong service wed,
Are a brighter escutcheon than aught else beside;
Then hurrah for the shipbuilding men of the Clyde!

The men of the Clyde, Glasgow's honour and pride,
THREE-TIMES-THREE for the black-squads that
   work on the Clyde!

Bibliography and further reading

Collections by poets included in this volume:

Anderson, Alexander, *Ballads and Sonnets* (London: Macmillan, 1879).

Bruce, George, *Poems and Songs* (Dundee: John Leng, 1886).

Campbell, Elizabeth, *Songs of My Pilgrimage*, intro. George Gilfillan (Edinburgh: Andrew Elliot, 1875).

Carnegie, David, *Lays and Lyrics from the Factory* (Arbroath: Thomas Buncle, 1879).

Donald, G. W., *Poems, Ballads and Songs* (Arbroath: Thomas Buncle, n.d. [1880]).

Donaldson, William, *The Queen Martyr, and Other Poems* (Elgin: J. McGillivray and Son, 1867).

Duthie, J. A. *Rhymes and Reminiscences* (Brechin: D. H. Edwards, Advertiser Office, 1912).

Geddes, James Y. *The Spectre Clock of Alyth and Other Selections* (Alyth: Thomas McMurray, 1886).

Johnston, Ellen, *Autobiography, Poems and Songs* (Glasgow: William Love, 1867).

McGonagall, William, *Collected Poems*, intro. Chris Hunt (Edinburgh: Birlinn, 2006).

Morrison, David H., *Poems and Songs* (Airdrie: Baird and Hamilton, 1870).

Nicholson, James, *Kilwuddie and Other Poems, with Life-Sketch and Portrait of the Author*, 4th edn (Glasgow: James McGeachy, 1895).

Nicolson, L. J., *Songs of Thule* (Paisley: Alexander Gardner, 1894).

Ogilvy, Dorothea, *Poems* (Edinburgh: Edmonston and Douglas, 1873).

Pindar, John, *Rambling Rhymes*, ed. Rev. A. M. Houston (Cupar: J. & G. Innes, Fife News, 1893).

Poute [Burgess, Alexander]. *The Book of Nettercaps, Being Genuine Poutery, Poetry and Prose* (Dundee: John Leng, 1875).

Smith, John ('Auld C'), *Poems and Lyrics* (Perth: Miller & Gall, Printed for the Author, 1888).

Syme, Henry ('Grandfather'), *Local Musings* (Dunfermline: A. Romanes, Press Office, 1876).

Tasker, David, *Musings of Leisure Hours* (Dundee: James P. Mathew, 1865).

Taylor, John, *Poems, Chiefly on Themes of Scottish Interest*, with introductory preface by W. Lindsay Alexander (Edinburgh: Andrew Stevenson, 1875).

Wallace, Margaret, *Emblems of Nature* (Coupar-Angus: William Culross, 1875).

Watt, James E., *Poetical Sketches of Scottish Life and Character* (Dundee: John Leng, 1880).

Works consulted:

Black, Aileen, *Gilfillan of Dundee* (Dundee: Dundee University Press, 2006).

Blair, Kirstie, '"Let the Nightingales Alone": Correspondence Columns, the Scottish Press, and the Making of the Working-Class Poet', *Victorian Periodicals Review* 47.2 (2014), pp. 188–207.

—. '"A Very Poetical Town": Newspaper Poetry and the Working-Class Poet in Victorian Dundee', *Victorian Poetry* 52 (2014), pp. 89–110. Special issue on 'Victorian Periodical Poetry', ed. Alison Chapman and Caley Ehnes.

—. 'McGonagall, "Poute" and the Bad Poets of Victorian Scotland', *The Bottle Imp* 14 (November 2013).

—. and Mina Gorji, eds *Class and the Canon: Constructing Labouring-Class Poetry and Poetics, 1750–1900* (Houndsmills: Palgrave, 2013).

Bold, Valentina, *James Hogg: A Bard of Nature's Making* (Bern: Peter Lang, 2007).

—. 'James Young Geddes (1850–1913): A Re-evaluation', *Scottish Literary Journal* 19.1 (1992), pp. 18–27.

Boos, Florence, ed., *Working-Class Women Poets in Victorian Britain: An Anthology* (Peterborough, ON: Broadview, 2008).

Brake, Laurel, Aled Jones and Lionel Madden, eds, *Investigating Victorian Journalism* (London: Macmillan, 1990).

Brown, D. Walker, *Clydeside Litterateurs* (Glasgow: Carter & Pratt, 1897).

Checkland, Olive and Sydney Checkland, *Industry and Ethos: Scotland 1832–1914*, 2nd edn (Edinburgh: Edinburgh University Press, 1989).

Cohen, Edward H., Anne R. Fertig and Linda Fleming, eds, *A Song of Glasgow Town: The Collected Poems of Marion Bernstein* (Glasgow: ASLS, 2013).

Cowan, R. M. W., *The Newspaper in Scotland: A History of its First Expansion 1815–1860* (Glasgow: George Outram, 1946).

Cox, Anthony, *Empire, Industry and Class: The Imperial Nexus of Jute, 1840–1940* (London: Routledge, 2013).

Cuthbertson, David, *The Life-History of Alexander Anderson, 'Surfaceman'* (privately printed, n.d.).

Donaldson, William, *Popular Literature in Victorian Scotland: Language, Fiction and the Press* (Aberdeen: Aberdeen University Press, 1986).

Edwards, D. H., ed., *One Hundred Modern Scottish Poets* (Brechin: D. H. Edwards, 1880).

—. ed., *Modern Scottish Poets* 14 vols [Second to Sixteenth Series] (Brechin: D. H. Edwards, 1881–1897).

Fergusson, Robert Menzies, *A Village Poet* (Paisley: Alexander Gardner, 1897).

Goodridge, John and Bridget Keegan, eds, *Nineteenth-Century English Labouring-Class Poets*, vol. III: 1860–1900 (London: Pickering & Chatto, 2006).

Gordon, Eleanor, *Women and the Labour Movement in Scotland, 1850–1914* (Oxford: Clarendon Press, 1991).

Griffin, Emma, *Liberty's Dawn: A People's History of the Industrial Revolution* (New Haven: Yale University Press, 2013).

Hewitt, Martin, *The Dawn of the Cheap Press in Victorian Britain: The End of the 'Taxes on Knowledge', 1849–1869* (London: Bloomsbury, 2014).

Hobbs, Andrew, 'Five Million Poems, or the Local Press as Poetry Publisher, 1800–1900', *Victorian Periodicals Review* 42 (2012), 488–92.

—. and Claire Januszewski, 'How Local Newspapers Came to Dominate Victorian Poetry Publishing', *Victorian Poetry* 52 (2014), pp. 65–87.

Houston, Natalie, 'Newspaper Poems: Material Texts in the Public Sphere', *Victorian Studies* 50 (2008), pp. 233–42.

Hughes, Linda, 'Poetry', in *The Routledge Handbook to Nineteenth-Century British Periodicals and Newspapers*, ed. Andrew King, Alexis Easley and John Morton (London: Routledge, 2016), pp. 124–37.

Jones, Aled, *Powers of the Press: Newspapers, Power and the Public in Nineteenth-Century England* (Aldershot: Ashgate, 1996).

Klaus, H. Gustav, *Factory Girl: Ellen Johnston and Working-Class Poetry in Victorian Scotland* (Frankfurt: Peter Lang, 1998).

Latto, William, *Tammas Bodkin, or the Humours of a Scottish Tailor*, 3rd edn (Edinburgh: John Menzies, 1868).

Lewis, Peter R., *Beautiful Railway Bridge of the Silvery Tay: Reinvestigating the Tay Bridge Disaster of 1879* (Stroud: Tempus, 2004).

Lindsay, William, *Some Notes: Personal and Public* (Aberdeen: W. W. Lindsay, 1898).

Livingstone, David, *The Last Journals of David Livingstone, in Central Africa*, ed. Horace Waller (New York: Harper & Brothers, 1875).

MacDiarmid, Hugh, *Scottish Eccentrics*, ed. Alan Riach (Manchester: Carcanet, 1993).

Mackay, Charles, 'Rouse, Brothers, Rouse!'. Broadside Ballads Online (Bodleian Library) Roud 13811: ballads.bodleian.ox.ac.uk/static/images/sheets/20000/16929.gif.

Maidment, Brian, 'Class and Cultural Production in the Industrial City: Poetry in Victorian Manchester', in *City, Class and Culture: Studies of Cultural Production and Social Policy in Victorian Manchester*, ed. A. J. Kidd and K. W. Roberts (Manchester: Manchester University Press, 1985), pp. 148–66.

Martin, George M., *Dundee Worthies* (Dundee: Dundee University Press, 2010 (first published 1934)).

Milne, John, *Selections from the Songs and Poems of the Late John Milne, Glenlivat* (Aberdeen: Free Press Office, 1871).

Murdoch, Alexander G., *The Scottish Poets, Recent and Living* (Glasgow: T. D. Morrison, 1883).

Pindar, John, *Autobiography* (Cupar: J. & G. Innes, Fife News, 1877).

Poems by the People (Edinburgh: John Menzies, 1869).

Reid, Alan, ed. *Bards of Angus and the Mearns* (Paisley: J. and R. Parlane, 1897).

Reid, Robert ('Rob Wanlock'). *Poems, Songs and Sonnets* (Paisley: Alexander Gardner, 1894).

Reilly, Catherine W., *Mid-Victorian Poetry 1860–1879: An Annotated Bibliography* (London: Mansell, 2000).

Rubery, Matthew, *The Novelty of Newspapers: Victorian Fiction After the Invention of the News* (Oxford: OUP, 2009).

Scott, Andrew Murray, *Dundee's Literary Lives vol 1: Fifteenth to Nineteenth Century* (Dundee: Abertay Historical Society, 2003).

Tomlinson, Jim, *Dundee and the Empire: 'Juteopolis' 1850–1939* (Edinburgh: Edinburgh University Press, 2014).

Vincent, David, *Literacy and Popular Culture: England 1750–1914* (Cambridge: Cambridge University Press, 1989).

Watson, Norman, *Poet McGonagall: the Biography of William McGonagall* (Edinburgh: Birlinn, 2010).

Whamond, Alexander, *James Tacket: A Humorous Tale of Scottish Life*, 3rd edn (Edinburgh: Seton and Mackenzie, 1877).

Whatley, Christopher A., Louise Miskell and Bob Harris, *Victorian Dundee: Images and Realities* (East Linton: Tuckwell Press, 2000).

—. and David B. Swinfen and Annette M. Smith, *The Life and Times of Dundee* (Edinburgh: John Donald, 1993).

Poems by subgenre

Poems by subgenre

Advertising verse: 56, 60, 63

Children, parenthood and domestic life: 19, 20, 27, 50, 64, 67, 105, 107, 108, 111, 115

Comic and satirical verse: 11, 12, 14, 15, 18, 26, 30, 31, 46, 51, 60, 72, 80, 81, 83, 98

Courtship, romance and marriage: 16, 17, 18, 78, 98, 106, 117

Emigration and labour overseas: 22, 54, 55, 66, 67, 71, 96, 116

Hardship and adversity: 19, 25, 38, 40, 43, 45, 50, 69, 84, 86, 87, 99, 105, 113

Industry, labour and the industrial town: 25, 27, 28, 34, 47, 68, 74, 75, 76, 82, 84, 86, 87, 104, 108, 113, 117, 118

Local events and affairs: 7, 12, 23, 24, 38, 51, 53, 58, 59, 68, 80, 91, 92

Poems about the *People's Journal* or *People's Friend*, addresses to editor: 4, 13, 14, 21, 44, 52, 61, 72, 79, 85, 97, 109

Poetic community and poems addressed to fellow-authors: 11, 13, 29, 31, 41, 42, 48, 52, 57, 65, 66, 81, 83, 114, 116

Politics (national and international) and foreign affairs: 6, 10, 11, 35, 37, 49, 88, 89, 90, 93, 94, 95, 99, 102, 103

Scottish history, heritage and landscape: 1, 2, 3, 9, 81, 99, 106, 110, 112

Self-improvement: 5, 8, 39, 61

Temperance: 19, 77, 101, 114

War and soldiering: 6, 54, 89, 90, 95, 102, 103

Women, work and family: 17, 28, 32, 33, 36, 62, 70, 73, 74, 75, 86, 87, 100, 104, 107, 111, 117